Discussions of William Blake

DISCUSSIONS OF LITERATURE

General Editor JOSEPH H. SUMMERS, Washington University

DISCUSSIONS

OF

WILLIAM BLAKE

Edited with an Introduction by

John E. Grant

THE UNIVERSITY OF CONNECTICUT

D. C. Heath and Company

BOSTON

CONTENTS

INTRODUCTION

PROBABLY no student begins his study of Blake without some awareness of a few poems like "The Lamb" and "The Tyger" which are almost as widely known as *Romeo and Juliet* or *Julius Caesar*. But as with Shakespeare, an initial acquaintance often proves to be misleading. The student suddenly discovers that a writer he had supposed to be pellucidly simple and probably naïve appears to be bewilderingly complicated in his art and disturbingly outspoken in his religious and social thought. There is no way to answer the question whether Blake's work is really "easy" or "hard" without suppressing half the truth. Blake himself implied that children could understand his work better than adults, but in the same letter he proclaimed "that which can be made Explicit to an Idiot is not worth my care." The evidence of posterity is equally equivocal. Millions of people know Blake's great "Jerusalem" hymn, "And did those feet in ancient time," whereas the number who have read *Jerusalem* itself with substantial understanding must be less than a hundred. One of the most perceptive of Blake's recent critics confesses that he does not know what "The Fly" means, but can a poem in iambic dimeter really be so difficult? Blake tells us that

> A Riddle or the Cricket's Cry
> Is to Doubt a fit Reply.

Is the Cricket's Cry easy or difficult to understand? Blake called such either/or questions "cloven fictions" and would doubtless have agreed with a recent poet that

> To ask the hard question is simple,
> The simple act of the confused will.

Blake's thought is parabolic, that is, poetic, as he tried to explain to a successful man who expected art to be agreeable and easy: "The wisest of the Ancients consider'd what is not too Explicit as the fittest for Instruction, because it rouses the faculties to act." Such a theory of art is the opposite of obscurantism, which values difficulty for its own sake; what Blake advocates is complexity for vision's sake.

Blake's ideas are most interesting when they challenge the proverbial philosophy of common sense. The extraordinary concreteness of Blake's conceptions draws the reader away from traditional dichotomies that dull mental precision and tend to regiment thinking. Such ready-made alternatives as originality and conventionality, good and evil, freedom and necessity, appearance and reality, the one and the many, even God and Man, are all treated by Blake as pragmatic antinomies rather than as metaphysical essences. That is, Blake had "theories" on all of these subjects, but the most accurate exposition of them must use figurative examples rather than discursive prose. If one wishes to understand Blake's ideas on "good and evil," a natural place to look is *The Marriage of Heaven and Hell*, which deals with the relationship between Angels and Devils. Blake does not simply invert the customary relationship, as has often been asserted, however. It is better to say that he transvalued good and evil, or that he went *beyond* these categories, but one should not confuse Blake with Nietzsche. The best brief answer is contained in the ironic action of the "Memorable Fancies" in *The Marriage* where the self-righteous Angels are ridiculed by the energetic Devils until they finally abandon their traditional errors. But this does not mean that there is no truth in conventional notions of goodness. It is only that we must imaginatively get *inside* good and evil, see their "human forms," before we can comprehend what they are.

Whether one accepts all of Blake's critiques is another matter. I have never met a "Blakean" in the strict sense of the word —a person in total agreement with Blake. But I have never known a person who had read much of Blake (or of Dante or Swift or Dostoyevsky) with understanding and yet remained indifferent to the largest problems the human mind is capable of imagining. True poets "educate" by drawing their readers out of premature complacency. Observe how Blake simultaneously challenges preconceptions in religion, philosophy, morality, and art in two forthright sentences:

The grandest Poetry is Immoral, the Grandest characters Wicked, Very Satan—Campaneus, Othello, a murderer, Prometheus, Jupiter, Jehovah, Jesus a wine bibber. Cunning and Morality are not Poetry but Philosophy; the Poet is Independent and Wicked; the Philosopher is Dependent and Good.

We have learned from the work of a number of recent scholars that Blake's unconventional ideas are not as unprecedented as they were formerly supposed to be. But the vigor and precision with which Blake speaks his mind make his polemical insights stand out even in the history of unorthodox ideas. Most of his statements remain as challenging now as they ever were. They have not aged like the radical polemics of recent and less vigorous iconoclasts such as Shaw and Wells. Blake's gnomic sayings, in their pith and clarity, resemble those of the Bible in that almost endless commentary seems necessitated by a very few words. I recall reading a good newspaper editorial-sermon based on the Blakean aphorism:

Art Degraded, Imagination Denied, War governed the Nations.

But Blake's simplest questions often go even more directly to the heart of the matter; as an antidote to political Doublethink, he asks a definitive riddle:

What is Liberty without Universal Toleration?

Almost every popular collection of Blake's work includes an account of his unspectacular life. Like Shakespeare's, Blake's life was absorbed into his work and one feels that he had no time to *be* a "personality" like any of the Johnsons, or Byron, or Wilde, or either of the Lawrences. That Blake *had* a personality, however, is indicated by the vivid anecdotes in Crabb Robinson's diary or, for that matter, by Blake's own letters. The legend that Blake was completely unknown to his important contemporaries can be corrected by the letters with which the following collection begins, but it is significant that Lamb did not know Blake's first name and that Coleridge only met Blake during the last years of his life. Tatham, on the other hand, actually knew Blake and gave an account of his character that is accurate and complete, if not profound. But his judgment of Blake's thought is made up of half-truths that had already become stereotypes during Blake's lifetime. If Blake "became wild and his theories wanted solidity," are we to suppose that he would have been wiser to remain tame and accept the laws of "Bacon, and Newton, and Locke"? "Prudence is a rich, ugly old maid courted by Incapacity."

The essays that follow the letters were all written during the past decade, and almost all are indebted to the three most important books of Blakean interpretation: S. Foster Damon's *William Blake: His Philosophy and Symbols* (1924 and 1958), probably still the most useful book for the student of Blake; Northrop Frye's *Fearful Symmetry: A Study of William Blake* (1947 and 1958), a brilliant account of Blake as thinker and artist; and David V. Erdman's *Blake: Prophet Against Empire* (1954), an intensive study of Blake's imaginative response to his own age. Hardly less important are Milton O. Percival's *William

Blake's Circle of Destiny (1938) and Joseph H. Wicksteed's *Blake's Vision of the Book of Job* (revised, 1924). Since each of these weighty books is best read as a whole, I have included no selections from them.

The first two essays in this collection, by Frye and Erdman, are valuable not only because they clarify key ideas and passages in Blake but also because they make explicit some of their authors' critical assumptions. One is constantly forced, in dealing with Blake, to define one's own position with increasing exactness. Blake's luxuriant symbolism leads the woolly or merely eclectic thinker astray and leaves him hopelessly lost. On the other hand, Blake's work is so integrated that the reader who masters any aspect of it simultaneously achieves a more secure grasp of Blake's whole system. The essay by Fisher is an example of how the solution of a narrow scholarly problem finally expands into a consideration of most of Blake's "philosophy." But comprehension of Blake's unique art of combined poetry and painting is no less important than conversance with his ideas. Frye's second essay provides a good introduction to this subject.

The last six essays represent various kinds of practical criticism. Adams provides an excellent approach to Blake's lyrics as well as an able discussion of that enigmatic poem "The Tyger." My own article considers the same poem from a different point of view and attempts to justify Blake's remarkable design for it. Van Doren demonstrates that the common reader who is sensitive both to poetry and to democratic values can speak authoritatively about the poem Coleridge selected as the best of Blake's *Songs* without alluding to Blake's "system." Sutherland makes progress with perhaps the most difficult shorter poem in English, while Nurmi ably expounds two of Blake's key ideas and gives a structural analysis of his most famous prophecy. Finally Kiralis provides a guide, in which each assertion is carefully documented, to basic symbols in the prophecies. Only through such coordinated precision can the interpreter correct and add to the excellent general accounts of the meaning of the prophecies presented in book-length studies.

The reader will discover that there are many differences of opinion in these essays about this most individualistic artist. The contrary approaches of Frye and Erdman, for example, do not imply basic disagreement, but it is easy to see why these critics might not concur about every particular problem. Adams and Grant see the Tyger differently, and there are other less manifest differences among the other critics. No doubt error as well as truth exists in Blake studies, but there can be neither a Blakean heresy nor a Blakean orthodoxy. Indeed, there are no essays to which I cannot imagine weighty objections. For example, Van Doren implies that it is a moot question whether the Black Boy will ever become "white." But there is no problem if one looks at the second illustration to the poem, for there the Black Boy has become white— in most versions, that is, for in at least one copy of the *Songs* he remains dark. Thirty years after he wrote the poem, Blake painted a Black Madonna to remind his white audience that God does not discriminate according to the conventional literary symbolism of black and white. Thus when we place the moot question in a larger perspective, we discover that the problem is first "solved" and then becomes moot again at a higher level. And there is a further question—has the poem no legitimate status apart from Blake's design? Blake tells us that "As the Eye sees, so is the Object."

For the student who aspires to master his subject so that he can go his own way without guides, I should like to make a final suggestion. Myth criticism, which sometimes appears to be a luxury when applied to other writers, is a necessity for the student of Blake, but one must always bear in mind the deceptive ease with which Blake uses mythic material. Although he almost never took over a myth unchanged (a fact that makes it difficult to annotate his work), the recognition of a mythic allusion in one of Blake's poems often acts as a key to an otherwise enigmatic passage. What the reader feels as a result of such a discovery is not the scholarly shock of recognition, but an imaginative shock of comprehension. For example, in order to understand "The Sunflower" one should know the classical myth of Clytie; in order to grasp the ideas at the end of "Auguries of Innocence" one must recognize an allusion to the Biblical Book of Jonah; in order to respond to the symbolism in "The Mental Traveller" it is useful to know the fate of the Norse god Loki; and in order not to misjudge the foot symbolism in the "Bard's Song" in *Milton* one should know the famous episode of the Sandals in the Indian epic, *The Ramayana*. But Blake's poetry is as free from the limits of time as it is from those of space. Even the work of later writers can be as relevant for a proper understanding as are these diverse "sources." The "Nurse's Song" of *Experience*, for example, communicates its horror most fully to the reader who is aware of the psychological interpretation of Henry James' *The Turn of the Screw*. The study of Blake's work thus engages one's total literary experience. Blake is the most archetypal of artists.

A List of Recent Criticism

Because of the variety and complexity of Blake's art, even the beginning student should attend more carefully to bibliographical problems than he needs to with most writers. Fortunately, there are excellent studies easily available and the serious student should consult them rather than trust to the potluck of a card catalogue in a college library. The basic guide to Blake studies through 1956 was written by Northrop Frye and is included in *The English Romantic Poets and Essayists: A Review of Research and Criticism*, edited by Carolyn Washburn Houtchens and Laurence Huston Houtchens (1957). This is an expansion of Frye's excellent Bibliographical Note (1951) to his Modern Library selection of Blake's writings. Since the Bicentennial year of 1957, however, Blake studies have proliferated so that there is already a serious need for the complete bibliography being compiled by G. E. Bentley, Jr., and Martin K. Nurmi, scheduled for publication in 1961. What follows is an interim report, designed to supplement the works cited in the various essays in this volume.

The standard reference text for Blake's literary work is Geoffrey Keynes' *The Complete Writings of William Blake with all the variant readings* (1957). Still in print, though somewhat less complete, is Keynes' *Poetry and Prose of William Blake* (reset 1939). A recent annotated edition of Blake's shorter writings is F. W. Bateson, ed., *Selected Poems of William Blake* (1957). Recent reproductions of Blake's paintings and graphic work include: Kerrison Preston, ed., *The Blake Collection of W. Graham Robertson* (1953); Geoffrey Keynes, ed., *The Pencil Drawings of William Blake: Second Series* (1956); Geoffrey Keynes, ed., *Engravings by William Blake: The Separate Plates* (1956); Geoffrey Keynes, ed., *Blake's Illustrations to the Bible* (1957); Martin Butlin, ed., *A Catalogue of the Works of William Blake in the Tate Gallery* (1957); and C. H. Collins Baker and R. R. Wark, eds., *Catalogue of William Blake's Drawings and Paintings in the Huntington Library* (Revised, 1957). Microfilms of six of Blake's books in the Fitzwilliam Museum, Cambridge, were issued in 1960 by Micro Methods, Ltd., Yorkshire, England. See also the editorial note on page 49, below.

Recent interpretive works on Blake's art include: Albert S. Roe, "A Drawing of the Last Judgment," *Huntington Library Quarterly*, XXI (1957), 35–55; George Wingfield Digby, *Symbol and Image in William Blake* (1957); Anthony Blunt, *The Art of William Blake* (1959).

Important recent critical books and essays include: Vivian de Sola Pinto, ed., *The Divine Vision: Studies in the Poetry and Art of William Blake* (1957) (the Bicentennial anthology of essays by eight scholars; consult especially the essays by Frye on *Milton* and Kiralis on *Jerusalem*); Northrop Frye, "Blake's Introduction to Experience," *Huntington Library Quarterly*, XXI (1957), 57–67; Northrop Frye, "Blake and Joyce," *The James Joyce Review*, I (1957), 39–46; Northrop Frye, "Blake After Two Centuries," *University of Toronto Quarterly*, XXVII (1957), 10–21; G. E. Bentley, Jr., "The Failure of Blake's *Four Zoas*," *Texas Studies in English*, XXXVII (1958), 102–113; Harold Bloom, "Dialectic in *The Marriage of Heaven and Hell*," PMLA, LXXIII (1958), 501–504; Karl Kiralis, "Joyce and Blake: A Basic Source for *Finnegans Wake*," *Modern Fiction Studies*, IV (1958), 329–334; and Robert F. Gleckner, *The Piper and the Bard: A Study of William Blake* (1959).

Still to appear are: a concordance of Blake's writings under the general editor-ship of David V. Erdman; S. Foster Damon's *Dictionary of Blake Symbols*; Geoffrey Keynes' *An Iconography of William Blake*; Keynes has also promised a catalogue raisonné of *The Paintings and Drawings of William Blake*, edited with Ruthven Todd. At least six other books, three by contributors to this volume, are also in prospect. The late P. F. Fisher's essay is part of a larger study; Hazard Adams will go on to treat all of Blake's major lyrics; Karl Kiralis is at work on a new commentary on *Jerusalem* which will include a chapter by A. S. Roe on the art of the book; Jean H. Hagstrum is investigating the problem of poetry and design in Blake; Miss Kathleen Raine is making a study of Blake and his sources; and G. M. Harper is about to publish his findings on Blake and Neoplatonism. The industry of Blakeans is almost equal to Blake's own.

JOHN E. GRANT

Discussions of William Blake

DISCUSSIONS OF LITERATURE

William Blake

Charles Lamb

Letter to Bernard Barton

May 15, 1824

DEAR B. B.,

. . . Blake is a real name, I assure you, and a most extraordinary man, if he be still living. He is the Robert [William] Blake, whose wild designs accompany a splendid folio edition of the "Night Thoughts," which you may have seen, in one of which he pictures the parting of soul and body by a solid mass of human form floating off, God knows how, from a lumpish mass (fac Simile to itself) left behind on the dying bed. He paints in water colours marvellous strange pictures, visions of his brain, which he asserts that he has seen. They have great merit. He has *seen* the old Welsh bards on Snowdon—he has seen the Beautifullest, the strongest, and the Ugliest Man, left alone from the Massacre of the Britons by the Romans, and has painted them from memory (I have seen his paintings), and asserts them to be as good as the figures of Raphael and Angelo, but not better, as they had pre-cisely the same retro-visions and prophetic visions with themself [himself]. The paint-ers in oil (which he will have it that nei-ther of them practised) he affirms to have been the ruin of art, and affirms that all the while he was engaged in his Water paintings, Titian was disturbing him, Ti-tian the Ill Genius of Oil Painting. His Pic-tures—one in particular, the Canterbury Pilgrims (far above Stothard's)—have great merit, but hard, dry, yet with grace. He has written a Catalogue of them with a most spirited criticism on Chaucer, but mystical and full of Vision. His poems have been sold hitherto only in Manuscript. I never read them; but a friend at my desire procured the "Sweep Song." There is one to a tiger, which I have heard recited, be-ginning:

> Tiger, Tiger, burning bright,
> Thro' the desarts of the night,

which is glorious, but, alas! I have not the book; for the man is flown, whither I know not—to Hades or a Mad House. But I must look on him as one of the most ex-traordinary persons of the age. Montgom-ery's book I have not much hope from. The Society, with the affected name, has been labouring at it for these 20 years, and made few converts. I think it was injudi-cious to mix stories avowedly colour'd by fiction with the sad true statements from the parliamentary records, etc., but I wish the little Negroes all the good that can come from it. I batter'd my brains (not butter'd them—but it is a bad *a*) for a few verses for them, but I could make nothing

From *The Letters of Charles Lamb & Mary Lamb*, ed. E. V. Lucas (New Haven, Yale University Press, 1935), II, 424–427. Reprinted by permission of the publisher.

of it. You have been luckier. But Blake's are the flower of the set, you will, I am sure, agree, tho' some of Montgomery's at the end are pretty; but the Dream awkwardly paraphras'd from B. . . .

Yours ever truly,

C. L.[1]

[1] E. V. Lucas' note:

William Blake was at this time sixty-six years of age. He was living in poverty . . . at 3 Fountain Court, Strand. Blake made 537 illustrations to Young's *Night Thoughts*, of which only forty-seven were published. Lamb is, however, thinking of his edition of Blair's *Grave*. The exhibition of his works was held in 1809, and it was for this that Blake wrote the descriptive catalogue. Lamb had sent "The Chimney Sweeper," in the *Songs of Innocence*, to James Montgomery for his *Chimney-Sweepers' Friend and Climbing Boys' Album*,

1824, a little book designed to ameliorate the lot of those children, in whose interest a society existed. Barton also contributed something. It was Blake's poem which had excited Barton's curiosity. Probably he thought that Lamb wrote it. Lamb's mistake concerning Blake's name is curious in so far as that it was Blake's brother Robert who in a vision revealed to the poet the method by which the *Songs of Innocence* were to be reproduced. He died in 1787. It might be added that Lamb's enthusiasm for Blake seems to have converted Barton, who, in 1830, was corresponding with John Linnell, the painter, about him.

"The Society with the affected name." The Society for Ameliorating the Condition of Infant Chimney-Sweepers.

"The Dream awkwardly paraphras'd from B." The book ended with three Climbing-Boys' Soliloquies by Montgomery. The second was a dream in which the dream in Blake's song was extended and prosified.

Samuel Taylor Coleridge

Letters to H. F. Cary and C. A. Tulk

TO H. F. CARY

6 Feby. 1818

. . . I have this morning been reading a strange publication—viz. Poems with very wild and interesting pictures, as the swathing, etched (I suppose) but it is said—printed and painted by the Author, W. Blake. He is a man of Genius—and I apprehend, a Swedenborgian—certainly a mystic *emphatically*. You perhaps smile at *my* calling another Poet, a *Mystic;* but verily I am in the very mire of commonplace common-sense compared with Mr. Blake, apo- or rather ana-calyptic Poet, and Painter!

TO C. A. TULK

Thursday Evening
[12 February 1818]

Dear Sir

. . . I return you Blake's poesies, metrical and graphic, with thanks. With this and the Book I have sent a rude scrawl as to the order in which I was pleased by the several poems. . . .

Blake's Poems.

I begin with my Dyspathies that I may forget them: and have uninterrupted space for Loves and Sympathies. Title page and the following emblem contain all the faults of the Drawings with as few beauties as could be in the compositions of a man who was capable of such faults + such beauties.—The faults—despotism in symbols, amounting in the Title page to the μισητόν, and occasionally, irregular unmodified Lines of the Inanimate, sometimes as the effect of rigidity and sometimes of exossation—like a wet tendon. So likewise the ambiguity of the Drapery. Is it a garment—or the body incised and scored out? The *Limpness* (= the effect of Vinegar on an egg) in the upper one of the two prostrate figures in the Title page, and the *eye*-likeness of the twig posteriorly on the second—and the strait line down the waistcoat of pinky gold-beater's skin in the next drawing, with the I don't know whatness of the countenance, as if the mouth had been formed by the habit of placing the tongue, not contemptuously, but stupidly, between the lower gums and the lower jaw—these are the only *repulsive* faults I have noticed. The figure, however, of the second leaf (abstracted from the *expression* of the countenance given it by something about the mouth and the interspace from the lower lip to the chin) is such as only a Master learned in his art could produce.

N.B. I signifies, It gave me pleasure. Ɪ, still greater—ƗƗ, and greater still. ⊙, in the highest degree, o, in the lowest.[1]

Shepherd Ɪ. Spring Ɪ (last Stanza Ɪ). Holy Thursday ƗƗ. Laughing Song Ɪ. Nurse's Song Ɪ. The Divine Image ⊙. The Lamb Ɪ. The little Black Boy ⊙: yea ⊙ + ⊙! Infant Joy ƗƗ. (N.b. for the 3 last lines I should wish—When wilt thou smile, or—O smile, O smile! I'll sing the while—For a Babe two days old does not, cannot *smile*—and innocence and the very truth of

[1] o means that I am perplexed and have no opinion.

From *Collected Letters*, ed. Earl Leslie Griggs, Vol. IV (Oxford, Clarendon Press, 1959), pp. 833–834, 836–838. Reprinted by permission of the publisher.

Nature must go together. Infancy is too holy a thing to be ornamented.)—Echoing Green I (the figures Ɇ, and of the second leaf ƗƗ). The Cradle Song I. The School boy ƗƗ. Night ☉. On another's Sorrow I. A Dream?—The little Boy lost I (the drawing Ɇ). The little boy found I. The Blossom o. The Chimney Sweeper o. The Voice of the ancient Bard o.

Introduction Ɇ. Earth's Answer Ɇ. Infant Sorrow I. The Clod and the Pebble I. The Garden of Love Ɇ. The Fly I. The Tyger Ɇ. A little Boy lost Ɇ. Holy Thursday I. P. 13, o. Nurse's Song o. The little girl lost and found (the ornaments most exquisite, the poem I). Chimney Sweeper in the Snow o. To Tirzah—and The Poison Tree I and yet o. A little girl lost o (I would have had it omitted—not for the want of innocence in the poem, but from the too probable want of it in many readers). London I. The sick Rose I. *The little Vagabond*—Tho' I cannot approve altogether of this last poem and have been inclined to think that the error which is most *likely* to beset the scholars of Emanuel Swedenborg is that of utterly demerging the tremendous incompatibilities with an evil will that arise out of the essential Holiness of the abysmal Aseity in the Love of the eternal *Person*—and thus giving temptation to weak minds to sink this Love itself into *good nature*, & yet still I disapprove the mood of mind in this wild poem so much less than I do the servile, blind worm, wrap-rascal scurf-coat of FEAR of the *modern Saints* (whose whole being is a Lie, to themselves as well as to their Brethren), that I should laugh with good conscience in watching a Saint of the new stamp, one of the Fixt Stars of our eleemosynary Advertisements, groaning in windpipe! and with the whites of his Eyes upraised at the *audacity* of this poem!—Any thing rather than *this* degradation [2] of Humanity, and therein of the Incarnate Divinity!

S. T. C.

[2] with which how can we utter "Our Father"?

Frederick Tatham

Letter to Francis Harvey

June 8, 1864.

DEAR SIR,

The MS you purchased of me was part of the possessions into which I came by legacy from Mrs. Blake, the widow of that extraordinary and excellent man, William Blake, Visionary, Poet and Painter, who also had a most consummate knowledge of all the great writers in all languages. To prove that, I may say that I have possessed books well thumbed and dirtied by his graving hands, in Latin, Greek, Hebrew, French, and Italian, besides a large collection of works of the mystical writers, Jacob Behmen, Swedenborg, and others. His knowledge was immense, his industry beyond parallel, and his life innocent and simple and laborious, far beyond that of most other men. Childlike, impetuous, fiery, indomitable, proud, and humble, he carried out a sort of purpose in his life which seemed only to produce what was invisible to the natural eye, to the despising of the things which are seen: he therefore became wild and his theories wanted solidity; but he was the most delightful and interesting man that ever an intellectual lover of art could spend a day with; and he died as he lived. He was much associated with many of the great men of the age in which he lived, and was meek and companionable with them. These things are to be deduced, and the great interest which the public have taken in him, by the several Biographies that have been published of him since his death—to which the reader and yourself had better be referred.

Believe me, dear Sir,

Very faithfully yours,

Frederick Tatham

From Geoffrey Keynes, "Blake's Library," *The* [London] *Times Literary Supplement*, November 6, 1959, p. 648. Reprinted by permission of Sir Geoffrey Keynes and the publisher.

Northrop Frye

Blake's Treatment of the Archetype

THE READER of Blake soon becomes familiar with the words "innocence" and "experience." The world of experience is the world that adults live in while they are awake. It is a very big world, and a lot of it seems to be dead, but still it makes its own kind of sense. When we stare at it, it stares unwinkingly back, and the changes that occur in it are, on the whole, orderly and predictable changes. This quality in the world that reassures us we call law. Sitting in the middle of the lawful world is the society of awakened adults. This society consists of individuals who apparently have agreed to put certain restraints on themselves. So we say that human society is also controlled by law. Law, then, is the basis both of reason and of society: without it there is no happiness, and our philosophers tell us that they really do not know which is more splendid, the law of the starry heavens outside us, or the moral law within. True, there was a time when we were children and took a different view of life. In childhood happiness seemed to be based, not on law and reason, but on love, protection, and peace. But we can see now that such a view of life was an illusion derived from an excess of economic security. As Isaac Watts says, in a song of innocence which is thought to have inspired Blake:

> Sleep, my babe; thy food and raiment,
>   House and home, thy friends provide;
> All without thy care or payment:
>   All thy wants are well supplied.

And after all, from the adult point of view, the child is not so innocent as he looks. He is actually a little bundle of anarchic will, whose desires take no account of either the social or the natural order. As he grows up and enters the world of law, his illegal desires can no longer be tolerated even by himself, and so they are driven underground into the world of the dream, to be joined there by new desires, mainly sexual in origin. In the dream, a blind, unreasoning, childish will is still at work revenging itself on experience and rearranging it in terms of desire. It is a great comfort to know that this world, in which we are compelled to spend about a third of our time, is unreal, and can never displace the world of experience in which reason predominates over passion, order over chaos, classical values over romantic ones, the solid over the gaseous, and the cool over the hot.

The world of law, stretching from the starry heavens to the moral conscience, is the domain of Urizen in Blake's symbolism. It sits on a volcano in which the rebellious Titan Orc, the spirit of passion, lies bound, writhing and struggling to get free. Each of these spirits is Satanic or devilish to the other. While we dream, Urizen, the principle of reality, is the censor, or, as Blake calls him, the accuser, a smug and grinning hypocrite, an impotent old man, the caricature that the child in us makes out of the adult world that thwarts him. But as long as we are awake, Orc, the lawless pleasure principle, is an evil dragon

From *English Institute Essays: 1950*, ed. Alan S. Downer (New York, Columbia University Press, 1951), pp. 170–196. Reprinted, with a few alterations and omissions, by permission of the author and the publisher.

bound under the conscious world in chains, and we all hope he will stay there.

The dream world is, however, not quite securely bound: every so often it breaks loose and projects itself on society in the form of war. It seems odd that we should keep plunging with great relief into moral holidays of aggression in which robbery and murder become virtues instead of crimes. It almost suggests that keeping our desires in leash and seeing that others do likewise is a heavy and sooner or later an intolerable strain. On a still closer view, even the difference between war and law begins to blur. The social contract, which from a distance seems a reasonable effort of cooperation, looks closer up like an armed truce founded on passion, in which the real purpose of law is to defend by force what has been snatched in self-will. Plainly, we cannot settle the conflict of Orc and Urizen by siding with one against the other, still less by pretending that either of them is an illusion. We must look for a third factor in human life, one which meets the requirements of both the dream and the reality.

This third factor, called Los by Blake, might provisionally be called work, or constructive activity. All such work operates in the world of experience; it takes account of law and of our waking ideas of reality. Work takes the energy which is wasted in war or thwarted in dreams and sets it free to act in experience. And as work cultivates land and makes farms and gardens out of jungle and wilderness, as it domesticates animals and builds cities, it becomes increasingly obvious that work is the realization of a dream and that this dream is descended from the child's lost vision of a world where the environment is the home.

The worker, then, does not call the world of experience real because he perceives it out of a habit acquired from his ancestors: it is real to him only as the material cause of his work. And the world of dreams is not unreal, but the formal cause: it dic-tates the desirable human shape which the work assumes. Work, therefore, by realizing in experience the child's and the dreamer's worlds, indicates what there is about each that is genuinely innocent. When we say that a child is in the state of innocence, we do not mean that he is sinless or harmless, but that he is able to assume a coherence, a simplicity and a kindliness in the world that adults have lost and wish they could regain. When we dream, we are, whatever we put into the dream, revolting against experience and creating another world, usually one we like better. Whatever in childhood or the dream is delivered and realized by work is innocent; whatever is suppressed or distorted by experience becomes selfish or vicious. "He who desires but acts not, breeds pestilence."

Work begins by imposing a human form on nature, for "Where man is not, nature is barren." But in society work collides with the cycle of law and war. A few seize all its benefits and become idlers, the work of the rest is wasted in supporting them, and so work is perverted into drudgery. "God made Man happy & Rich, but the Subtil made the innocent, Poor." Neither idleness nor drudgery can be work: real work is the creative act of a free man, and wherever real work is going on it is humanizing society as well as nature. The work that, projected on nature, forms civilization, becomes, when projected on society, prophecy, a vision of complete human freedom and equality. Such a vision is a revolutionary force in human life, destroying all the social barriers founded on idleness and all the intellectual ones founded on ignorance.

So far we have spoken only of what seems naturally and humanly possible, of what can be accomplished by human nature. But if we confine the conception of work to what now seems possible, we are still judging the dream by the canons of waking reality. In other words, we have quite failed to distinguish work from law, Los from Urizen, and are back where we started. The real driving power of civilization and prophecy is not the mature mind's sophisticated and cautious adaptations of the child's or the dreamer's desires: it comes from the original and innocent form of those desires, with all their reckless disregard of the lessons of experience.

The creative root of civilization and prophecy can only be art, which deals not only with the possible, but with "probable impossibilities"—it is interesting to see Blake quoting Aristotle's phrase in one of his marginalia. And just as the controlling idea of civilization is the humanizing of nature, and the controlling idea of prophecy the emancipation of man, so the controlling idea of art, the source of them both, must be the simultaneous vision of both. This is apocalypse, the complete transformation of both nature and human nature into the same form. "Less than All cannot satisfy Man"; the child in us who cries for the moon will never stop crying until the moon is his plaything, until we are delivered from the tyranny of time, space, and death, from the remoteness of a gigantic nature and from our own weakness and selfishness. Man cannot be free until he is everywhere: at the center of the universe, like the child, and at the circumference of the universe, like the dreamer. Such an apocalypse is entirely impossible under the conditions of experience that we know, and could only take place in the eternal and infinite context that is given it by religion. In fact, Blake's view of art could almost be defined as the attempt to realize the religious vision in human society. Such religion has to be sharply distinguished from all forms of religion which have been kidnapped by the cycle of law and war, and have become capable only of reinforcing the social contract or of inspiring crusades.

When we say that the goal of human work can only be accomplished in eternity, many people would infer that this involves renouncing all practicable improvement of human status in favor of something which by hypothesis, remains forever out of man's reach. We make this inference because we confuse the eternal with the indefinite: we are so possessed by the categories of time and space that we can hardly think of eternity and infinity except as endless time and space, respectively. But the home of time, so to speak, the only part of time that man can live in, is now; and the home of space is here. In the world of experience there is no such time as now; the present never quite exists, but is hidden somewhere between a past that no longer exists and a future that does not yet exist. The mature man does not know where "here" is: he can draw a circle around himself and say that "here" is inside it, but he cannot locate anything except a "there." In both time and space man is being continually excluded from his own home. The dreamer, whose space is inside his mind, has a better notion of where "here" is, and the child, who is not yet fully conscious of the iron chain of memory that binds his ego to time and space, still has some capacity for living in the present. It is to this perspective that man returns when his conception of "reality" begins to acquire some human meaning.

The Sky is an immortal Tent built by the Sons of Los:
And every Space that a Man views around his dwelling-place
Standing on his own roof or in his garden on a mount
Of twenty-five cubits in height, such space is his Universe:
And on its verge the Sun rises & sets, the Clouds bow
To meet the flat Earth & the Sea in such an order'd Space:
The Starry heavens reach no further, but here bend and set
On all sides, & the two Poles turn on their valves of gold. . .

If the vision of innocence is taken out of its eternal and infinite context, the real here and now, and put inside time, it becomes either a myth of a Golden Age or a

Paradise lost in the past, or a hope which is yet to be attained in the future, or both. If it is put inside space, it must be somewhere else, presumably in the sky. It is only these temporal and spatial perversions of the innocent vision that really do snatch it out of man's grasp. Because the innocent vision is so deep down in human consciousness and is subject to so much distortion, repression, and censorship, we naturally tend, when we project it on the outer world, to put it as far off in time and space as we can get it. But what the artist has to reveal, as a guide for the work of civilization and prophecy, is the form of the world as it would be if we could live in it here and now.

Innocence and experience are the middle two of four possible states. The state of experience Blake calls Generation, and the state of innocence, the potentially creative world of dreams and childhood, Beulah. Beyond Beulah is Eden, the world of the apocalypse in which innocence and experience have become the same thing, and below Generation is Ulro, the world as it is when no work is being done, the world where dreams are impotent and waking life haphazard. Eden and Ulro are, respectively, Blake's heaven or unfallen world and his hell or fallen world. Beulah is the world of the lover and the beloved, Generation the world of the subject and the object, and Ulro the world of the ego and the enemy, or the obstacle. This is, of course, one world, looked at in four different ways. The four ways represent the four moods or states in which art is created: the apocalyptic mood of Eden, the idyllic mood of Beulah, the elegiac mood of Generation, and the satiric mood of Ulro. These four moods are the tonalities of Blake's expression; every poem of his regularly resolves on one of them.

For Blake the function of art is to reveal the human or intelligible form of the world, and it sees the other three states in relation to that form. This fact is the key to Blake's conception of imagery, the pattern of which I have tried to simplify by a table.[1] Let us take the word "image" in its vulgar sense, which is good enough just now, of a verbal or pictorial replica of a physical object. For Blake the real form of the object is what he calls its "human form." In Ulro, the world with no human work in it, the mineral kingdom consists mainly of shapeless rocks lying around at random. When man comes into the world, he tries to make cities, buildings, roads, and sculptures out of this mineral kingdom. Such human artifacts therefore constitute the intelligible form of the mineral world, the mineral world as human desire would like to see it. Similarly, the "natural" or unworked form of the vegetable world is a forest, a heath, or a wilderness; its human and intelligible form is that of the garden, the grove, or the park, the last being the original meaning of the word Paradise. The natural form of the animal world consists of beasts of prey: its human form is a society of domesticated animals of which the flock of sheep is the most commonly employed symbol. The city, the garden, and the sheepfold are thus the human forms of the mineral, vegetable, and animal kingdoms, respectively. Blake calls these archetypes Golgonooza, Allamanda, and Bowlahoola, and identifies them with the head, heart, and bowels of the total human form. Below the world of solid substance is a chaotic or liquid world, and the human form of that is the river or circulating body of fresh water.

Each of these human forms has a contrasting counterpart in Ulro, the world of undeveloped nature and regressive humanity. To the city which is the home of the soul or City of God, the fallen world opposes the city of destruction which is doomed through the breakdown of work described by Ezekiel in a passage quoted by Blake as "pride, fullness of bread and abundance of idleness." Against the image of the sheep in the pasture, we have the im-

[1] See the next page.

age of the forest inhabited by menacing beasts like the famous tiger, the blasted heath or waste land full of monsters, or the desert with its fiery serpents. To the river which is the water of life the fallen world opposes the image of the devouring sea and the dragons and leviathans in its depths. Blake usually calls the fallen city Babylon, the forest Entuthon Benython, and the dead sea or salt lake Udan Adan. Labyrinths and mazes are the only patterns of Ulro; images of highways and paths made straight belong to the world informed with intelligence.

The essential principle of the fallen world appears to be discreteness or opacity. Whatever we see in it we see as a self-enclosed entity, unlike all others. When we say that two things are identical, we mean that they are very similar; in other words "identity" is a meaningless word in ordinary experience. Hence in Ulro, and even in Generation, all classes or societies are aggregates of similar but separate individuals. But when man builds houses out of stones, and cities out of houses, it becomes clear that the real or intelligible form of a thing includes its relation to its environment as well as its self-contained existence. This environment is its own larger "human form." The stones that make a city do not cease to be stones, but they cease to be separate stones: their purpose, shape, and function is identical with that of the city as a whole. In the human world, as in the work of art, the individual thing is there, and the total form which gives it meaning is there: what has vanished is the shapeless collection or mass of similar things. This is what Blake means when he says that in the apocalypse all human forms are "identified." The same is true of the effect of work on human society. In a completely human society man would not lose his individuality, but he would lose his separate and isolated ego, what Blake calls his Self-

EXPERIENCE		CATEGORY	INNOCENCE	
Individual Form	*Collective Form*		*Collective Form*	*Individual Form*
sky-god (Nobodaddy)	aristocracy of gods	(1) Divine	human powers	incarnate God (Jesus)
a) leader and high priest (Caiaphas)	tyrants and victims	(2) Human	community	a) one man (Albion)
b) harlot (Rahab)				b) bride (Jerusalem)
dragon (Covering Cherub)	beasts of prey (tiger, leviathan)	(3) Animal	flock of sheep	one lamb (Bowlahoola)
tree of mystery	forest, wilderness (Entuthon Benython)	(4) Vegetable	garden or park (Allamanda)	tree of life
a) opaque furnace or brick kilns	a) city of destruction (Sodom, Babylon, Egypt)	(5) Mineral	city, temple (Golgonooza)	living stone
b) "Stone of Night"	b) ruins, caves			
(not given)	salt lake or dead sea (Udan Adan)	(6) Chaotic	fourfold river of life	"Globule of Blood"

hood. The prophetic vision of freedom and equality thus cannot stop at the Generation level of a Utopia, which means an orderly molecular aggregate of individuals existing in some future time. Such a vision does not capture, though it may adumbrate, the real form of society, which can only be a larger human body. This means literally the body of one man, though not of a separate man.

Everywhere in the human world we find that the Ulro distinction between the singular and the plural has broken down. The real form of human society is the body of one man; the flock of sheep is the body of one lamb; the garden is the body of one tree, the so-called tree of life. The city is the body of one building or temple, a house of many mansions, and the building itself is the body of one stone, a glowing and fiery precious stone, the unfallen stone of alchemy which assimilates everything else to itself, Blake's grain of sand which contains the world.

The second great principle of Ulro is the principle of hierarchy or degree which produces the great chain of being. In the human world there is no chain of being: all aspects of existence are equal as well as identical. The one man is also the one lamb, and the body and blood of the animal form are the bread and wine which are the human forms of the vegetable world. The tree of life is the upright vertebrate form of man; the living stone, the glowing transparent furnace, is the furnace of heart and lungs and bowels in the animal body. The river of life is the blood that circulates within that body. Eden, which according to Blake was a city as well as a garden, had a fourfold river, but no sea, for the river remained inside Paradise, which was the body of one man. England is an island in the sea, like St. John's Patmos; the human form of England is Atlantis, the island which has replaced the sea. Again, where there is no longer any difference between society and the individual, there can hardly be any difference between society and marriage or between a home and a wife or

child. Hence Jerusalem in Blake is "A City, yet a Woman," and at the same time the vision of innocent human society.

On the analogy of the chain of being, it is natural for man to invent an imaginary category of gods above him, and he usually locates them in what is above him in space, that is, the sky. The more developed society is, the more clearly man realizes that a society of gods would have to be, like the society of man, the body of one God. Eventually he realizes that the intelligible forms of man and of whatever is above man on the chain of being must be identical. The identity of God and man is for Blake the whole of Christianity: the adoration of a superhuman God he calls natural religion, because the source of it is remote and unconquered nature. In other words, the superhuman God is the deified accuser or censor of waking experience, whose function it is to discourage further work. Blake calls this God Nobodaddy, and curses and reviles him so much that some have inferred that he was inspired by an obscure psychological compulsion to attack the Fatherhood of God. Blake is doing nothing of the kind, as a glance at the last plate of *Jerusalem* will soon show: he is merely insisting that man cannot approach the superhuman aspect of God except through Christ, the God who is Man. If man attempts to approach the Father directly, as Milton, for instance, does in a few unlucky passages in *Paradise Lost*, all he will ever get is Nobodaddy. Theologically, the only unusual feature of Blake is not his attitude to the person of the Father, but his use of what is technically known as pre-existence: the doctrine that the humanity of Christ is co-eternal with his divinity.

There is nothing in the Ulro world corresponding to the identity of the individual and the total form in the unfallen one. But natural religion, being a parody of real religion, often develops a set of individual symbols corresponding to the lamb, the tree of life, the glowing stone, and the rest. This consolidation of Ulro symbols Blake calls Druidism. Man progresses toward a free and equal community, and regresses toward tyranny; and as the human form of the community is Christ, the one God who is one Man, so the human form of tyranny is the isolated hero or inscrutable leader with his back to an aggregate of followers, or the priest of a veiled temple with an imaginary sky-god supposed to be behind the veil. The Biblical prototypes of this leader and priest are Moses and Aaron. Against the tree of life we have what Blake calls the tree of mystery, the barren fig tree, the dead tree of the cross, Adam's tree of knowledge, with its forbidden fruit corresponding to the fruits of healing on the tree of life. Against the fiery precious stone, the bodily form in which John saw God "like a jasper and a sardine stone," we have the furnace, the prison of heat without light which is the form of the opaque warm-blooded body in the world of frustration, or the stone of Druidical sacrifice like the one that Hardy associates with Tess. Against the animal body of the lamb, we have the figure that Blake calls, after Ezekiel, the Covering Cherub, who represents a great many things, the unreal world of gods, human tyranny and exploitation, and the remoteness of the sky, but whose animal form is that of the serpent or dragon wrapped around the forbidden tree. The dragon, being both monstrous and fictitious, is the best animal representative of the bogies inspired by human inertia: the Book of Revelation calls it "the beast that was, and is not, and yet is."

Once we have understood Blake's scheme of imagery, we have broken the back of one of the main obstacles to reading the prophecies: the difficulty in grasping their narrative structure. Narrative is normally the first thing we look for in trying to read a long poem, but Blake's poems are presented as a series of engraved plates, and the mental process of following a narrative sequence is, especially in the later poems, subordinated to a process of comprehending an inter-related pattern of im-

ages and ideas. The plate in Blake's epics has a function rather similar to that of the stanza with its final alexandrine in *The Faerie Queene:* it brings the narrative to a full stop and forces the reader to try to build up from the narrative his own reconstruction of the author's meaning. Blake thinks almost entirely in terms of two narrative structures. One of these is the narrative of history, the cycle of law and war, the conflict of Orc and Urizen, which in itself has no end and no point and may be called the tragic or historical vision of life. The other is the comic vision of the apocalypse or work of Los, the clarification of the mind which enables one to grasp the human form of the world. But the latter is not concerned with temporal sequence and is consequently not so much a real narrative as a dialectic.

The tragic narrative is the story of how the dream world escapes into experience and is gradually imprisoned by experience. This is the main theme of heroic or romantic poetry and is represented in Blake by Orc. Orc is first shown us, in the "Preludium" to *America,* as the libido of the dream, a boy lusting for a dim maternal figure and bitterly hating an old man who keeps him in chains. Then we see him as the conquering hero of romance, killing dragons and sea monsters, ridding the barren land of its impotent aged kings, freeing imprisoned women, and giving new hope to men. Finally we see him subside into the world of darkness again from whence he emerged, as the world of law slowly recovers its balance. His rise and decline has the rotary movement of the solar and seasonal cycles, and like them is a part of the legal machinery of nature.

Blake has a strong moral objection to all heroic poetry that does not see heroism in its proper tragic context, and even when it does, he is suspicious of it. For him the whole conception of κλέα ἀνδρῶν [brave deeds of heroes] as being in itself, without regard to the larger consequences of brave deeds, a legitimate theme for poetry, has been completely outmoded. It has been outmoded, for one thing, by Christianity, which has brought to the theme of the heroic act a radically new conception of what a hero is and what an act is. The true hero is the man who, whether as thinker, fighter, artist, martyr, or ordinary worker, helps in achieving the apocalyptic vision of art; and an act is anything that has a real relation to that achievement. Events such as the battle of Agincourt or the retreat from Moscow are not really heroic, because they are not really acts: they are part of the purposeless warfare of the state of nature and are not progressing towards a better kind of humanity. So Blake is interested in Orc only when his heroism appears to coincide with something of potentially apocalyptic importance, like the French or American revolutions.

For the rest, he keeps Orc strictly subordinated to his main theme of the progressive work of Los, the source of which is found in prophetic scriptures, especially, of course, the Bible. Comprehensive as his view of art is, Blake does not exactly say that the Bible is a work of art: he says "The Old & New Testaments are the Great Code of Art." The Bible tells the artist what the function of art is and what his creative powers are trying to accomplish. Apart from its historical and political applications, Blake's symbolism is almost entirely Biblical in origin, and the subordination of the heroic Orc theme to the apocalyptic Los theme follows the Biblical pattern.

The tragic vision of life has the rhythm of the individual's organic cycle: it rises in the middle and declines at the end. The apocalyptic theme turns the tragic vision inside out. The tragedy comes in the middle, with the eclipse of the innocent vision, and the story ends with the re-establishment of the vision. Blake's major myth thus breaks into two parts, a Genesis and an Exodus. The first part accounts for the existence of the world of experience in terms of the myths of creation and fall. Blake sees

no difference between creation and fall, between establishing the Ulro world and placing man in it. How man fell out of a city and garden is told twice in Genesis, once of Adam and once of Israel—Israel, who corresponds to Albion in Blake's symbolism, being both a community and a single man. The Book of Genesis ends with Israel in Egypt, the city of destruction. In the Book of Exodus we find the state of experience described in a comprehensive body of Ulro symbols. There is the fallen civilization of Egypt, destroyed by the plagues which its own tyranny has raised, the devouring sea, the desert with its fiery serpents, the leader and the priest, the invisible sky god who confirms their despotic power, and the labyrinthine wanderings of a people who have nothing but law and are unable to work. Society has been reduced to a frightened rabble following a leader who obviously has no notion of where he is going. In front of it is the Promised Land with its milk and honey, but all the people can see are enemies, giants, and mysterious terrors. From there on the story splits in two. The histories go on with the Orc or heroic narrative of how the Israelites conquered Canaan and proceeded to run through another cycle from bondage in Egypt to bondage in Babylon. But in the prophecies, as they advance from social criticism to apocalyptic, the Promised Land is the city and garden that all human effort is trying to reach, and its conqueror can only be the Messiah or true form of man.

The New Testament has the same structure as the Old. In the life of Jesus the story of the Exodus is repeated. Jesus is carried off to Egypt by a father whose name is Joseph, Herod corresponds to Pharaoh, and the massacre of the innocents to the attempt to exterminate the Hebrew children. The organizing of Christianity around the twelve disciples corresponds to the organizing of the religion of Israel among twelve tribes, the forty days wandering of Jesus in the desert to the forty years of Israel, the crucifixion to the lifting of the brazen serpent on the pole, and the resurrection to the invasion of Canaan by Joshua, who has the same name as Jesus. From there on the New Testament splits into a historical section describing the beginning of a new Christian cycle, which is reaching its Babylonian phase in Blake's own time, and a prophetic section, the Book of Revelation, which deals with what it describes, in a phrase which has fascinated so many apocalyptic thinkers from Joachim of Floris to Blake, as the "everlasting gospel," the story of Jesus told not historically as an event in the past, but visually as a real presence.

The characters of Blake's poems, Orc, Los, Urizen, Vala, and the rest, take shape in accordance with Blake's idea of the real act. No word in the language contains a greater etymological lie than the word "individual." The so-called undivided man is a battle-ground of conflicting forces, and the appearance of consistency in his behavior derives from the force that usually takes the lead. To get at the real elements of human character, one needs to get past the individual into the dramatis personae that make up his behavior. Blake's analysis of the individual shows a good many parallels with more recent analyses, especially those of Freud and Jung. The scheme of the Four Zoas is strikingly Freudian, and the contrast of the Orc and Los themes in Blake is very like the contrast between Jung's early book on the libido and his later study of the symbols of individuation. Jung's anima and persona are closely analogous to Blake's emanation and specter, and his counsellor and shadow seem to have some relation to Blake's Los and Spectre of Urthona.

But a therapeutic approach will still relate any such analysis primarily to the individual. In Blake anything that is a significant act of individual behavior is also a significant act of social behavior. Orc, the libido, produces revolution in society: Vala, the elusive anima, produces the social code of *Frauendienst* [service of women]; Urizen, the moral censor, produces the reli-

gion of the externalized God. "We who dwell on Earth can do nothing of ourselves," says Blake: "everything is conducted by Spirits." Man performs no act as an individual: all his acts are determined by an inner force which is also a social and historical force, and they derive their significance from their relation to the total human act, the restoration of the innocent world John Doe does nothing as John Doe: he eats and sleeps in the spirit of Orc the Polypus: he obeys laws in the spirit of Urizen the conscience; he loses his temper in the spirit of Tharmas the destroyer; and he dies in the spirit of Satan the death-impulse.

Furthermore, as the goal of life is the humanization of nature, there is a profound similarity between human and natural behavior, which in the apocalypse becomes identity. It is a glimmering of this fact that has produced the god, the personalized aspect of nature, and a belief in gods gradually builds the sense of an omnipotent personal community out of nature. As long as these gods remain on the other side of nature, they are merely the shadows of superstition: when they are seen to be the real elements of human life as well, we have discovered the key to all symbolism in art. Blake's Tharmas, the "id" of the individual and the stampeding mob of society, is also the god of the sea, Poseidon the earth-shaker. His connection with the sea is not founded on resemblance or association, but, like the storm scene in *King Lear,* on an ultimate identity of human rage and natural tempest.

In the opening plates of *Jerusalem* Blake has left us a poignant account of one such struggle of contending forces within himself, between his creative powers and his egocentric will. He saw the Industrial Revolution and the great political and cultural changes that came with it, and he realized that something profoundly new and disquieting was coming into the world, something with unlimited possibilities for good or for evil, which it would tax all his powers to interpret. And so his natural desire to make his living as an engraver and a figure in society collided with an overwhelming impulse to tell the whole poetic truth about what he saw. The latter force won, and dictated its terms accordingly. He was not allowed to worry about his audience. He revised, but was not allowed to decorate or stylize, only to say what had to be said. He was not allowed the double talk of the sophisticated poet, who can address several levels of readers at once by using familiar conceptions ambiguously. Nothing was allowed him but a terrifying concentration of his powers of utterance.

What finally emerged, out of one of the hottest poetic crucibles of modern times, was a poetry which consisted almost entirely in the articulation of archetypes. By an archetype I mean an element in a work of literature, whether a character, an image, a narrative formula, or an idea, which can be assimilated to a larger unifying category. The existence of such a category depends on the existence of a unified conception of art. Blake began his prophecies with a powerfully integrated theory of the nature, structure, function, and meaning of art, and all the symbolic units of his poetry, his moods, his images, his narratives and his characters, form archetypes of that theory. Given his premises about art, everything he does logically follows. His premises may be wrong, but there are two things which may make us hesitate to call them absurd. One is their comprehensiveness and consistency: if the Bible is the code of art, Blake seems to provide something of a code of modern art, both in his structure of symbols and in his range of ideas. The other is their relationship to earlier traditions of criticism. Theories of poetry and of archetypes seem to belong to criticism rather than to poetry itself, and when I speak of Blake's treatment of the archetype I imply that Blake is a poet of unique interest to critics like ourselves. The Biblical origin of his symbolism and his apocalyptic theory of perception have a great deal in common with the theory of anagoge which underlies the poetry of Dante, the main structure of which survived through the Renaissance at least as late as Milton. Blake had the same creative powers as other great poets, but he made a very unusual effort to drag them up to consciousness, and to do deliberately what most poets prefer to do instinctively. It is possible that what impelled him to do this was the breakdown of a tradition of criticism which could have answered a very important question. Blake did not need the answer, but we do.

The question relates to the application of Blake's archetypes to the criticism of poetry as a whole. . . .[2]

The difficulty of a "private mythology" is not peculiar to Blake: every poet has a private mythology, his own formation of symbols. His mythology is a cross-section of his life, and the critic, like the biographer, has the job of making sure that what was private to the poet shall be public to everyone else. But, having no theory of archetypes, we do not know how to proceed. Blake supplies us with a few leading principles which may guide us in analyzing the symbolic formation of poets and isolating the archetypal elements in them. Out of such a study the structure of literature may slowly begin to emerge, and criticism, in interpreting that structure, may take its rightful place among the major disciplines of modern thought. There is, of course, the possibility that the study of Blake is a long and tortuous blind alley, but those who are able to use Blake's symbols as a calculus for all their criticism will not be much inclined to consider it.

The question that we have just tried to answer, however, is not the one that the student of Blake most frequently meets. The latter question runs in effect: you may show that Blake had one of the most pow-

[2] Here Mr. Frye briefly discusses problems of literary scholarship which he takes up in more detail in his *Anatomy of Criticism* (Princeton, 1957).—Ed.

erful minds in the modern world, that his thought is staggeringly comprehensive and consistent, that his insight was profound, his mood exalted, and his usefulness to critics unlimited. But surely all this profits a poet nothing if he does not preserve the hieratic decorum of conventional poetic utterance. And how are we to evaluate an utterance which is now lucid epigram and now a mere clashing of symbols, now disciplined and lovely verse and now a rush of prosy gabble? Whatever it is, is it really poetry or really great and good poetry? Well, probably not, in terms of what criticism now knows, or thinks it knows, about the canons of beauty and the form of literary expression.

Othello was merely a bloody farce in terms of what the learned and acute Thomas Rymer knew about drama. Rymer was perfectly right in his own terms; he is like the people who say that Blake was mad. One cannot refute them; one merely loses interest in their conception of sanity. And critics may be as right about Blake as Rymer was about Shakespeare, and still be just as wrong. We do not yet know whether literature and criticism are forms or aggregates: we know almost nothing about archetypes or about any of the great critical problems connected with them. In Dante's day critics did know something about the symbols of the Bible, but we have made little effort to recover that knowledge. We do not know very much even about genres: we do not know whether Blake's "prophecy" form is a real genre or not, and we certainly do not know how to treat it if it is. I leave the question of Blake's language in more competent hands, but after all, even the poets are only beginning to assimilate contemporary speech, and when the speech of *Jerusalem* becomes so blunt and colloquial that Blake himself calls it prosaic, do critics really know whether it is too prosaic to be poetic, or even whether such an antithesis exists at all? I may be speaking only of myself, for criticism today is full of confident value-judgments, on Blake and on everyone else, implying a complete understanding of all such mysteries. But I wonder if these are really critical judgments, or if they are merely the aberrations of the history of taste. I suspect that a long course of patient and detailed study lies ahead of us before we really know much about the critical problems which the study of Blake raises, and which have to be reckoned with in making any value-judgment on him. Then we shall understand the poets, including Blake, much better, and I am not concerned with what the results of that better understanding will be.

David V. Erdman

Blake: The Historical Approach

"I HAVE imposed on myself . . . grossly," wrote a schemer who had tried to impose on Blake but had mistaken his man, "I have imposed on myself . . . grossly in believing you to be one altogether abstracted from this world, holding converse with the world of spirits!" The miracle is common, but it is not exactly gross.

Blake himself encouraged it. "My abstract folly hurries me often away while I am at work," he told Thomas Butts, the muster clerk who bought his paintings, "carrying me over Mountains & Valleys, which are not Real, in a Land of Abstraction where Spectres of the Dead wander." A more straightforward person, or Blake in a more forthright record, might have said: I find it difficult to keep busy at this miniature portrait of Mrs. Butts,[1] because my mind wanders to the battlefield where men are dying, and then I see in my mind's eye the spirits of the contending powers.

We do not impose on ourselves if we believe that Blake held converse with the world of spirits, but we do if we think of either the poet or his spirits as "altogether abstracted from this world." As an observer of his own introspection, Blake understood the process of abstraction better than that; he knew that "it is impossible to think without images of somewhat [something] on this earth." At the age of twenty-six he saw Lunardi's first English demonstration

of lighter-than-air craft (unless he was one of the few hapless Londoners who did not come out of their houses that day), and he knew that balloon navigators take some earth with them for ballast. When Blake soared, he did not expect to escape from the world of Bacon and Newton and Pitt, but to change its laws of gravity: "I . . . with my whole might chain my feet to the world of Duty & Reality," he explained; "but . . . the faster I bind, the better is the Ballast, for I, so far from being bound down, take the world with me in my flights."

We now understand this about Blake, in the sense that we recognize that he kept his sanity in spite of what he called "Nervous Fear" at the terrors of the times he lived in. "Fires inwrap the earthly globe," he wrote in 1793, "yet man is not consum'd." We may also understand it as a clue to his meaning, in the sense that Blake always kept his visions oriented in time and space, always knew where the sun was rising and what his horizons were. A person who wanted to escape the world altogether would not bother about horizons. But Blake never expected to get rid of his Urizen; he hoped only to teach him to be elastic and responsive as "the bound or outward circumference of Energy"—he hoped only to change Urizen from a workmaster to a schoolmaster who would recognize his own limitations and never bind fast the infant "joys & desires." Blake did not like the *status quo*, but he loved England's green and pleasant land. He did not

[1] To be exact, Blake was occupied with other work for Butts when he wrote this letter; the miniature of Mrs. Butts was his chore the following year.

From *English Institute Essays: 1950*, ed. Alan S. Downer (New York, Columbia University Press, 1951), pp. 197–223. Reprinted, with a few revisions by the author, by permission of the author and the publisher.

like the "turrets & towers & domes Whose smoke destroy'd the pleasant gardens, & whose running kennels Chok'd the bright rivers"; but his program was reconstruction, not emigration; he welcomed the "golden Builders" who were expanding London's suburbs. He stood "in London's darkness" when he wrote "of the building of Golgonooza, & of the terrors of Entuthon."

I heard in Lambeth's shades.
In Felpham I heard and saw the Visions of Albion.
I write in South Molton Street what I both see and hear
In regions of Humanity, in London's opening streets.

To William Blake, Time and Space were "Real Beings," and history was a very real, if "emblematic," texture.

II

The aim of the historical approach is to approximate Blake's own perspective, to locate, as nearly as we can, the moment and place in which he stood, to discover what he saw and heard in London's streets —what loomed on the horizon and what sounds filled the air.

The value of doing this for Blake's lyric poems may be open to question. For example, the "London" of Songs of Experience is a successful general symbol. In the lines

In every voice, in every ban,
The mind-forg'd manacles I hear,

everyone will agree that the phrase "mindforg'd manacles" is an improvement in many ways over the rejected earlier wording, "german forgèd links." And since we can do pretty well with the poem in contexts of our own manufacture or out of our own experience, some people will doubt the value of pursuing the clue of the rejected reading, "german forgèd," to discover that when Blake wrote the poem there was alarm among freeborn Englishmen that German George, the King of England, might be preparing to bring in "subsidized Hessians and Hanoverians" "to cut the throats of Englishmen," by way of following up the reiterated royal "ban" or Proclamation against Seditious Writings, the intent of which was to put manacles on such men as Paine and Blake.[2] Nevertheless, the poem does gain poignancy when read as a cry of anguish from a city in the toils of antijacobinism. And our footnote does at least discourage the assumption that Blake meant to say that the victims of tyranny are victims simply of manacles forged in their own minds. We see that he was writing about thought control as well as controlled thoughts.

Again, "The Tyger" is everyone's private possession and an inexhaustible general symbol. Yet it is possible for us to enlarge our view of its cosmic blacksmithery by considering those points at which the images of "The Tyger" touch the images of Blake's French Revolution and The Four Zoas. In a synoptic vision of the defeat of royal armies, as at Yorktown and at Valmy, Blake says "the stars threw down their spears." At the climax of "The Tyger" he uses the same words. We can at least observe, if we wisely hesitate to draw conclusions, that Blake speaks of the vindication of the American and French revolutions in the same terms that he uses to suggest the vindication of the creation of the tiger.

In short, the Songs of Experience are well-nigh perfect crystals in themselves, and yet as critics of their essential force and brilliance—and of course as literary historians—we gain by knowing that they were created in the Year One of Equality, in the time of the birth of the French Re-

2 F. W. Bateson (Selected Poems of William Blake [London 1957], p. 127) reads: "In every execration or curse (not in every prohibition)." But this is to rely on a meaning for which the O.E.D. depends rather heavily on its reading of this line in Blake. Blake may be punning on two meanings of "ban" but the context of forged manacles suggests the meaning (literal and figurative) of governmental or ecclesiastical proclamation or prohibitory edict, illustrated in O.E.D. from Paradise Lost and Coleridge's Friend and Burke (in 1790 against Paine).

public and the London Corresponding Society.

The value of applying historical research to the avowedly prophetic and manifestly historical writings, on the other hand, should be beyond question. Yet not merely the difficulty of the task, but the sophisticated tradition through which Blake has come to us and which still directs our attention largely another way, have thus far prevented its being attempted in any thorough fashion.

Consider how the neglect of historical particulars impedes the progress of Professors Sloss and Wallis, the almost indefatigable editors of *William Blake's Prophetic Writings,* in their pursuit of the wandering Zoas. On the assumption that history and Blake's kind of "prophecy" are unrelated, they omit his *French Revolution* from their canon and with it many a passage that could shed light on later symbols. And when, in Blake's "long resounding, strong heroic verse," they come upon remarks about "War on the Rhine & Danube," they note in passing that Blake may be referring to the Napoleonic Wars. But these editors treat the wars of Urizen and Luvah as altogether abstract, for they have snipped off the clue thread that the poet provided when he said "Luvah is France" and they have neglected the trail that leads back from Urizen to George the Third, via the canceled plates of *America.* For example, at one point in *The Four Zoas,* near the end of Night I, aggressive Urizen, after having brooded "Eternal death to Luvah" and threatened a long war, suddenly reverses his field:

But Urizen, with darkness overspreading all the armies,
Sent round his heralds, secretly commanding to depart
Into the north. Sudden, with thunder's sound, his multitudes
Retreat from the fierce conflict . . .
Mustering together in thick clouds, leaving the rage of Luvah
To pour its fury on himself & on the Eternal Man.

"Points like this which do not explain themselves," say the editors, "can receive no light from without." I am afraid we must apply to the editors themselves, as well as to Urizen's armies, the lines which immediately follow: "Sudden down fell they all together into an unknown Space, Deep, horrible, without End."

This can happen to any of us on our way through *The Four Zoas,* and I do not mean to sound lofty. But the historical approach tells us that Night I contains a survey of the diplomatic and military relations between Britain and France up through 1799 and that at this point we have come to Britain's ill-fated Netherlands campaign, during which 36,000 men marched out and 20,000 marched back very precipitately, after fierce conflict, leaving the rage of Luvah or Napoleon to vent its fury on himself and on humanity ("the Eternal Man"). Napoleon was in a mood to do so, because he had just come through his coup of 18th Brumaire, which is described by Blake as a transformation of form from human to reptilian.[3]

I do not mean to imply that everything comes clear with the application of a little current history. In Blake's writings, as he has warned us, "there are many angles," and even the historical angle is never constant. The bard prefers to "walk up & down in 6,000 years," transposing furiously, translating the acts of Robespierre into those of Moses or abstracting the British heroes into their spiritual forms or telescoping together the Biblical and modern rebellions of slaves against Pharaohs in "dark Africa."

Sometimes we can understand a good deal of Blake's argument without paying much attention to his historical referents

[3] According to Linnell, by the way, Blake had an explanation from "some public man—ambassador, or something of the sort, that the Bonaparte of Italy was killed, and that another was somehow substituted from the exigent want of the name, who was the Bonaparte of the Empire." Gilchrist, p. 327. It is not clear whether Linnell or some other friend of Blake is being quoted.

or even being aware of them. A great deal of Blake criticism, some of it very valuable in literary and philosophical insight, gets along famously in the swirling vortex of Blake's oratory without attending to what, in the narrowest literal sense, he is talking about, or, to put the matter another way, without asking just precisely which historical persons or events have appeared to Blake as manifestations of eternal archetypes. The increasing interest in Blake's social thought, however, and in his excitement about the industrial revolution which did—and the social revolution which did not—take place while he was writing, now makes imperative the clearest possible definition of his minute particulars, especially of the dates and contexts of those works in which he deals with the history of his own times.

We speak loosely of all Blake's difficult works as "prophetic," yet in so figurative a sense that it is not customary to look for any literal message for the times—even in those two poems he himself called prophecies: *America, a Prophecy, 1793*, and *Europe, a Prophecy, 1794*. Yet Blake defined the nature of prophecy quite literally as an honest man's warning that "if you go on So, the result is So." And the warning of *America* is plain enough: that if kings such as Albion's Prince repeat against the Republic of France, in 1793, the crusade that failed against the Republic of America, they will reach the end of their rule over the people, who are "the strong."

The warning of *Europe*, in 1794, is more veiled and less specific in its prediction. But in its own language it is directed to Pitt and Parliament. It traces the steps leading to Britain's declaration of war in February, 1793, and describes the effect of the "gagging acts" of the following year. And its warning is that the trumpet of British power has marked the end of all royal power, for the war now raging is Armageddon, and the bloody sun now rising in France is the light of Christ's Second Com-

ing. The peaceful child of 1789 seemed easy to wrap in swaddling clothes, but the "terrible Orc" of the embattled Republic will brook no counterrevolutionary attempt to crucify him. "The bloodthirsty people across the water," as Blake put it crudely in his notebook, "Will not submit to gibbet & halter."

If this interpretation can be demonstrated (and I believe that my chapter which does so is pretty securely based), how is it possible that with only one exception that I know of (Jacob Bronowski) critics have mistaken the obviously historical part of *Europe, a Prophecy* for a summary of events leading up to the French Revolution of 1789, a matter scarcely prophetic in any immediate sense? The answer is partly that even Mr. Schorer, with all his interest in the social theme, has been so busy dispelling the fogs of mysticism around Blake that he has left it to those who follow to explore the cleared ground. A more implicit difficulty is the fog in Blake's style itself. Nowhere is his private nomenclature more puzzling than in *Europe*; nowhere is there more sly shifting from one level of discourse to another, more difficulty with ambiguities of punctuation and sudden changes of pace. Yet once we have separated the central narrative (lines 60–150 and 198–206) from the surrounding mythological framework (which reaches from the morning of Christ's Nativity to the day of his Second Coming) we are dealing with an orderly sequence of events which can be fitted into the calendar of secular history as soon as we can date some of the minute particulars.

An example will illustrate the sort of detective work that can be done and that flows logically from the recognition that Blake's prophecy really deals with current events—and from an awareness that Blake, in dealing with current politics, is not altogether apart from the main stream of eighteenth-century political satire. Miss Miles has discovered a major source of Blake's language in the language of social satire.[4] In a recent note in *The Art Quarterly* (Spring, 1949) I have called attention to Blake's use of themes in the political caricatures of James Gillray. In the text of *Europe* Blake describes a groveling "Guardian of the secret codes" in flight from Westminster Hall or the Houses of Parliament. He does not draw a picture of the incident, but in Gillray's caricatures there are two, "The Fall of the Wolsey of the Woolsack" and "Sin, Death and the Devil," published in May and June, 1792, which is acceptable as the year "before the trumpet blew" if we take the trumpet as Pitt's declaration of war against France. Both prints commemorate Pitt's ousting from his cabinet of the Lord High Chancellor Thurlow, Keeper of the Seal and Guardian of the King's Conscience. In the second print, which is a parody of Fuseli and of Milton, Thurlow is the Devil, Pitt is Death, and the Queen (for Pitt was a Queen's man at the time) is Sin, carrying the key to the backstairs and all our woe.[5]

Pitt, who had been trying to rid himself of the formidable Thurlow for some time, found his opportunity when the chancellor ridiculed Pitt's Sinking Fund Bill as the work of "a mere reptile of a minister" and told Parliament that no bill should attempt to bind future governments. The grain of sedition in this remark must have seemed infinitesimal even in 1792. But Pitt, counting on his own indispensability at a time when he had filled the royal mind with constitutional alarm, asked the king to dismiss his Guardian, and the king obliged.

Blake treats the episode as a sign that the revolutionary world crisis has singed even the great Guardian of British law:

---

[4] See Josephine Miles, "The Language of William Blake," *English Institute Essays: 1950*, pp. 141–169. Revised as Chapter 5 of *Eras & Modes in English Poetry* (Berkeley and Los Angeles, 1957).
[5] Here, too, is a key to Blake's emphasis in *Europe* on the cruelty of queens, pre-eminently the cruelty of the Queen of Heaven, who desires "That Woman, lovely Woman, may have dominion" through the code of "Sin," and who regards Rintrah (Pitt) as her knight-errant.

Above the rest the howl was heard from Westminster louder & louder;
The Guardian of the secret codes forsook his ancient mansion,
Driven out by the flames of Orc; his furr'd robes & false locks
Adhered and grew one with his flesh, and nerves & veins shot thro' them.
With dismal torment sick, hanging upon the wind, he fled
Groveling along Great George Street thro' the Park gate: all the soldiers
Fled from his sight: he drag'd his torments to the wilderness.

The "howl . . . louder & louder" of the judge driven out by the flames of rebellion may echo the "Irregular Ode" in the *Rolliad*, in which Thurlow on an earlier occasion is depicted as warning "every rebel soul" to tremble, as he grows "profane" with a "louder yet, and yet a louder strain."

Blake's particulars are unambiguous. The street that led from Westminster Hall, the mansion of the law, to St. James's Park was Great George Street. Blake's description of the chancellor in his dismal torment is as informed as the account in Thurlow's standard biography, where we read of his drive through the park to St. James's Palace to surrender the Seal, his dejection as "a solitary outcast," and his "diminished consequence" when seen "without his robes, without his great wig." There is no mistaking Blake's allusion to this unique event. In the whole span of time his poem might conceivably allude to, the only ermined justice driven out of Westminster was Baron Thurlow. Sloss and Wallis, it is true, conjectured that "this passage may be a reference to the London riots of . . . 1780, when the mob . . . burned Lord Mansfield's house." But this was poor guesswork. A simple check discloses that Mansfield's house was nowhere near Westminster or Great George Street or any park and that none of the fires of 1780 was in Westminster. This guess, missing the date by twelve years, demonstrates both the haphazard nature of Blake research when it has been a matter of seeking him in the material world and the sort of misleading commentary that still hedges Blake's historical clues from sight.

Much more is at stake, of course, than the right reading of a few historical allusions. Only when the central historical theme of *Europe* is cleared of misconceptions can we bring into focus the symbolism of the "Preludium" and of the mythological framework that encloses the central narrative, and only then can we see and properly appreciate the subtle use of Miltonic allusions there—and the architectural brilliance of the whole poem. But these are not matters for a hasty exposition.

In my book [*Blake: Prophet Against Empire* (Princeton, 1954)] I show that a similar bringing into focus is possible for Blake's three epics, *The Four Zoas, Milton,* and *Jerusalem,* although these are not dated prophecies of the same sort as *America* and *Europe.*

III

I have been dwelling on the importance of the historical approach, and thus far my examples have been largely in the category of "light from without." For the rest of my time I want to talk about a method of reading Blake's "Visionary or Imaginative" language for clues or "Ulro Visions" which he himself supplies—for visions, that is, of the ultimate material starting-points of his visions. This method may be described as the reduction of Blake's fourfold vision to single vision. This is what I do when I say Rintrah "is" William Pitt, or Albion "is" the people of England. It is what Blake does when he says, "Luvah is France." So long as we recognize that we are dealing with only one side of Blake's fourfold, it is legitimate to do this—especially since the other sides are incomplete without this one, which is the ballast that keeps his balloon navigable.

I am well aware that Blake, in his impatience with people who would see only with the eye and attend only to the ballast and not the flight, asserted "for My Self that I

do not behold the outward Creation & that to me it is hindrance . . . it is as the dirt upon my feet." But to a detective or "Watch Fiend" like the historical scholar, the dirt upon Blake's feet is a good clue: it tells us where he has been walking. (Most of it upon Blake's feet is that gray clay known locally as "London stone.") You are familiar with the rest of the passage:

"When the Sun rises, do you not see a round disk of fire somewhat like a Guinea?" O no, no, I see an Innumerable company of the heavenly host crying, "Holy, Holy, Holy is the Lord God Almighty!" I question not my Corporeal . . . Eye. . . . I look thro' it & not with it.

Read backward, as I am suggesting for purposes of orientation, Blake's vision of an innumerable company singing Holy Holy "is" a sunrise.

When Blake writes to Flaxman, "The kingdoms of this World are now become the Kingdoms of God & His Christ, & we shall reign with him for ever & ever. The reign of Literature & the Arts commences," he is responding to rumors of peace between the kingdoms of France and Britain *just as he responded to the sunrise* (I quote a letter of October, 1801, but he used almost the same language at similar news a year earlier). Toward the end of the same letter he states more simply the hope "that France & England will henceforth be as One Country and their Arts One" and that he can soon go to Paris "to see the Great Works of Art." This simple and profound hope underlies much of the yearning in Blake's prophecies for an end to "the war of swords" or "corporeal war" and a commencement of the time of "intellectual war" when "sweet Science reigns." We impose on ourselves—yes, grossly—if we neglect the connection here between vision and history.

My point about method is that we can often work back from vision to starting-point if we but grant that the vision has a starting-point, is a vision "of" something. To Dr. Trusler, who told Blake "Your

Fancy . . . seems to be in the other world, or the World of Spirits," Blake retorted: "I see Every thing I paint In This World, but Everybody does not see alike." Sometimes Blake's way of seeing what he paints is curiously close to the ways of Erasmus Darwin.

Fuseli, introducing Blake's designs to an orthodox audience, called attention to a quality of "taste, simplicity, and elegance" in Blake's "wildness." Miss Miles tells us that the major materials of Blake's language are those of mid-eighteenth-century poetry. And she makes the salutary observation that many of Blake's language habits which may have seemed unique are properly defined as *extensions* of eighteenth-century practice. With regard to some of the obscurities of Blake's figurative language, I suggest that they will often yield up their literal meanings when we approach them as the product of an exuberant *extension* of eighteenth-century practice in ornamental periphrasis, or Poetic Diction.

Blake enjoyed referring, in a letter, to his wife's ocean bathing as "courting Neptune for an Embrace." In his poems he liked to refer to the ear as "the Gate of the Tongue." And he liked to take away the scaffolding of his conceit, too: he crossed out manuscript readings which made it clear that by the tongue's gate he meant the "auricular nerves." The gate of my tongue is your ear, your "auricular nerves," ultimately your reason; it is not simply what my nerves do that make my speech incoherent, but the effect of the closing up of your inlets of soul. Urizen is your reason, not mine. In *The Four Zoas* a kind of Della Cruscan periphrasis is used in descriptions of battle. An iron gun is a "black bow" which shoots "darts of hail" or "arrows black." A smoking gun is a "cloudy bow." A cavalry charge under cover of artillery fire comes out like this: "Spur, spur your clouds Of death! . . . Now give the charge! bravely obscur'd With darts of wintry hail! Again the black bow draw!"

The one who fires the first shot is the one who doth "first the black bow draw." When a Zoa and his Emanation are separated by the mischance of war, they do not say, "Farewell for the duration," but "Return, O Wanderer, when the day of Clouds is o'er."

In Blake's day the newspapers still referred to British soldiers as "the sons of Albion," and so does Blake. Often the Sons and Daughters of Albion represent the various institutions and vocations of English men and women. When the Daughters are at their "Needlework" they represent the textile trades. They strip wool ("Jerusalem's curtains") from sheep ("mild demons of the hills"), and the cellars and garrets where they work are "the dungeons of Babylon." When Blake walks about London "among Albion's rocks & precipices" and looks into Albion's "caves of solitude & dark despair," he is walking through the narrow cobbled streets and looking into dark shops and tiny hovels—"the caves of despair & death" in "the interiors of Albion's Bosom." In the neoclassical tradition employed by Darwin, labor is done by gnomes and nymphs. In Blake it is done by demons and spectres. When young men and women enter apprentice slavery or the army, they are "taking the spectral form." Blake the journeyman engraver is the "spectre" of Blake the poet.

For a concentrated exercise in this materialistic method of reading Blake's "emblematic texture," let us study some of the passages in which Blake is looking at himself at work, engraving or etching on polished copper plates with engraving tools or with varnish and nitric acid (aqua fortis). Here the material referents are palpable, and the differences between matter and manner stand out plain.

Blake's best known reference to the etching process, which he employed in all his "Illuminated Printing," is found in *The Marriage of Heaven & Hell.*

On the abyss of the five senses, where a flat sided steep frowns over the present world, I saw a mighty Devil folded in black clouds, hovering on the sides of the rock. With corroding fires he wrote the following sentence now perceived by the minds of men, & read by them on earth.

The abyss into which Blake is looking is the mirrorlike surface of his copper plate. When he focuses on the surface itself, he sees a flat sided rock. When he looks into the mirror world and orients toward *that* as real, then the "present world" is beneath it, and the flat surface is a steep cliff overhanging the present world. The mighty Devil folded in black clouds and hovering on the sides of the rock is the mirror image of Blake in his black suit pouring aqua fortis ("corroding fires") onto the copper to destroy the abyss except where he has written with impermeable ink or varnish.[6] His sentence, appearing on the plate in reverse, is only perceived by the minds of men when it is printed and reversed back from the abysmal state. The relationship between the mirror image and the direct image symbolizes the relationship between the vision conveyed to "minds" and the physical sentence on the copper. Thus a full understanding of this passage depends on—or begins with—our visualizing the rudiments of the process: once we "see" that, we can proceed to explore the further connotations of "the abyss of the five senses." [7]

For the process of line engraving we may turn to *The Four Zoas*, where we will find a Spectre who "drave his solid rocks before Upon the tide." The tide is the pond-like surface of the plate, upon which the engraving Spectre lodges the bits of copper gouged out by the graver as he pushes it forward with his hand—driving "his solid rocks before Upon the tide."

Here again is the abyss which is not an abyss, the apparently solid surface which opens to infinite meaning—represented by an apparently non-solid tide or abyss which supports rocks or a rock.

The pushing of the graver (or etching needle) makes channels for the ink, and since these channels are technically called furrows, the most obvious metaphor is that of plowing. The complaint that the poet's children have been "plow'd and harrow'd" for another's profit is a complaint that Blake's drawings have been engraved (and etched) by Schiavonetti for his profit.[8] All the plowing mentioned in the prophetic works is not engraving, of course. But sometimes even the direct description of agriculture contains an implied comparison to the poet's own manner of earning his bread.

Wisdom is sold in the desolate market where none come to buy,
And in the wither'd field where the farmer plows for bread in vain.

Blake had English famine years in mind when he wrote this. But he had also recently plowed for bread in vain, metaphorically, in the sense that he had engraved forty-three plates for an edition of Young's *Night Thoughts* which none had come to buy.

But let us turn to a passage where the focus is, both literally and metaphorically, on the plowing which is engraving. Here the "weeping" of "clods" in "the plowed furrow" suggests that Blake, like his fellow craftsmen, is resorting to "the engraver's best auxiliary, aquafortis," [9] which makes

---

[6] In conventional intaglio etching the plate would be covered with a blackened ground, but for his relief etching Blake worked directly on the polished surface.

[7] I say the rudiments of the process. Notice that Blake keeps secret his actual method of getting words onto the plate. [See Ruthven Todd, "The Techniques of Blake's Illuminated Printing," *Print* (1948).—Ed.]

[8] Schiavonetti's "etchings" for *The Grave* combined intaglio etching and engraving, while much "line engraving," including Blake's journeywork, employed intaglio etching for foliage and background.

[9] Some people "imagine that the curves, lines, hatchings . . . in a line engraving are produced by a slow and laborious operation . . . but the hard manual work involved in the production of the furrows or ditches in the metal, has been almost entirely superseded, since the days of Albert Dürer . . . by the use of the engraver's best auxiliary, aquafortis." Andrew Tuer, *Bartolozzi and His Works*, I, 80.

the bits of copper dissolve. And the "many" who speak are, according to the context, the multiple eyes of God, that is, of Blake's imagination. "Many conversed on these things as they labour'd at the furrows," says Blake, meaning that many ideas occurred to him as his eyes and imagination attended to the lines he was engraving.

The passage I have begun to quote, *Jerusalem 55*, contains another reminder that these material aspects of Blake's meaning are but the dirt on his feet, or, as he puts it here, but

> as the moss upon the tree, or *dust upon the plow,*
> Or as the sweat upon the labouring shoulder, or as the chaff
> Of the wheat-floor or as the dregs of the sweet wine-press.
> Such are these Ulro Visions: for tho' we sit down

—"we" are the Eyes speaking about themselves, "the Human Organs" who can at will contract "into Worms or Expand . . . into Gods,"—

> for tho' we sit down within
> The plowed furrow, list'ning to the weeping clods till we
> Contract or Expand Space at will; or if we raise ourselves
> Upon the chariots of the morning, Contracting or Expanding Time,
> Every one knows, we are One Family, One Man blessed for ever.

Blake is speaking about the unity of life in the Imagination which denies the limitations and divisions accepted by the eyes that see only matter. But our concern at the moment is with the dust and the sweat. What the eyes say is this: We may focus on the furrow being engraved, until we look through that and see a world in a grain of copper; or we may look out the window and in imagination follow the sun ("raise ourselves Upon the chariots of the morning") until we see past, present, and future Time. In that way we see the unity of all space and all time.

Through the wrong end of the telescope

we (I mean you and I, now) can see William Blake, sweating at "the meer drudgery" of engraving, and accomplishing "not one half of what I intend, because my Abstract folly hurries me often away while I am at work."

The difference between engraving and relief etching, we must understand, represented the difference between the hack work Blake had to do for a living and the prophetic work he did "to lay up treasures in heaven" and as a soldier of the imagination. His Spectre did most of the plowing and could boast that his labor was necessary to put a world "underneath the feet of Los" and bring a smile of hope to "his dolorous shadow" of a wife. Many a time, declared the surly Spectre, his engraving kept them all from "rotting upon the Rocks" and put "spungy marrow" into the prophet's "splinter'd bones." Yet Blake longed to rise above the "meer drudgery" of engraving, longed to escape this Spectre's power and cast him "into the Lake," perhaps into the very tide upon which he drave his solid rocks.

The writing and etching of his own poems, on the other hand, was done by Los, bard and prophet, "without Fatigue." With corrosive fires he burnt apparent surfaces away to reveal the "eternal lineaments" of truth.[10] Or he would "pour aqua fortis on the Name of the Wicked & turn it into an Ornament & an Example." Or, in his favorite imagery, he would forge "under his heavy hand the hours, The days & years" of Tyranny, and thus bind the wicked "in chains of iron."

This shift of image from etcher to blacksmith, from worker with acid on copper to worker with iron and steel in fire, was

---

[10] I suppose we may look upon Blake's reading of the Bible in the infernal sense as a heretical blossom of that medieval exegetical tradition according to which, as Mr. Robertson has pointed out, the aim of the wise man is to cut away the *cortex or integumentum* and reveal the nucleus of inner meaning. The tradition reaches Blake, of course, by way of the Protestant mystics and euhemerist antiquaries.

essential for the connotations of cosmic bardic power. In "The Tyger" Blake could scarcely have written: What the hand dare seize the acid-bottle? An engraver's shop did have a small anvil for leveling, and a hand-bellows for drying, copper plates. But the blacksmith's mighty hammer, anvil, tongs, chain, and furnaces of intellectual war were far more effectual equipment for a bard in competition with the dark Satanic mills which were producing "ramm'd combustibles" and "molten metals cast in hollow globes, & bored Tubes in petrific steel" (Wilkinson's new process for making cannon barrels was to bore them from solid cast steel). There was also the emotional identification with the working artisan rather than with the more isolated intellectual worker, who might talk about books and pen and paper. Los, as blacksmith, could quite legitimately "wipe the sweat from his red brow." Ultimately Blake pictured him as assisted by a thousand laboring sons, because Blake knew that a multitude of furnaces and fellow laborers, a whole intellectual movement, would be needed to build the new Jerusalem, when free men, "Young Men of the New Age," inherited "the Ruin'd Furnaces of Urizen."

Another strong symbol of effective energy is the printing press, especially in its apocalyptic analogue, the human wine press "call'd War on Earth." The figure of the printer, however, does not compare in power to that of the blacksmith. In the preface to *Jerusalem* Blake prays in humble fashion that his own "types" shall not be "vain." But only once, in *Milton*, is the press of Los specifically called a "Printing-Press," and even there our attention is quickly shifted to a fiercer image. As the poet "lays his words in order above the mortal brain," his types are compared to the steel teeth of a cogwheel which "turn the cogs of the adverse wheel."

At one point in *Jerusalem* Blake does speak of the publication of paper books, when he refers to the pages of a pamphlet against war as "leaves of the Tree of Life." But here he is referring, not to his own fire-seared labors, which he expects to have read only by "future generations," but to the milder and more ephemeral publications of men "scarcely articulate."

In the passage I refer to (*Jerusalem* 45–46), a considerable speech or sermon by someone called "Bath" is spoken of as a sheaf of pages and handed to someone called "Oxford, immortal Bard" with a request that Oxford write an introduction to the public—or so I interpret the following: "Oxford, take thou these leaves of the Tree of Life; with eloquence That thy immortal tongue inspires, present them to Albion: Perhaps he may receive them, offer'd from thy loved hands." Here is a pretty concrete situation, and it ought certainly to yield up its literal meaning to an assiduous Watch Fiend. Both prongs of our historical method must be employed. On the one hand we must establish the historical context of *Jerusalem* by pinning down various kinds of internal evidence. This I have done fairly thoroughly and have found that *Jerusalem* deals with the latter phase of the Napoleonic wars and that the poem's central prophetic theme is a plea to Albion and his Sons not to pursue the war with France to mutual ruin or to make a vengeful peace that would destroy the freedom and national brotherhood of the two nations. On the eve of Waterloo the latter probability weighs on Blake's mind: "What can I do to hinder the Sons of Albion from taking vengeance? or how shall I them perswade?" In the earlier speech by Bath, he fears for Albion's own destruction.

We must on the other hand examine Blake's hyperbole to see what kind of literal statement the eloquence of Bath and Oxford can be reduced to. Translated into ordinary language, Bath's speech is an anti-war tract addressed to the people of England ("O Albion") alluding to the abolition of the slave trade, a Parliamentary measure enacted in 1807, and inveighing against imperial selfhood or British national pride: "however high Our palaces and cities and however fruitful are our fields, In Selfhood we are nothing." The remark that Bath speaks "in midst of Poetic Fervor" suggests that the author of the tract has been currently engaged in writing verse, and the statement that Bath is one who "first assimilated with Luvah in Albion's mountains" means, within the framework of date and theme established for *Jerusalem,* that he was one of the first British intellectuals to preach peace with France in the present period, that is, since the renewal of war in 1803.

Armed with these clues, my assistant, Martin Nurmi, soon found the preacher-poet of Bath by looking into a bibliography of works written in that city. In 1808, shortly after the passage of the Abolition Bill, the Reverend Richard Warner published *A Letter to the People of England: on Petitioning the Throne for the Restoration of Peace.* In the same year he published such evidence of "Poetic Fervor" as *Bath Characters* and *Rebellion in Bath, an Heroico-Odico-Tragico-Comico Poem.* As for Warner's being one who "first assimilated with Luvah," in 1804 he startled Bath and London with the publication of a fast-day sermon entitled *War Inconsistent with Christianity,* which advocated that Englishmen refuse to bear arms even in case of an invasion by Napoleon. Reviewed widely and heatedly, Warner's sermon went into four editions within a few months and continued to be reissued throughout the war. In *Bath Characters* Warner caricatures himself thus:

> Dick preaches foul DEMOCRACY;
> And forces luckless loyal sinners,
> To hear his rant, and spoil their dinners

—or so his foes say. But "On the *broad basis*" he'll rely "Of GENUINE CHRISTIANITY."

"Stripped of its Oriental dress," says Warner in his Fast Sermon, "the declaration of CHRIST may fairly be taken as a direct and unequivocal reprehension of hostile violence, both in individuals and states." "However brilliant the successes are with which their arms shall be crowned; whatever acquisitions of territory conquest may unite to their ancient empire . . . WAR is the GREATEST CURSE with which a nation can be afflicted, and . . . all its imaginary present advantages, or future contingent benefits, are but as 'dust in the balance,' and as 'chaff before the wind.'" Warner's sentiments are undoubtedly those of Blake's "voice of Bath."

In his 1808 *Letter to the People* Warner's alarm that the "national spirit . . . is graduating into a spirit of lawless ambition, and aggressive violence" parallels Bath's concern lest Albion should "slay Jerusalem in his fearful jealousy," and on the other hand his warning, "Be *expeditious* . . . lest the concluding scene of the war be performed upon your own shores; lest [Britain's] peaceful plains exhibit those horrors which the nations of the continent have so long and so largely experienced," suggests the tenor of Bath's urgency: "his [Albion's] death is coming apace . . . for alas, we none can know How soon his lot [the lot of Jesus or of Luvah-France] may be our own."

None of the Warner pamphlets I have seen discusses the slave trade, although in the *Letter* a passing reference to the "deliverers of Africa, the friends of the poor," may have been enough to prompt Bath's lines. Nor have I yet encountered—though I do not despair of doing so [11]—any of Warner's "leaves" with an introduction by an Oxford poet saying, "In mild perswasion," something like this:

> Thou art in Error, Albion, [in] the Land of Ulro. . . .
> Reason not on both sides. Repose upon our bosoms.

[11] I have still (in 1960) not found a pamphlet introduced by "Oxford"; perhaps Blake's friend "Edward, the bard of Oxford" was simply handing out copies of Warner's pamphlet with appropriate verbal comment.

Peter F. Fisher

Blake and the Druids

THE CONTEXT of Blake's treatment of Druidism was primarily his own particular vision of human history, but much of what he had to say was understandably connected with traditional sources and the theories of contemporary antiquarians. The theories of antiquarians such as Bryant, Davies, and Stukeley have received more attention, since they happen to be in the main stream of scholarly research, and the traditional sources a good deal less. Of these traditional sources, references in classical authors have been noticed, but practically nothing has been said about that large body of folklore containing the remains of Welsh bardism. No one could deny that this material was a mixture of ancient tradition and later additions, but this very fact would have attracted Blake, and may have moved him to add another 'moment' to the life of the bardic tradition with his "Welch Triades" at the beginning of his *Descriptive Catalogue of* 1809.[1] To establish the relationship between the traditional sources of Druidism and Blake's own use of the term in *Milton* and *Jerusalem* will involve considerable reference to some of the theories of the antiquarians, relevant statements in classical authors, and especially his conception of natural religion. For him history was the field of recurrent attempts to wake up human conscience, both individual and social. Each

attempt was a new vision finally reduced by the dead weight of self-interest and misunderstanding to some system of accepted beliefs with its conventional morality and its sacrificial rites. Bardic tradition provided him with an apt symbol of what history was about and also with a convenient foil for his gospel of vision.

Blake did not actually mention the immediate source of this interest in bardism, but some of the triads had been collected and translated by Edward Williams and were to be found as an appendix to a collection of his poems published in 1794. Williams called himself a "Bard according to the Rights and Institutes of the Bards of the Island of Britain," and claimed that his triads were translated from the Silurian or most ancient dialect.[2] The 'triad' itself was said to be the most common of all aphoristical forms used by the bards, since it was constructed on the basis of certain fixed and unalterable principles where the connections of its parts were related to one another simply and concisely. The form was evidently used for oral instruction in that lore which the Druids refused to commit to writing.[3] These particular triads

[1] H. N. Frye (*Fearful Symmetry* [Princeton, 1947], p. 173) refers to Blake's 'triads' as imitations or adaptations in the fashion of the day. They certainly are not to be found in Williams' collection at the back of his *Poems, Lyrical and Pastoral* (London, 1794, Vol. II).

[2] Williams, I, xx: "The Silurian differs in many particulars from the Biblical dialect of modern writers. To attempt an investigation of the true sense of the very obscure term *Abred* would have required a longer dissertation than I had room for; and probably, my abilities would have failed me."

[3] *Ibid.*, II, 225. Cf. Caesar, *De Bello Gallico*, VI, xiii. Caesar also noted that the institution (*disciplina*) was said to have originated in Britain. See *Jerusalem*, II, 27, Pref., where Blake calls Albion the "Parent of the Druids."

From *Journal of English and Germanic Philology*, LVIII (October 1959), 589–612. Reprinted by permission of the journal and the estate of the author.

were selected from a manuscript collection by Llewelyn Sion, a Bard of Glamorgan, about 1560. Of this particular manuscript, Williams claimed to have a transcript, and the original collection was said to have been made from various manuscripts of great antiquity. To such a collection as that of Williams, Blake probably referred in his *Descriptive Catalogue* when he wrote of having "in his hands poems of the highest antiquity." [4]

Blake's attitude toward Druidism was likely influenced and, in many ways, perhaps formed by such fragments and the commentaries on them. He first saw Druidism as the "Patriarchal Religion" which, in its completed cycle, exemplified every aspect of an inspired, prophetic faith, and later, of a degenerate cult. Part of this outlook was taken from the antiquarians who, like Bryant and Davies, emphasized the civilization and learning of the Ancient Britons and also an original unity of language, culture, and religion. [5]

There was understandably a great deal of accommodation to Christian belief in these traditions. The traditional chronology (*amseryddiaeth*) gave some support to antiquarian theory which was already trying to expand the scope of Genesis without actually contradicting it. Druidic chronology was divided into three main dispensations: from creation to the sixth century B.C. was the first; from the sixth century to the third century A.D., the second; and the third was the Christian. These contributions of Celtic enthusiasts and of the antiquarians confirmed Blake's conviction that all antiquities could be traced to one source—a prophetic and inspired faith.

The antiquities of every Nation under Heaven, is no less sacred than that of the Jews. They are the same thing, as Jacob Bryant and all antiquaries have proved . . . . All had originally

one language, and one religion: this was the religion of Jesus, the everlasting Gospel. Antiquity preaches the Gospel of Jesus. [6]

The kind of "Antiquity" to which Blake referred was a universal, "Druidic" antiquity where his own conception of genius and inspiration at first flourished and then suffered a decline.

Blake's identification of the original, universal culture with Druidism was supported by both Davies and Stukeley, but the traditional sources for it went back to bardic legends and classical authors. Davies cited Diogenes Laertius' opinion that the "philosophy of Greece originated in the Celtae." [7] Abaris, a priest of Apollo among the Druidic Hyperboreans, was said to have visited Pythagoras for the ostensible purpose of taking back to one of the northern temples the gold which he had collected. An actual exchange of doctrine was implied, and the most durable of the Greek philosophic schools whose founder had learned from Egyptian priests, Persian Magi, the Brahmans of India, and the initiates of Samothrace was also directly connected with British Druidism. The Pythagoreans

---

[6] *Ibid.*: "The British Antiquities are not in the Artist's hands; all his visionary contemplations, relating to his own country and its ancient glory, when it was, as it again shall be, the source of learning and inspiration." Milton (*Doctrine and Discipline of Divorce*, in *Works* [New York, 1932], III, 376) mentioned the Druids as those "by whom this Island was the Cathedrall of Philosophy to France."

[7] Edward Davies, *Celtic Researches* (London, 1804), p. 184. Cf. *Mythology and Rites of the British Druids* (London, 1809), sec. II, p. 123: "The mythology of the Britons was of a character somewhat more antique than that of the Greeks and Romans, as we find it in their best writers." Diogenes Laertius traced the beginnings of philosophy to related sources which included the Persian Magi, the Chaldeans, the Indian gymnosophists, and the Druids (*De Clarorum Philosophorum Vitis*, proemium). See also Pliny, *Historia Naturalis*, XVI, 95; XXIV, 62–63; XXIX, 12. Cf. Milton, *Areopagitica*, *Works* (Columbia ed.), IV, 339: "Writers of good antiquity, and ablest judgement have bin perswaded that ev'n the school of Pythagoras, and the Persian wisdom took beginning from the old Philosophy of this Island."

---

[4] Blake, No. V: *The Ancient Britons.*
[5] *Ibid.*: "The Britons (say historians) were naked civilized men, learned, studious, abstruse in thought and contemplation; naked, simple, plain in their acts and manners; wiser than after-ages."

emphasized this latter connection more than any of the others, for they said that Pythagoras himself was the incarnation of the Hyperborean Apollo, and inferred that the most Greek of Greek gods had originated in Britain. No wonder Blake called Greek philosophy "a remnant of Druidism." [8] Diodorus Siculus, out of Hecataeus and other sources, said that the Britons worshipped Apollo above all other gods, and that they had a special regard for the Greeks—particularly the Athenians and the Delians. Abaris was supposed to have renewed the ancient league of friendship with the Delians.

It is not surprising that these classical references to British Druidism were exploited to the full by the antiquarians who laboured with enthusiasm at the task of demonstrating Blake's own thesis: "All things Begin & End in Albion's Ancient Druid Rocky Shore." [9] That part of their work which included classical culture was buttressed by the evidence of ancient writers,

but the link with Hebraic tradition required more ingenuity. Stukeley did not hesitate to claim that the Druids came to Britain as a Phoenician colony as soon as Tyre was founded, during the life of Abraham. They brought with them the customs and beliefs of the patriarchal religion and even the technical details of sacred architecture.

I must prepare the reader for a right understanding of our Druid edifices, by informing him, that Stonehenge, and all other works of this nature in our island, are erected by the most ancient measure call'd a cubit, which we read of in the holy scripture and in ancient profane authors. I mean the same individual measure, call'd the Hebrew, Egyptian, Phoenician cubit; most probably deriv'd from Noah and Adam. 'Tis the same that the pyramids of Egypt and other of their works are projected upon; the same as that of Moses's tabernacle, Solomon's temple, &c., and we may reasonably pride ourselves in possessing these visible monuments of the old measure of the world.[10]

Davies went still further and quoted an ingenious friend of his who suggested that Menyw, the first man of the Druidic tradition, was identical with Menu (*Manu*) of the Indian *Veda*. He even extended the conjecture to include Minos, king of Crete, who became one of the judges at the court of Pluto whose worship by the Druids of Gaul Caesar noticed. Both Menu and Minos, however, were finally made to refer to the patriarch Noah.[11]

Blake made use of all this in much the same spirit as Dante made use of Thomistic philosophy and the astronomy of Ptolemy. If he had been a Greek, he would have

[8] *Jerusalem*, III, 52, Pref. The story of Abaris is first recorded by Herodotus (*Historiae*, IV, 36) ; other references are Porphyry's life of Pythagoras and Iamblichus (*De Pythagorica Vita*, xix, xxviii). Abaris was said to have travelled over the whole world, without food, carrying an arrow which he later showed Pythagoras. By means of this arrow, he claimed to have passed through inaccessible places and expelled pestilence from cities on the way. He lived in temples and was never seen to eat or drink. Davies (*Celtic Researches*, p. 183) connected the arrow with the wheat straw used by the Druids in the rites of Apollo and Diana, and also suggested that 'arrow' ($\delta \tau \sigma \tau o s$) was a play on the word 'think' (Ep. $\delta \tau \omega$), so that what Abaris really conveyed was his doctrine. Stukeley (*Abury* [London, 1743], pp. 96–97) even supposed the arrow to be some kind of instrument like a magnetic needle. See Diodorus Siculus, *Bibliotheca Historica*, II, 47. Finally, the encircling of the globe by Abaris could refer to the mystical journey of the soul around the Circle of Inchoätion (*abred*) before attaining the Circle of Felicity.

[9] *Jerusalem*, II, 27, Pref. *Milton*, I, 6, 25. The fact that Blake associated the "Religion of Jesus" with an original Druidism should surprise no one who has noticed Stukeley's title of 'patriarchal Christianity' for the larger theme of his work (*Abury*, pp. i–ii).

[10] William Stukeley, *Stonehenge* (London, 1740), p. 6. Cf. *A Descriptive Catalogue &c.*, No. V: *The Ancient Britons*: "Adam was a Druid, and Noah . . ."

[11] Davies also claimed that Arthur was one of the titles of Noah to whose deification he attributed the development of pagan myth (*Mythology and Rites of the British Druids*, sec. III, p. 187). Blake's association of Arthur with Albion could be traced to Davies, along with Atlas, who is called a Hyperborean (cf. Hesiod, *Theogony*, 736). For the connection between Menu, Minos, and Druidism, see sec. III, p. 197. See also Caesar, *De Bello Gallico*, VI, xviii.

found the navel of the world at Delphi. For one who was never tired of emphasizing that the journey to Eden started from the ground under one's feet, and that the most visionary perspective included the geography of one's own country, antiquarian theory provided accommodating material. It was clear that Bryant and Davies concentrated on the more favourable aspects of Druidic culture—aspects which Blake used to establish his account of the fall of man and the impact of prophetic inspiration on the subsequent history of man's fallen societies. An indication of the relationship Druidism bore to the elaboration of this original pattern was to be found in *A Descriptive Catalogue* (particularly Nos. IV and V) where Gray's bard, the last of the Druids, was placed beside a description of the last "Battle of King Arthur" (Albion) and the rout of his forces (disorganization of Albion's faculties, the "Zoas"). Here Blake was associating inspiration and the divine vision with Druidism. However, he later came to treat Druidism pejoratively— in the last two books of *Jerusalem*—as the degenerate effect of man's fallen historical destiny on original prophetic inspiration.[12] Druidism became the symbol of the outer husk of an earlier vision, and such a translation of the triads as that of Williams must have provided him with material for evaluating both husk and vision.

Williams himself was the zealous prophet of what he considered an expression of the true faith. He ridiculed Gray's *Bard* as an example of the literary confusion of a "savage Scandinavian Mythology" with British antiquities. The charge was obviously that of an enthusiastic purist who could see nothing but good in the Druidic tradition. It was perhaps because of this that he resented the appropriation of ancient British lore by the "Gothic" revival. However, the tradition had itself undergone various changes which made it difficult to decide how much of an authentic original was to be found in the synopsis of Llewelyn Sion in the first place. The selections which Williams chose gave no evidence of the interest noticed by classical writers in the theology of a pantheon of gods. Caesar, for instance, described the Druids as interested in disputes concerning the power of the gods, and added that they paid particular honours to Mercury whom they considered the inventor of all arts. After Mercury, he went on to say, they worshipped Apollo, Mars, Jupiter, and Minerva like other nations. Strabo, the geographer, cited the authority of Artemidorus that in "an island close to Britain," presumably Ireland, Ceres and Proserpine were venerated with rites similar to those of Samothrace.[13] By calling himself, on his title page, "Bard according to the Rights and Institutes of the Bards of the Island of Britain," Williams might be said to lose the objectivity of the editor, and become an apologist for the triads he was translating.

Along with the polemic of the apologist and the voice of the prophetic bard, he also mixed the ardor of the republican revolutionary—a combination which would not prove unappealing to Blake. He spoke of his intention of going to America to escape the injustice of laws which were not "made equally for the poor as for the rich."

[12] Cf. Frye, p. 175; Joseph Wicksteed, *William Blake's "Jerusalem"* (London, 1953), p. 57. This same ambivalent outlook (which is far from being equivocation) may be seen in his remarks on the antiquities of the Jews. On the one hand, he called the laws of the Jews "the basest & most oppressive of human codes" (*Annotations to Watson's "Apology for the Bible,"* p. 25), and on the other, spoke of the "Return of Israel" as a "Return to Mental Sacrifice & War" (*Jerusalem*, II, 27) — a return to the original prophetic religion of inner struggle and search.

[13] Strabo, *Geographica*, IV, 4; Caesar, *De Bello Gallico*, VI, xiv–xvii. These references were also cited by Davies (sec. II, pp. 88–89). Williams (II, 202) admitted that his outline was what had been refined by Christianity "in which the Bards adopted nothing that was averse to their Ancient Theology, but rather confirmed the truth of it." Milton (*Mansus*, ll. 42–43) described the Druids as a race "busied with the holy rites of the gods (*sacris operata deorum*)."

Another motive is to ascertain the truth of an opinion, prevalent in Wales, on good authority, that there are still existing, in the interior parts of the American Continent, the remains of a Welsh Colony that went over there in the twelfth Century under the conduct of Madoc, the son of Owen Gwynedd, Prince of Wales.[14]

Southey's poem came as a later illustration of the legendary unity between Britain and America which formed part of the source for Blake's development of Albion as "Patriarch of the Atlantic." There was also his conception of a prehistoric "Atlantic continent"—the basis of both cultures— and he made use of the Atlantic ocean to represent the flood which destroyed an original civilization of the world. To Blake, however, the 'flood' was ultimately synonymous with the 'fall.' The real origin of cultivated life lay in his "Atlantic Mountains where Giants dwelt in Intellect"—the paradise state of Eden far beyond the "stony Druids" and the "Creation that groans, living on Death." [15] But while he made use of the materials of Celtic myth to communicate his own vision, Williams tried to ac-

commodate the triads of Bardism to Christian doctrine.

Aside from ignoring any reference to those parts of the tradition which might be interpreted as polytheistic, Williams was faced with a conception of reincarnation which, in one form or another, held a central position in the Druidic system.

I have in one passage mentioned a *qualified sense* in which the Christian Bards and Druids believed the Metempsychosis: this was, that the depraved soul of man passes in a state beyond the grave into progressive modes of existence corresponding with the nature of Earthly worms and brutes, into whom, in the literal sense, the Aboriginal or Patriarchal Druids believed it passed. Taliesin places this probationary, divestigating, or purifying Metempsychosis in the Hell of Christianity, whence the soul gradually rises again to Felicity, the way for it having been opened by Jesus Christ.[16]

Blake's outlook, expressed explicitly at the end of *Jerusalem*, that all lives, through the process of time, came to the realization of a full "Humanity" was in striking contrast to the Druidic conception of a ladder of ascent from the subhuman to the superhuman. This very ladder seemed to infer that man had been something else, and was about to become something else, and it tended to make man turn aside from the realization of his human existence. He was to find the source and order of life elsewhere—either beneath, in the forces of nature, or beyond, in the ideal of divine perfection. Both routes distracted him from himself and the field of his actual experience. Blake saw in Druidism the prototype of all systematic theology which attempted to explain the paradoxes of spiritual life in the rational terms of fallen man and his world of nature.

[14] Williams, I, xii; II, 64 n. The material for Southey's *Madoc* was taken from William Robertson's *History of America* published in 1777. Southey's story of a Celtic adventurer who founded a settlement in mythical 'Aztlan'—the ancestral home of the Aztecs—and was finally made to fight for his life at the foot of the stone of sacrifice suggested the common origin of both Aztec and Druidic sacrificial rites. Blake spoke equally of the "reared Rocks of Albion's Sons" (*Jerusalem*, II, 43, 82) and the "Rocks of the Altars of Victims in Mexico" (*ibid.*, 7).

[15] *Jerusalem*, II, 50, 1–7. See this fragment to the Countess of Egremont:

> My designs unchang'd remain.
> Time may rage but rage in vain.
> For above Time's troubled Fountains
> On the Great Atlantic Mountains,
> In my Golden House on high,
> There they Shine Eternally.

Cf. *Jerusalem*, II, 36, 38–39. G. M. Harper ("Blake's Neo-Platonic Interpretation of Plato's Atlantis Myth," *JEGP*, LIV [January 1955], 72–79) traces this and other references to Thomas Taylor's commentaries on Plato.

[16] Williams, I, xx–xxi. He later claimed that the doctrine of metempsychosis most clearly vindicated divine justice (II, 194 n.). "It is sufficiently countenanced by many passages in the New Testament, and was believed by many of the Primitive Christians, and by the Essenes amongst the Jews." Cf. Job 33: 29–30; Malachi 4: 5; Matthew 11: 13–14; 17: 10–13; Mark 9: 11–13; John 9: 2–3.

Druidism, according to Blake, gradually degenerated into man's first attempt to let theory take the place of reality, and theorizing, the place of realizing, so that the fallen condition became more comfortable and apparently more secure. He called the Indian systems of thought "Abstract Philosophy," and the systems of Pythagoras and Plato, "Abstract Law," to express the progressive reduction of inspired insight to some absolutely logical scheme.[17] The traditional theory of reincarnation, like the orthodox Christian doctrine of election and reprobation, provided an absolute rule of thumb for what was relative in actual human experience. Both were attempts to reduce insight beyond the fallen perspective to dogmatic form, and both left out the other side of the paradox which even ordinary experience suggested. What is given in experience is always unique, and at the same time, always a repetition of everything like it, but this does not necessarily mean that everything is predetermined once and for all or that everything is bound to repeat itself. The circle of recurrence was identity in motion, in process, so that the temporal cycle was, as Blake came to see it, the 'analogy' of eternal identity. One of his definitions of character was what could be repeated with infinite variety but could neither be surpassed nor changed into something else,

for we see the same characters repeated again and again, in animals, vegetables, minerals, and in men; nothing new occurs in identical existence; Accident ever varies, Substance can never suffer change nor decay.[18]

[17] *The Song of Los*, ll. 18–19.
[18] *A Descriptive Catalogue &c.*, No. III. Needless to say, Blake nowhere gave any support to the change of human into animal existences implied by the literal interpretation of the Pythagorean tradition. Williams (II, 197) reflected the Druidic belief in subhuman and superhuman progressions, and spoke of a falling away from good and a return to it through "a succession of animal existences." Thomas Taylor in his translation of Proclus' *Theology of Plato* (London, 1816, I, 1 n.) quoted that particular philosopher's commentary (V, 329D–E) on Plato's *Timaeus* (42B–C) with

The truth underlying the reincarnation of character and that underlying the unique individuality of each character formed part of this visionary analogy which Blake tried to establish between time and eternity throughout his prophetic books. What was perceived as periodic and successive was seen from the temporal point of view, and what was perceived as unique and simultaneous was seen from the eternal point of view. Both points of view coincide in the moment of vision when the paradox was resolved, and everything was seen to be eternal.[19]

The problem of presenting a unified vision of temporal periodicity had become clarified for Blake while writing what he finally called *The Four Zoas*. It was probably during this part of his life that he read Williams or encountered the bardic triads in some form. Whatever he found in them to disagree with, they must have struck him as authentic in the same sense that he considered Macpherson and Chatterton authentic. He was not the least interested in documentary authenticity, but rather in the authentic original as it survived and was recreated continually in the human mind.[20] The authentic original of Druidism which developed systematically from the central notion of cyclical recurrence was deeply involved with Blake's theme of creation, redemption, and judgment in *The Four Zoas*. The writing of this

reference to human souls descending into brute animals, and concluded that the rational essence of man could by no means become the soul of a savage animal. "For a brutal nature is not a brutal body but a brutal life." See Blake's *Vision of the Last Judgment*, p. 79.
[19] Cf. *The Laocoön Group:* "All that we See is Vision, from Generated Organs gone as soon as come, Permanent in The Imagination, Consider'd as Nothing by the Natural Man."
[20] *Annotations to Wordsworth's "Poems,"* pp. 364–65: "I Believe both Macpherson & Chatterton, that what they say is Ancient Is so." See also *Annotations to Watson's "Apology for the Bible,"* pp. 15–16: "As if Public Records were True! Impossible; for the facts are such as none but the actor could tell."

work made clear a distinction he later used in *Milton* and *Jerusalem*—a distinction between inspired, prophetic religion which united temporal process and eternal identity in one vision and its recurring distillate, "Natural Religion," which abstracted temporal process and the wheel of becoming into a false kind of absolute identity expressed in the form of theological dogma. In these later works, he called the first the "Everlasting Gospel," and the second, "Druidism."

In *The Four Zoas*, he began with the conception of the cyclical pattern of natural necessity called the "Circle of Destiny" —in *Jerusalem*, "Divine Analogy"—and the problem of temporal recurrence dominated the work.[21] Like the Druids, he recognized the larger cycle which contained man's historical destiny from Adam to Luther and included what he later called the "Twenty-seven Heavens" and their "Churches." He also recognized the lesser lunar cycle which contained man's individual destiny from birth to rebirth and included the phases of life outlined in *The Mental Traveller*. Most important, however, was the constant interplay of life and death, joy and sorrow, pleasure and pain, the one contrary living off the other, yet never completely absorbing it. As in Swedenborg, Blake found in Druidism a deep-rooted tendency to eliminate one contrary in favour of the other and to regard this process as the moral triumph of good over evil.

All modes of existence which are necessarily as numerous as Divine Conception can make them, will forever remain in existence with no other change than that of being thoroughly divested of all their Evils, and continue eternally as beautiful varieties in the Creation, which without this numerosity of externalities would not possess perfect beauty.[22]

[21] *The Four Zoas*, I, 71–102; *Jerusalem*, II, 49, 56–59; IV, 85, 3–13.
[22] Williams, II, 202. Blake even spoke of suffering as necessary (H. Crabb Robinson, *Diary* [Boston, 1869], p. 27). "There is suffering in heaven, for where there is the capacity of enjoyment, there is also the capacity of pain." The painless, effortless

The moral judgment abhors a paradox, but it is only in paradox that the recurrent nature of life and its unique identity can both be understood. To fall short of this paradox is to become committed to the half-truths of formal logic and dogmatic theology where, to get a final answer, it is necessary to eliminate the contrary aspect of every problem.

The inability to sustain the paradox of the contraries was, in effect, a submission to the cloven fiction of two exhaustive alternatives to every problem—in this instance, that of recurrence and identity. Druidism which stood for a view of eternal identity in terms of temporal succession was typical of all natural religions according to Blake. On the other hand, the everlasting gospel was the vision of the circle of time contained by eternal identity as the substantial form underlying every possibility. Orthodox Christian doctrine had come to accept as limited a view of the problem as Druidism, and Augustine's attack on the whole cyclical theory which he attributed to the failure of logic to grasp the nature of infinity could as easily be turned against his own doctrine of special creation and predestination.[23] On the level of accepted doctrine, Christianity obviously regarded the theory of cycles as a contradiction of the historical principle inherent in Scripture—the progressive disclosure of the spirit of truth. It also objected to the repetition of typical or characteristic individuals and events as contrary to the unique character of personal identity and historical situations.

As a professed Christian, Blake was careful to distinguish between the visionary sig-

paradise of the faithful could only be pleasant, or even endurable, as an impossible dream. Cf. *Marriage of Heaven and Hell*: "Without Contraries is no progression. Attraction and Repulsion, Reason and Energy, Love and Hate, are necessary to Human existence."
[23] Augustine, *De Civitate Dei*, xii, 18–22; v, 9–10. The rejection of the theory of cycles (*circuitus temporum*) was an early characteristic of Christian thought (see Origen, *Contra Celsum*, iv, 68).

nificance of periodicity and the crass naturalism with which it was later interpreted by both the Druidic and classical traditions. But he continued to accept the notion of cyclical recurrence as one of the contraries involved in the relationship between identity and process. In *Jerusalem,* he clearly indicated that the "Circle of Destiny" of his *Four Zoas* was to be understood as an analogy which served to express the seer's visionary experience of the polarity of the unique and the periodic. He gave no indication of trying to reconcile these two contraries on the level of doctrine at all. It was probably not until *Milton* and *Jerusalem* that he finally succeeded in liberating himself from his own "Circle of Destiny," so that he saw it as "Divine Analogy."

Within the context of *The Four Zoas,* however, Blake described the attempt of man's natural reason to encompass the fallen world of space and time in terms of cyclical repetition. Urizen was the "Mental Traveller" who united the larger cycle of human history to the individual cycle of human life—one whose contrary was no longer a female counterpart but the earth's "bosom of clay" created in the void.

When wearied, dead he fell, his limbs repos'd in
  the bosom of slime;
As the seed falls from the sower's hand, so Urizen
  fell, & death
Shut up his powers in oblivion; then as the seed
  shoots forth
In pain & sorrow, so the slimy bed his limbs
  renew'd.
At first an infant weakness; periods pass'd; he
  gather'd strength,
But still in solitude he sat; then rising, threw
  his flight
Onward, tho' falling, thro' the waste of night &
  ending in death
And in another resurrection to sorrow & weary
  travel.[24]

In addition, Urizen was represented bearing with him his books which remained un-

consumed after each periodic death and resurrection. The continuity of experience and a final "perfect recollection" was also emphasized by traditional Bardism.

Man, on arriving at a state above Humanity, recovers the perfect recollection of all former modes of existence, and to eternity retains it.[25]

Blake never supposed that man could surpass his human identity, although he could realize it to an extent which included an eternal progression. There were references, however, to what Shelley might have called pre-existence and to "former modes of existence." In a letter to Flaxman, sent from Felpham on 21 September 1800, he wrote:

I look back into the regions of Reminiscence & behold our ancient days before this Earth appear'd in its vegetated mortality to my moral vegetated Eyes. I see our houses of Eternity which can never be separated, tho' our Mortal vehicles should stand at the remotest corners of heaven from each other.

Crabb Robinson mentioned a sense in which Blake claimed to have been, or to have been with, Socrates.[26]

All these references tend to show that the Druids took their analogy from the cyclical order of nature and applied it to human destiny as a part of that order. Blake took his analogy from his own vision of human existence and applied it to the circle of time or what he meant by 'nature.' In other words, 'nature' to the Druid and the Deist was the basic reality containing a scale of being including man, but to Blake, 'nature' was the lowest degree in a scale of visionary perception which man himself contained. He came to see in Druidism the original of contemporary Deism with its remote, unapproachable Deity whose laws were to be found in the natural order. After the complimentary remarks of his *Descriptive Catalogue,* he made use of "Druidism" as the most perverse form the "Religion of Generation" could take to destroy

---

[24] *The Four Zoas,* VI, 159–66. Urizen's fall, it will be noted, took the form of a spiral whirling in "unresistible revolutions" (l. 154).

[25] Williams, II, 198.
[26] Quoted by Alexander Gilchrist, *Life of William Blake* (Everyman ed., London, 1942), p. 333.

human conscience in the person of Jerusalem.[27] In spite of Williams' denial of any
connection between Druidism and natural
religion and the antiquarians' praise of it
as the religion of the patriarchs, Blake saw
in its isolation of the Deity and its exalta-
tion of him into the Supreme Moral Agent
the root of the worst of all tyrannies—one
based on the apparently reasonable and benevolent demands of the natural man's
ideals. So interpreted, nature and natural
laws became the "Stone of Trial" and the
"Stone of Torture" to balance the scale of
moral justice between good and evil for
the human victim in this best of all possible worlds.

The victimization of man, in Blake's
opinion, followed the immemorial pattern
of the deterioration of religious discipline
from internal effort to external pressure,
and finally, to the kind of adjustment to social order and natural necessity required by
the Deist. Such a deterioration was the inevitable result of virtue ceasing to mean "a
man's leading propensity" and becoming a
synonym for an acceptable pattern of behaviour. Correction of behaviour according
to some pattern or code tended to become
increasingly negative, and eventually cul-
minated in the ritual murder of criminals
in the name of moral virtue. Blake considered the whole process negative and therefore vicious, however necessary the expe-
dient and however good the intention. Morality was a concession to the ways of this
world and the natural man's substitute for
conscience.

While we are in the world of Mortality we Must
Suffer. The Whole Creation Groans to be de-
liver'd; there will always be as many Hypocrites
born as Honest Men, & they will always have
superior Power in Mortal Things. You cannot
have Liberty in this World without what you
call Moral Virtue, & you cannot have Moral
Virtue without the Slavery of that half of the

[27] *Jerusalem*, I, 7, 63–64. Williams (II, 199) con-
sistently referred Druidic doctrine to divine revelation. "Bardism always refers its origin to *Divine
communications*, and never talked of, I know not
what, *Religion of Nature*."

Human Race who hate what you call Moral
Virtue.[28]

Those who hated what was called moral
virtue were those whose morality took the
inner form of conscience.

Conscience in those that have it is unequivocal.
It is the voice of God. Our judgment of right &
wrong is Reason.[29]

As the abiding ethical principle, forgiveness of sins represented to Blake the eternal
process of regeneration as against the purely temporal process of moral justification
with its calculated balancing of ethical deb-
its and credits. Forgiveness of sins was the
characteristic feature of the activity of conscience, just as self-righteous condemna-
tion tended to become the negative activity of the moral judgment.

What finally reunited regenerate man
(Albion) to his eternal sense of values (Jerusalem) or his conscience was the recognition of the distinction between the religion of generation represented as "Druidic" and the religion of regeneration called
the "Everlasting Gospel." It took Albion
from the beginning to the end of *Jerusalem*
to see the difference between them, and in
the process, explore the depths of Ulro—
"meer Nature or Hell." The three states of
Ulro were called "Creation, Redemption &
Judgment," [30] and they formed the infernal

[28] *Vision of the Last Judgment*, pp. 92–95. "In
Hell all is Self Righteousness; there is no such
thing there as Forgiveness of Sin; he who does
Forgive Sin is Crucified as an Abettor of Criminals, & he who performs Works of Mercy in Any
shape whatever is punish'd &, if possible, destroy'd, not thro' envy or Hatred or Malice, but
thro' Self Righteousness that thinks it does God
Service, which God is Satan."
[29] *Annotations to Watson's "Apology for the
Bible,"* p. 2. Blake's marginalia to this particular
book reflect his attitude to the pretensions of any
rationale of morality. Cf. p. 117: "The Gospel is
Forgiveness of Sins & has No Moral Precepts;
these belong to Plato & Seneca & Nero." See also
Jerusalem, III, 61, 17–27.
[30] *Jerusalem*, II, 36, 41–42. Reuben is called (ll.
23–24) the "Vegetative Man," and Merlin is "his
Immortal Imagination." "Ulro," probably an ana-
gram of 'rule' or 'ruler,' is the natural state of

counterparts of those which led on to eternal life: Generation, Beulah, and Eden. The difference between the kind of universal outlook implied by the infernal states and that implied by the others was the difference between an outlook dedicated to outer conformity and one disciplined to inner fulfillment. The three states of Ulro were three stages in the individual's relationship to the ruler of this world conceived as the supreme moral agent and judge—a cosmic version of Orwell's Big Brother. The other three states, however, were stages in the individual's progressive realization of his "Human Existence." Generation was the state into which he was born and in which he dare not remain or he would consolidate in it and fall into Ulro. It was the state of nature as seen by the visionary imagination, just as Ulro was nature without vision. It was, in fact, human life seen as a living process within the circle of time—with its problems, contradictions, and constant change. Beulah was the state in which these problems and contradictions disappeared—"where Contrarieties are equally True." [31] It was the state where the individual had put to rest the natural "Selfhood" without having fully realized his "Human Existence"—a state significantly associated with the Quietists such as Fénelon and Teresa, rather than the prophets. Finally, there was Eden, the "land of life," where the "Human Existence" was fully realized, and time could be seen from the standpoint of eternity.

How, then, did Blake's "states" compare with the "circles" of Druidism found in Williams? For, according to the tradition of the Welsh Druids, there were three "Circles of existence."

There are three Circles (or states) of existence: the *Circle of Infinity*, where there is nothing but God, of living or dead, and none but God can traverse; the *Circle of Inchoätion*, where all things are by Nature derived from Death; this circle has been traversed by man; and the *Circle of Felicity*, where all things spring from Life; this man shall traverse in Heaven.[32]

At first glance, the three circles of Druidism would seem to correspond to Blake's states: Generation, Beulah, and Eden, but the most notable features of his outlook were missing. First of all, there was no evident conviction that all existence must be seen as human to some degree, since man could not hope to understand anything from a viewpoint other than his own. Secondly, struggle and search, the mental warfare of eternity, was understood as an unfavourable aspect of the lowest circle of existence—as belonging to death rather than life.[33] Finally, Blake's notion that man contained both creator and creature in himself, along with heaven and hell, was apparently avoided in favour of a disciplined resignation to an absolute code of imposed conditions.

Blake obviously thought that Druidism had come to sacrifice life to its conditions. Every 'religion' was prone to take this degenerate form—a form which was usually

---

"Single vision" (*Letter to Thomas Butts*, 22 November 1802) associated with Newton and mere spatial extension. See also *Annotations to Swedenborg's "Divine Love and Wisdom,"* pp. 195–96.
[31] *Milton*, II, 30, 1. For references to the states of existence, see D. J. Sloss and J. P. R. Wallis, *The Prophetic Writings of William Blake* (Oxford, 1926), II, 134–37; 151–52; 162–63; 234–35.

[32] Williams, II, 241. "Infinity," Williams points out, is a translation of *Ceugant*, which "in its etymological sense, signifies the *Circle of Vacuity*; in its metaphysical acceptation, here, it signifies the immense void beyond the bounds of the material Creation, into which none but the Deity can penetrate." Another translation would be "closing circumference," reminding one of Urizen's compasses. "Inchoätion" is a translation of *abred* (*ab*, 'from,' and *rhed*, a 'course'), which presumably referred to the transmigration of the soul. *Gwynfyd* (or *Gwynvyd*) meant the 'white' world, and was usually translated the "Circle of Felicity."
[33] The static nature of the Circle of Infinity was in marked contrast to Blake's "Mental War" in eternity (*Jerusalem*, II, 43, 31–32).

And the two Sources of Life in Eternity, Hunting and War,
Are become the Sources of dark & bitter Death & of corroding Hell.

expressed as a code of rules or laws. He therefore emphasized that the source of the good life lay in individual struggle and search rather than in conformity to an established set of regulations. But the God of the Welsh Triads would seem to be a Supreme Regulator like Plato's Divine Geometer and Priestley's Watchmaker—one for whom the correct conditions of life were more important than life itself.

The three regulations of God towards giving existence to every thing: to annihilate the power of evil, to assist all that is good, and to make discrimination manifest, that it might be known what should and what should not be.[34]

The deification of conditions which included natural, social, and moral laws amounted to a deification of the nature of things seen by man's limited perceptions in his present degree of development. This meant that man fell from Generation into Ulro—the net of conditions which, when accepted as final, Blake called "Nature," "Natural Morality," and "Natural Religion." In opposition to the deification of life's conditions, he chose to deify human life itself, or rather, human existence, since he did not worship what man usually was, but what it was in him to be. "For everything that lives is Holy." He found it necessary to restore the priority of life over its functions, conditions, and especially its ideals. In the prophetic books, man's fallen state was attributed to the fact that his "Human Existence" was asleep, and his faculties and the conditions of his life had usurped control over him. To emphasize law at the expense of life would keep Albion asleep forever.

For Blake conscience was the actual criterion of moral rectitude, the living law as distinct from the law of the members which was the rule of temporal conditions. He did not suppose it possible to get rid of the outer law of nature and society, but he did object to giving this kind of legal sanction a dignity beyond immediate necessity. The very worst that could happen was to give

such legal sanctions and conventions an absolute moral authority by basing them on a divine decree. By this means morality acquired a prerogative beyond conscience and tended to supersede and finally destroy it. As Blake put it, Jerusalem who was Albion's conscience was then "Offer'd up to Holiness" in the interests of "Natural Religion."[35] Druidism became the original example of the destruction of conscience in the name of morality and religion. The Druidic rite of human sacrifice was the central symptom of a disintegrating society where all sacrifice was regulated from without and the sacrificial victim was the scapegoat for society's ills. The sacrifice of the victim was a parody of self-sacrifice, just as the self-righteous virtue of the moralist was a parody of conscience. Blake thought of the "Patriarchal Religion" as one of self-sacrifice which later declined

From willing sacrifice to Self, to sacrifice of (miscall'd) Enemies For Atonement.[36]

Sacrifice which was not self-sacrifice was both useless and criminal.

Bardic tradition, as Williams reported it, made every effort to justify the sacrificial rites of the Druids. The sacrifice of animals was considered a means of advancing them along the path of development.

[34] Williams, II, 240.

[35] *Milton*, I, 19, 46–48:

> Come, bring with thee Jerusalem with songs on the Grecian Lyre!
> In Natural Religion, in experiments on Men
> Let her be Offer'd up to Holiness!

See also *Annotations to Watson's "Apology for the Bible,"* p. 3: "If Conscience is not a Criterion of Moral Rectitude, What is it?" Blake's conception of conscience or honesty was also involved with his attack on Locke's denial of innate ideas and the whole notion of a merely natural and experimental scheme of knowledge. Cf. *Annotations to Reynolds's "Discourses,"* p. 58: "The Man who says that we have No Innate Ideas must be a Fool & Knave, Having No Con-Science or Innate Science."

[36] *Jerusalem*, II, 28, 20–21. Compare Blake's reference to "Justice" and "Truth" in line 23 with Williams' sixteenth aphorism (II, 199).

The sacrifice of animals, which were always those of the least ferocity of disposition, was a religious co-operation with Divine Benevolence, by raising such an animal up to the state of Humanity, and consequently expediting his progress towards Felicity; it was not to appease, we know not what, *Divine wrath,* a thing that cannot possibly exist; the idea of which is of all others, the most blasphemously disgraceful to the Deity.[37]

The sacrifice of human life, on the other hand, was regarded as a cooperative effort between the sacrificers and the victim, based on a doctrine of moral compensation.

Man, having been guilty of crimes that are punishable by Death, must be so punished; and by giving himself up a voluntary victim to Death, being conscious of deserving it, does all that lies in his power to compensate for his crimes. . . .[38]

The notion of compensation and of a rule distinct from individual conscience tended to separate self-sacrifice from the moral judgment and allow the moralist to concentrate on the sacrifice of others. Blake noticed this tendency, and Druidism became the symbol of life as trial and experiment where the object of experiment was always another. He saw that the whole doctrine of moral compensation was too easily twisted by self-deceit into an excuse for vengeance in the name of the social order and into a cloak for personal jealousy. Blake's symbol of "Druid Law" was used to uncover the negative effects of the scales of moral justice in the hands of Rahab, the goddess of Nature. In her was brought together the perverse poison of mutual accusation and judgment in the infested spectre of fallen man's inner life.

The Jealousies became Murderous, uniting together in Rahab
A Religion of Chastity, forming a Commerce to sell Loves,
With Moral Law an Equal Balance not going down with decision.

[37] Williams, II, 199.
[38] *Ibid.,* p. 199. A later authority (J. Williams ab Ithel, *Barddas* [London, 1862], I, lxix) referred to the doctrine of *eneidvaddeu* which placed the soul in a better state when, by the act of conscious atonement, it had compensated for its crimes.

Therefore the Male severe & cruel, fill'd with stern Revenge,
Mutual Hate returns & mutual Deceit & mutual Fear.[39]

Blake made Druidism into a comprehensive symbol of all the perversities of fallen existence which were respectably hidden in the "Religion of Generation." What made Druidism the cult of the world from which all 'worldly' religions came was its attempt to consolidate the original voice of the prophet into the fixed ritual and rule of the priest. The terms which had not been final for the seer became final in the name of an organized cult, and the conditions of life and worship were rendered invariable in the interests of an established clergy. This always produced, according to Blake, cruelty in the name of a benevolent concern for the victim's welfare, and he represented the human race in the person of Albion being sacrificed by his daughters in the temple of "Natural Religion." The "Divine Vision" was lost, and the human form of man's possibilities was altered, so that his perceptions were dissipated into the "Indefinite Becoming" of natural process.[40]

[39] *Jerusalem,* III, 69, 33–37. Providentially, the temporal universe, according to Blake, was so constructed that error caused the least possible suffering to the sinner (II, 31, 30–34):

I could not dare to take vengeance, for all things are so constructed
And builded by the Divine hand that the sinner shall always escape,
And he who takes vengeance alone is the criminal or Providence.
If I should dare to lay my finger on a grain of sand
In way of vengeance, I punish the already punished.

For the theme of revenge, see also III, 63, 39–41; 66, 38–39. Cf. *Annotations to Watson's "Apology for the Bible,"* p. 25.
[40] *Jerusalem,* III, 66, 1–56. The union, in Blake's use of imagery, between cruelty and a benevolent, even experimental, interest in the victim might be compared with Tacitus' charge (*Annals,* XIV, 30) that the Druids used prisoners for purposes of divination, "for they considered it lawful to offer the blood of captives on their altars, and to consult the gods by means of the nerves of men (*et*

Druidism became the composite symbol of fallen man's preoccupation with a natural security at the expense of a greater human adventure.

Blake treated the decline from the "Patriarchal Religion" to "Druidism" as fundamentally a degeneration in man's powers of perception, and hence, a falling off of his imaginative genius which integrated perception and was the root of his very existence. He had become less than himself—a mere wraith or "Spectre"—and in so doing, had ceased to think of the universe as the field of intelligent agency or as a 'Cosmic Man.' Humanity had become something in between God and nature—a something which partook of both but was neither. The original myth of the Cabalistic Adam Kadmon or 'Grand Man,' who was the archetypal principle of intelligent agency in the universe, had given way to the naturalistic view of man as merely a constituent factor in the cosmic process. Blake placed the roots of the former tradition in the 'period' before Adam or in the state before the creation of the natural man. Speaking "to the Jews" in his preface to the second chapter of *Jerusalem*, he referred their ancestry to the patriarchs who were the first Druids.

> Your Ancestors derived their origin from Abraham, Heber, Shem and Noah, who were Druids, as the Druid Temples (which are the Patriarchal Pillars & Oak Groves) over the whole Earth witness to this day.
> You have a tradition, that Man anciently contain'd in his mighty limbs all things in Heaven & Earth: this you received from the Druids.[41]

The myth of the Giant Man was not developed in Williams' version of the triads, but instead, there was the conception of a gradual progression from the "lowest point of

existence" to the state of felicity—a progression which stopped short of the circle of *"Ceugant"*—the eternal 'Void' of the Deity. Blake objected to the disembodied Absolute or any nonhuman abstraction of Deity as the false vision of unattainable perfection, and he placed this "Central Void" in opposition to the "Divine Vision" of Christ.[42]

His conception of the Deity was certainly not, however, what is usually called "anthropomorphic"—the projection of fallen man's subjective idiosyncrasies. It was connected with the fact that the beginning and end of anything can never supersede its essential origin, and the ultimate extent of man's possibilities must be the fulfillment of his "Humanity." Luvah's statement concerning the human faculties applied to the whole question of human aspirations and ultimate aims: "Attempting to be more than Man We become less."[43] The attempt to

---

[41] *Jerusalem*, II, 27.

hominum fibris consulere deos fas habebant)." The same tendency prevailed in ecclesiastical Christianity. Cf. *Notes Written on the Pages of "The Four Zoas"*: "Christ's Crucifix shall be made an excuse for executing Criminals."

[42] *Ibid.*, II, 30, 19–20. See Williams, II, 240–41: "All animated Beings are subject to three Necessities: a beginning in the Great Deep (lowest point of existence), Progression in the Circle of Inchoätion, and Plentitude in Heaven, or the Circle of Felicity; without these things nothing can possibly exist but God. Three things are necessary in the Circle of Inchoätion: the least of all animation, and thence the beginning; the materials of all things, and thence increase, which cannot take place in any other state; the Formation of all things out of the dead mass, hence discriminate individuality." The Druidic "Circles," however, appeared as the creations of a superhuman Deity for whom progression took place, while Blake's "states" were the creations of a "Divine Humanity" in whom progression was the realization of an individual existence. Cf. *Jerusalem*, II, 35, 9–10:

> In Me all Eternity
> Must pass thro' condemnation and awake beyond the Grave.

[43] *The Four Zoas*, IX, 709. Williams (II, 197) spoke of the accommodation of the Deity to the life of man. "Finite Beings can never comprehend Infinity; they cannot conceive any thing of God, but as something external to themselves individually different, and, consequently, *finite*. The Deity for this reason, though in himself *infinite*, manifests himself to *finite* comprehensions as a *finite being*, as in the Person of Jesus Christ, &c." Cf. *Annotations to Swedenborg's "Divine Love and*

surpass the balanced fulfillment of one's actual capabilities was characteristic of the perverse will of the natural man who wished to be superior to his neighbour and to all men. One of the main sources of unbalanced development, in Blake's opinion, lay in the primary use of the rational faculty to encompass man's present limitations of perception and on them establish the limits of the entire universe. This was precisely what Urizen was trying to do in the sixth Night of *The Four Zoas* when, like the typical eighteenth-century philosopher, he sought the basis of his life by examining the limitations of his faculties. At the very commencement of his journey around the worlds of man's fallen faculties, he encountered Blake's version of the three fates, the threefold representation of Vala, Goddess of Nature. They wore the three colours of the three orders of Druidic priests, and represented respectively the presiding, attracting, and conducting powers reflected in natural process.[44] In this way, Druidism was

connected with the initial stages of man's fall from innocence through the birth of a rational set of moral values based on a definitive system of nature.

Blake did not suppose, however, that the primitive Druids, whom he had called "wiser than after-ages," were less than the "ancient Poets" who had formed the basis of an original priesthood in his *Marriage of Heaven and Hell*. In fact, the Bardic Triads gave the same priority to original 'genius' as he did. By 'genius' he had meant the "true Man" from which his outward form was derived and to which every intellectual and physical activity could ultimately be traced. It was the 'whatness' in man, and underlay the form of anything. Most important, the "Poetic Genius" was the universal source of forms in the species and the individual. It was the faculty which experienced, or what he called the "Imagination"—the basic root of the total imagery of experience.[45] As the "Spirit of Prophecy," his conception of 'genius' could be compared with what the Druids had called *awen*. Although neoclassical terminology and poetic diction clearly affected Williams' translation of the "Poetic Triades" or "Triades of Song" (*Trioedd Cerdd*) there was much Blake could still appreciate.

The three final intentions of Poetry: accumulation of Goodness; enlargement of the Understanding; and what increases Delight.[46]

But this original emphasis on genius was finally corrupted, according to tradition, along with the institutes of the Bards, by the Scots, Irish, Bretons, and even the Germans. Bardism survived in its pure form only among the Welsh.

Williams' attitude was ultimately sectari-

Wisdom," p. 24: "That there is but one Omnipotent, Uncreate & God I agree, but that there is but one Infinite I do not; for if all but God is not Infinite, they shall come to an End, which God forbid." See also p. 11: "Man can have no idea of any thing greater than Man, as a cup cannot contain more than its capaciousness. But God is a man, not because he is so perceiv'd by man, but because he is the creator of man."

[44] *The Four Zoas,* VI, 8–19. This is a threefold representation of the "Daughters of Albion" who dismember him (*Jerusalem,* III, 66, 17–34) and reduce his vision to that of the corporeal senses. The "Eldest Woman" whose name is written on her forehead (l. 18) obviously suggests the Babylon of Revelation (17: 5). The three orders of Primitive Bards, according to Williams (II, 230–31) were Bards, Ovates (or Euvates), and Druids. The last of these was the chief, and it was the Druid (*Derwydd*) who dressed in white as a symbol of truth and sanctity. The Ovate (*Ofydd*) wore green like the vegetation of the earth, and the Bard (*Prifardd*), blue, the colour of heaven. See also Edward Jones, *Musical and Poetical Relicks of the Welsh Bards* (London, 1794; 2nd ed.), pp. 2–9. Strabo (*Geographica,* IV, 197) called the Bards chanters and poets, the ovates, sacrificers and physiologists, and the Druids, moral philosophers.

[45] *All Religions Are One.* Cf. Williams, II, 232: "Without three qualifications no one can be a Bard: a poetical genius [*awen wrth gerdd*]; the knowledge of Bardic institutes; and irreproachable morals." The orders of the original Bards (p. 231) were determined by genius (*awen*), exertion (*ymgais*), and incident (*dichwain*).

[46] Williams, II, p. 256. For the corruption of Bardism see p. 248.

an, although his view that Britain had been the original seat of the Patriarchal Religion was certainly shared by Blake. Neither one adopted the legend reported by Geoffrey of Monmouth, who claimed the authority of Taliesin, the celebrated bard of the fifth century, for the story of Trojan Brutus. Blake's use of Arthur, however, probably did come from the emphasis given him by the successors of Geoffrey, but his reference to the existence of genuine Bards in the fifth century could refer to Williams' mention of Meugant, Merlin, and Taliesin who were said to have lived around that time.[47] Apart from these references, his "Druidic" period covered all but the last quarter of the "Circle of Destiny" with its historical perspective stretching over 6,000 years—beginning with Adam and ending with Luther. Original Druidism, indeed, began even before Adam and included the first two "Eyes" of God within the cycle of seven from Lucifer to Jesus.[48]

The "Twenty-seven Heavens & their Churches" provided Blake with his cyclical calendar of history graduated according to the separate attempts to reestablish communication between time and eternity. Within this context, Druidism stretched from Adam to Terah the father of Abraham who "was called to succeed the Druidical age, which began to turn allegoric and mental signification into corporeal command, whereby human sacrifice would have depopulated the earth." [49] The "Churches" and their respective "Heavens" were ways

of ordering popular belief and social practice, but the "Eyes" of God were the ways God was 'seen' or understood by each succeeding epoch. In *The Four Zoas*, the "Eyes" took the form of "Guards" sent to sacrifice themselves for Satan—Blake's symbol for the opacity of man's fallen perception. The Patriarchal Religion began with the first two—Lucifer and Molech—who were of the pre-Adamite age before the corporeal senses had become completely consolidated as fallen man's only avenues of perception. Between the Elohim who created Adam and Pachad whose name meant 'fear' was Blake's "Druidical age," succeeded by the worship of Jehovah by the "Church" of Abraham and the children of the promise.

Druidism as a symbol in the prophetic books began to be developed in the later additions to *The Four Zoas*. The sources which Blake actually mentioned were Milton and Jacob Bryant. If the internal evidence be considered sufficient to assume that he also knew something of Davies and Stukeley, there is certainly as much to suggest that he had seen Williams' collection of "Welsh Triades" or some such collection. The use he made of the triadic form to describe the last battle of Arthur significantly united the characteristics of the four human faculties or "Zoas" to the fall of his own Arthur who was the Giant Albion.

In the last Battle that Arthur fought, the most Beautiful was one
That return'd, and the most Strong another: with them also return'd
The most Ugly, and no other beside return'd from the bloody Field.

The most Beautiful, the Roman Warriors trembled before and worshipped:
The most Strong, they melted before him and dissolved in his presence;
The most Ugly they fled before with outcries and contortions of their Limbs.[50]

The reference, as he explained, was to the human faculties represented by the "Zoas":

---

[47] *A Descriptive Catalogue &c.*, No. V. Blake's reference to the "remains of those naked Heroes in the Welch Mountains" was connected with the reign of Arthur and the account of ancient British history given by Milton. Milton's evident belief in the accusations of the Romans (*History of Britain*, Book II, *Works*, Columbia ed., x, 51) made him call the Druids "Progenitors not to be glori'd in." See Williams, II, notes to 1–3; 5–7.

[48] *The Four Zoas*, VIII, 398–406; *Milton*, I, 13, 17–29; *Jerusalem*, III, 55, 30–33. For the twenty-seven heavens and their churches, see *Milton*, II, 37, 35–43; *Jerusalem*, III, 75, 10–22. Cf. Zechariah 9: 10; Revelation 4: 5.

[49] *A Descriptive Catalogue, &c.*, No. V.

[50] Sloss and Wallis, II, facing 302.

pathos or emotion (Luvah), sublimity or power (Tharmas), limitation or reason (Urizen), and vision or existence (Los) who was Arthur (Albion) himself. The battle was the "Intellectual Battle" mentioned at the beginning of *The Four Zoas;* it was the fall of the Giant Man, the Adam Kadmon of the Cabala, whose collapse from unity into diversity brought about the creation of the universe. For his Giant Man, Blake used the figure of Albion and the myth derived from the ancient Cabalistic tradition which he traced to the origins of Druidism.[51] He related the stories of Arthur to such a conception, and in the traditional death and promised return of the King, he saw the fall of man and his final redemption. Malory's own account of Arthur's epitaph suggested this same theme of death, transformation, and return.

Yet some men say in many parts of England that King Arthur is not dead, but had by the will of our Lord Jesu into another place; and men say that he shall come again, and he shall win the holy cross. I will not say it shall be so, but rather I will say, here in this world he changed his life. But many men say that there is written upon his tomb this verse: *Hic jacet Arthurus, Rex quondam Rexque futurus.*[52]

The statement that Arthur "changed his life" in "this world" contained Blake's notion of regeneration working in and through the entire cycle of birth and death.

However, his final treatment of Arthur in *Jerusalem* was typical of his treatment of Druidism as a whole. In the scornful speech

of Vala, declaring the natural man's utter dependence on the "Female Will" of Mother Nature, she described both priest and king as the false front of the fallen "Worm" in his futile attempt to establish the natural analogy of an eternal society. Arthur became the symbol of the dream of imperial power which would prove an enforced imitation of the real communion of eternity.[53] He even became, in company with Satan and Cain, an infernal counterpart to the inspired ruler such as Moses or David and the states of existence they represented.[54] It was not that Blake condemned the effort to establish an analogy of eternal existence in time, for the whole of the temporal order was a "Divine Analogy." As he had said in *The Marriage of Heaven and Hell,* "Eternity is in love with the productions of time." But inspiration from eternity must remain the true basis of these productions, and the temporal order of things should not be made—in the spirit of the builders of Babel and their utopian successors—the basis and end of its own productions. "Eden" was the point where the productions of time and the life of eternity met. Blake claimed to be "an inhabitant of that happy country," and his professed aim was to unite the world of generation, through Eden, to its eternal source.

---

[51] *Jerusalem,* II, 27: "Albion was the Parent of the Druids, & in his Chaotic State of Sleep, Satan & Adam & the whole World was Created by the Elohim." In his *Descriptive Catalogue,* the "Triple Elohim" (cf. *Milton,* I, 13, 22) became the threefold life of man represented by the three Britons. The awakening of Arthur (Albion) "with tenfold splendor" probably refers to the ten *sephiroth* of the Cabalistic "Tree of Life" representing the full extent of what Blake called "Human Existence."
[52] Malory, *Morte d'Arthur,* XXI, vii.

[53] *Jerusalem,* III, 64, 12–17. The use of Arthur by Blake suggests an association with Alexander, whose legendary fame probably influenced Geoffrey of Monmouth's description of Arthur. See J. S. P. Tatlock, *The Legendary History of Britain* (Berkeley & Los Angeles, 1950), p. 312. As a precedent for Arthur, Alexander's search for imperial hegemony would reflect the search of man for the universal community of an earthly paradise enforced and maintained by the sword. Blake associated this ideal of enforced political community with the ideal of "Moral Virtue"—the basic cause of war—and with its principal protagonists: "the Alexanders & Caesars, the Lewis's & Fredericks" (*Jerusalem,* III, 52). For Blake's association of Druidism with a society cut off from eternity, see *Jerusalem,* III, 66, 1–15.
[54] *Ibid.,* III, 73, 35–42.

Northrop Frye

Poetry and Design in William Blake

THE ABILITY to paint and the ability to write have often belonged to the same person; but it is rare to find them equally developed. Most people so gifted have been either writers who have made a hobby of painting, like D. H. Lawrence, or painters who have made a hobby of writing, like Wyndham Lewis. When the two are combined, one usually predominates. It is not uncommon for poets who can draw to illustrate their poems, like Edward Lear; nor is it uncommon for painters who can write to provide inscriptions to their paintings, like Rossetti. In a world as specialized as ours, concentration on one gift and a rigorous subordination of all others is practically a moral principle. Mr. Eliot uses the word "schizophrenia" even about the attempt to write both poetry and philosophy. Blake, it is clear, had a different attitude, and the reasons for his different attitude are of some interest.

Besides being a poet and painter, Blake was a professional engraver and a tireless and versatile experimenter in a great variety of media. He was an artisan or craftsman who was an expert in an important minor art as well as two major ones. His political sympathies were anarchist and revolutionary. The combination of talents and outlook reminds us of William Morris, and as the French Revolution wore on into Napoleonic imperialism, Blake came more and more to anticipate Morris in his view of the social function of art. Like Morris, he felt that revolutionary action would only go from one kind of slavery to another unless it were directed toward the goal of a free and equal working society. Like Morris, he believed that real work and creative activity were the same thing, and that as long as society supported a class of parasites, work for the great majority of people would be perverted into drudgery. And so, like Morris, he came to feel that the essential revolutionary act was in the revolt of the creative artist who is also a manufacturer, in the original sense of one who works with his hands instead of with automata. And as the tendency of a class-ridden society is to produce expensive luxuries for the rich and shoddy ugliness for the poor, the true manufacturer should present his work as cheaply and as independently of commerce and patronage alike as possible.

The creative producer, then, has to imitate, on a necessarily limited scale, the mass-producing methods of commerce. Also, a revolutionary break with both patronage and commercial exploitation is only possible if some revolutionary new method of production is discovered. Blake made at least three attempts to develop his own means of production. First, and most important to students of literature, was his discovery of the engraving process which he used for most of his poems. It is clear that Blake expected this process to be more efficient and less laborious than it was: he expected, in short, that it would make him independent of publishers as well as of patrons, so that he could achieve personal independence as both poet and painter at a single blow. A character in his early satire, *An Island in the Moon*, speaks of printing off two thousand copies of engraved works

From *The Journal of Aesthetics and Art Criticism*, X (September 1951), 35–42. Reprinted by permission of the author and the journal.

in three volumes folio, and selling them for £100 apiece. Next came an attempt at large-scale reproduction of prints by means of a millboard, but the millboard proved too fragile for more than a few copies, and the variety of results it produced was too unpredictable. He was still dependent on patrons and connoisseurs to do the work he wanted to do, and on publishers' commissions to keep himself alive the rest of the time. Finally Blake turned to another idea on a much bigger scale: he thought he might gain government support for the arts if he could start a revival of fresco-painting on the walls of public buildings. The chief commercial disadvantage of fresco, Blake thought, was that the original painting had to remain as long as the wall it was painted on did, and he proposed that frescoes should be painted, not directly on the plaster, but on canvas stretched over the plaster, so that they could be taken off and changed. After he had worked out what he thought was a practicable method of painting such "portable frescoes," he held the one exhibition of his life in 1809, to introduce it to the public. The fate of this exhibition is well known, though it is seldom realized that its primary object was to advertise, not Blake, but a new instrument of production that would initiate a social revolution.

It is natural that Blake, whose main source of income was illustrating books, should at first think of his own poems as constructed on the same principle as the illustrated book, an alternation of text and design. In the passage from *An Island in the Moon* already quoted, he speaks of making every other plate a high finished print. An early prophecy called *Tiriel* survives in a manuscript and a group of twelve separate illustrations, about the same number of plates that would be needed for the text. Fortunately for us, however, Blake began his experiments with aphorisms and lyrics which took only a single plate apiece, and so hit very early on a form in which text and design are simultaneously present

and contrapuntally related. From the start Blake avoids all devices that would tend to obscure either text or design at the expense of the other. In illuminated books we often find what we may call the tradition of hieroglyphic, in which the verbal sign itself becomes a picture, such as the ornamented capitals of medieval manuscripts or the tortuous decorations of the Book of Kells. There is nothing of this in Blake: occasionally the shoots and tendrils of the design are entangled with the longer letters of the text, but that is all. The words are left alone to do their own work. The only exception I can think of is the heading to *The Book of Los*, where Urizen is shown wrapped up in a net inside the letter O of "Los," and even this is intended as a joke.

More surprising than the independence of the words from the design is the independence of the design from the words. Blake's age, after all, was the age of the pictorial Slough of Despond known as "historical painting," in which the painter was praised for his grasp of archaeology and the history of costume and for the number of literary points he could make. Again, the *Songs of Innocence and Experience* are in the direct tradition of the emblem-books: they are by far the finest emblem-books in English literature. But the typical emblem is a literary idea to begin with: its design takes its form, not from pictorial laws, but from the demands of the verbal commentary, and it is allegorical in a way that Blake's lyrics never are. In Blake the poem does not point to the picture, as it regularly does in the emblem. On the other hand, the design is not, like most illustrations, an attempt to simplify the verbal meaning. The Songs of Innocence are not difficult poems to read, and one might expect them to be made even easier, at least for children, by being put into a picture-book. Perhaps even Blake expected this. But when we contemplate the great spiral sweep that encircles "The Divine Image," or the passionate red flower that explodes over "Infant Joy," or the marching horizontal lines of "Holy

Thursday," we can see that, so far from simplifying the text, the design has added a new dimension of subtlety and power.

In the earliest prophecies, *The Book of Thel* and *Visions of the Daughters of Albion*, text and design approach one another rather tentatively. In *Thel* the design is always at the bottom or the top of the page, but in the Visions the text is occasionally broken in the middle, and an important step has been taken toward the free interpenetration of the two which belongs to Blake's mature period. In the early prophecies there is often an unequal balance between the amount Blake has to say in each of the two arts. Thus *The Marriage of Heaven and Hell* is in literature one of Blake's best known and most explicit works, but for that very reason it is less successful pictorially. The text predominates too much, and what design there is follows the text closely and obviously. So much so, in fact, that some of the marginal decorations become a rather irritating form of punctuation. Thus on Plate 11 the words "whatever their enlarged & numerous senses could percieve" are followed by a little drawing of a bird; the words "thus began Priesthood" are followed by a black serpentine spiral, and the words "at length they pronounc'd that the Gods had order'd such things" are followed by tiny kneeling figures. On the other hand, *The Book of Urizen* is pictorially one of Blake's greatest works: here there is no plate without a major design on it, and there are ten plates without text. Blake here seems to be trying to forget about the poem, which with its short lines sits awkwardly on the plate in double columns. It is clear that there were pictorial as well as poetic reasons for the long seven-beat line of Blake's prophecies.

The finest of the earlier prophecies, as far as the balance between verbal and pictorial elements is concerned, are undoubtedly the "continent" poems, *America, Europe,* and *The Song of Los,* the last of these divided into two parts called "Africa" and "Asia." After 1795 Blake began to meditate a prophecy of epic proportions, and between then and 1800 he undertook two colossal projects which enabled him to work out the archetypes of his verbal and pictorial systems respectively, on an epic scale. Each of these was a dream of nine nights: one was the great unfinished poem, *The Four Zoas,* which never reached the engraving process, but was left in a manuscript full of extraordinary sketches; the other was his illustrated edition of Young's *Night Thoughts.* The fascination that Young's poem clearly had for Blake was not due to Young so much as to the fact that Young's poem was based, like Blake's own symbolism, on the Bible. Throughout Blake's illustrations we can see how he infallibly goes to the Biblical archetype which gives what point and direction there is to Young's narrative. It was from his work on Young that Blake gained a co-ordinated vision of the leviathan, the four "Zoas" of Ezekiel, the Great Whore with her beast, and the other essential elements of his later symbolism. The final fruits of his effort were the two great poems *Milton* and *Jerusalem,* in fifty and one hundred plates respectively, after which Blake turned his main attention away from poetry.

It is difficult to convey adequately the sense of the uniqueness of Blake's achievement in these engraved poems. In the Preface to *Jerusalem* Blake speaks with pride of having developed a free and unfettered verse, but he hardly seems to notice that he had at the same time perfected a far more difficult and radical form of mixed art, for which there is hardly a parallel in the history of modern culture. The union of musical and poetic ideas in a Wagner opera is a remote analogy; but the poetry is not independent of the music in Wagner as it is of the painting in Blake. Blake seems to have worked on his text and his pictorial ideas simultaneously: this is clear from the manuscript of *The Four Zoas,* where the pencil sketches in the margins indicate that Blake did not think in terms of a poem to be written first and decorated afterward, but, from the beginning, in terms of a narrative sequence of plates.

Blake felt that his conception of outline was one which held all the arts together, and his engraving technique does a great deal to prove his case. The stamped designs produced by a relief etching on metal, in which the details stand out from surrounding blank space, give us something of the three-dimensional quality of sculpture. On the other hand, the tremendous energy of Blake's drawings with their swirling human figures makes them of particular interest to dancers and students of ballet, even if more sedentary observers merely find them out of drawing. About the color it is more difficult to speak. After reading what Blake has to say about the subordinating of color to outline in painting, we are not surprised to find that there is no fixed color symbolism in the designs: every copy is colored differently. At the same time, as he developed confidence and scope, he began to move toward the luminous splendors of the golden city that was the end of his vision. "A word fitly spoken," says the Book of Proverbs, "is like apples of gold in pictures of silver." Such ideas were entirely unbefitting to Blake's station in life. The text of the only surviving colored copy of *Jerusalem* is in a strong orange which looks like a poor man's substitute for the golden letters he doubtless dreamed of.

The designs play a great variety of roles in relation to the words, besides that of direct illustration. The natural symbols lend themselves admirably to pictorial metamorphosis, and the process is simplified by the fact that the symbols of experience are often direct parodies of those of innocence. Vines with grapes, ears of wheat, and a profusion of green leaves sprout from the tree of life; brambles, thorns, thistles, dead trees, and tangles of roots belong to the tree of mystery. In Plate 75 of *Jerusalem* a row of angels, with haloes around their bodies, make a line of intersecting circles, the "wheels within wheels" of Ezekiel's vision. At the bottom of the page the same

rhythm is picked up and parodied by a picture of Rahab and Tirzah caught in the rolling coils of serpents.

I have spoken of the analogy between Wagner and Blake, and some of Blake's pictorial symbols incorporate ideas in a way that reminds one of Wagner's technique of the leitmotif. Thus it is one of Blake's doctrines that we see the sky as a huge concave vault because we see it with eyes that are imprisoned in a concave vault of bone. The title page of *The Book of Urizen* depicts Urizen himself, the fallen reason of man, and it therefore endeavors to give a concentrated impression of befuddled stupidity. The picture is built up in a series of rounded arches. Urizen sits crouching in the foetus posture that Blake regularly uses for mental cowardice, and two great knees loom out of the foreground. His skull and bushy eyebrows are above; behind his head are the two tables of the law, each with a rounded top; behind them is the arch of a cave, the traditional symbol since Plato of blinded vision, and over the cave droops a dismal willow branch, an imp of the tree of mystery.

Occasionally, though rarely, the design comments ironically on the text, if an ironic touch in the text permits it. Thus the ninth plate of *America* contains the speech of the terrified reactionary angel of Albion denouncing the rebellious Orc as "Blasphemous Demon, Antichrist, hater of Dignities," and so on. The design shows a graceful spreading tree with birds of paradise sitting on its branches; underneath are a ram and some children asleep, sunk in the profound peace of the state of innocence. A much more frequent type of comment, and one which also is sometimes ironic, is a pictorial reference or quotation, generally to the Bible. *The Marriage of Heaven and Hell* concludes with a portrait of Nebuchadnezzar going on all fours. Nebuchadnezzar is not mentioned in the text, but the prophecy deals with the overthrow of senile tyranny, and Nebuchadnezzar, the tyrant of Babylon who becomes a monstrous animal, first cousin to behemoth and leviathan, is for Blake a central symbol of the kind of thing he is attacking. The great picture of Albion before the cross of Christ, which concludes the third part of *Jerusalem*, is a more familiar example. It is more common, however, to have the designs focus and sharpen the verbal symbolism. Thus the poem *Europe*, if we had only the text, would seem an almost perversely intellectualized treatment of the theme of tyranny and superstition. It is when we look at the plates depicting famine, war, and pestilence that we realize how acutely aware of human misery Blake always is.

In the longer poems there is, of course, a good deal of syncopation between design and narrative. At the bottom of Plate 8 of *Jerusalem* is a female figure harnessed to the moon: the symbol is not mentioned in the text until Plate 63. The effect of such devices is to bind the whole poem together tightly in a single unit of meaning. And here, perhaps, we come closest to the centre of the aesthetic problem that Blake's achievement raises. The words of a poem form rhythms which approach those of music at one boundary of literature, and form patterns which approach those of painting at the other boundary. To the rhythmical movement of poetry we may give the general name of narrative; the pattern we may call the meaning or significance. The Renaissance maxim *ut pictura poesis* thus refers primarily to the integrity of meaning which is built up in a poem out of a pattern of interlocking images. When Spenser begins the last canto of the Legend of Temperance with the words "Now gins the goodly frame of Temperance fairly to rise," he means that, in addition to the narrative, a unified structure of meaning has been built up which can be apprehended simultaneously, like a painting, or, to follow Spenser's image, like a building. Such a passage shows the principle of *ut pictura poesis* in action.

When we think of "meaning" we usually think of something to be expressed in gen-

eral propositions. But the units of poetry are images rather than ideas, and a poem's total meaning is therefore a total image, a single visualizable picture. Not many rhetorical critics pursue their image-linking to this ultimate point. They usually remain close to the texture of the poem, engaged in the detailed study of the poetic equivalents of the technique of brush and palette knife. The critic who can only express meaning in terms of propositions has to stop his interpretation of the poem at the point of fitting it into the background of a history of ideas.

But it is possible to go farther, and it is only when literary critics stand back far enough to see the imagery as one pattern that they are in a position to solve the problems of structure, of genre, and of archetype. The meaning of, for instance, Spenser's *Mutabilitie Cantoes* is not the conflict of being and becoming, which is only an aspect of its content. Its meaning is the total structure of its imagery, and this structure is a spherical, luminous, ordered background with a dark mass thrusting up defiantly in the central foreground: the same structural archetype that we find at the opening of *The Book of Job*. The propositional content of Blake's *Europe* could be expressed somewhat as follows: the root of evil and suffering is the fallen nature of man; this fallen nature is a part of physical nature; this deification has polluted Western culture from the sky-gods of Greece and Rome to the gravitational universe of Newton. But its poetic meaning, its total image, is given us by Blake himself in his frontispiece to the poem, the famous picture of the Ancient of Days, the bearded god whose sharp cruel compasses etch the circumference of the human skull and of the spherical universe which is its objective shadow.

Blake's prophecies are in the tradition of the Christian epic, and the meaning or total image of the Christian epic is the apocalypse, the vision of reality separated into its eternal constituents of heaven and hell. At the time that he was completing his epic prophecies, Blake was preoccupied by the pictorial vision of the Last Judgement. He has left us the magnificent picture reproduced as Plate 4 of Darrell Figgis's book on Blake's paintings, and an elaborate commentary for a still larger design of which nothing else remains. After this, Blake tended to make the picture the unit of a new kind of non-verbal narrative, and so turned from poetry to the sequences of his Milton, Bunyan, Dante, and Job illustrations.

The only complete edition of Blake's engraved poems is in the third volume of *The Works of William Blake* edited by Ellis and Yeats and published by Bernard Quaritch in 1893. This edition was a heroic publishing effort, and it showed the true spirit of scholarship, as it must have lost a great deal of money. But it is increasingly difficult to obtain, and the reproductions, which are in black and white and done from lithographs, a rather greasy medium that failed to interest Blake himself, are not very satisfactory, to put it mildly. There are passable color reproductions of the lyrics and a few of the shorter prophecies, but so far as I know there has been no good edition, with or without color, of *America, Europe, Milton,* or *Jerusalem*.[1] There are even editions

of the lyrics which have been illustrated by other people. For one reason or another, many literary students of Blake have only the vaguest notion of what sort of pictorial basis underlies his poetry. A good many foolish ideas about Blake have resulted from staring at the naked text. The notion that he was an automatic writer is perhaps the most absurd of these: the notion that his prophecies offer only the dry bones of a vision that died within him runs it a close second. We spoke at the beginning of the specialized nature of modern culture; and a man who possesses so much interest for students of religion, philosophy, history, politics, poetry, and painting will be chopped by his critics into as many pieces as Osiris. It is all the more necessary to correct the tendency to identify blinkered vision with directed vision by trying to expose oneself to the whole impact of Blake at once.

---

[1] In addition to the Ellis and Yeats reproductions, one may call attention to the Muir color facsimiles of the illuminated books done mostly in the 1880's. These are often better than the ones in Ellis and Yeats, but they were produced in small editions and even large libraries rarely have many of them. Mr. Frye also alludes to the Dent facsimiles, 1927–1932, of *The Marriage of Heaven and Hell, The First Book of Urizen,* and *Visions of the Daughters of Albion.* An invaluable guide to original copies, as well as a list of facsimiles, is contained in Geoffrey Keynes and Edwin Wolf

2nd, *William Blake's Illuminated Books: A Census* (New York, 1953).

An important project of making excellent reproductions was begun in 1949 by the Trianon Press for the William Blake Trust. Volumes so far published include:

> *Jerusalem* (color), 1951
> *Jerusalem* (black and white), 1952
> *Songs of Innocence* (color), 1954
> *Songs of Innocence and of Experience* (color), 1955
> *The Book of Urizen* (color), 1958
> *Visions of the Daughters of Albion* (color), 1959
> *The Marriage of Heaven and Hell* (color), 1960

One wishes that more libraries would acquire this beautiful series because the reproductions, at their best, are almost forgeries.—Ed.

Hazard Adams

Reading Blake's Lyrics: "The Tyger"

THE immensely complicated pattern of symbolism in Blake's prophetic books has been called a "system." To do so is inaccurate, for "system" suggests the possibility of effective reduction of meaning and tends to ally it with occultist systems of correspondences. Unfortunately no other word is quite adequate; therefore in the following discussion I shall adopt the word and qualify its use. What I shall call the "system" is expressible only as a poetically coherent cluster of metaphor—coherent, that is, within itself, and also in relation to traditions or conventions of symbolic correspondence which lie beyond the pattern as it is expressed by Blake. The system itself has only an ideal existence. "Expressions" of it are really only strivings toward it. My purpose is to argue that a striving toward expression of this system (a view of the world as metaphor, as Wallace Stevens might have put it) is the basis of all Blake's work, the early lyrics and the late prophecies. Such a view, though in practice it has been held by many commentators on Blake, has never, I believe, been defended in theory against the popular view of the good poem as a comparatively independent entity. If one is to hold my theory, it ceases to be surprising that very few commentaries on single poems by Blake (those outside of books on the whole body of Blake's work) have been successful in expressing what is felt about the greatness of individual poems. It is furthermore no surprise that the best essays on Blake's lyrics seem constantly in danger of expanding in the direction of book-length statements. The true Blakean feels that to explain a single line of Blake he must somehow explain all of him, and in at least one sense he is correct.

The view I hold—that in effect Blake's early poems strive to express the same system that the later prophetic books approach—seems to violate our sense of temporal order. Many scholars would prefer to argue that it is folly to seek out Blake's "sublime allegory" in poems written presumably before that allegory was fully expressed. I do not wish to deny Joseph Wicksteed's contention that Blake's later work must be applied to the earlier with the greatest of care.[1] To practice too much caution, however, is to assume that Blake's symbolism is more private than it really is and that it is the product of slow development. From Blake's point of view the latter is at least a dubious assumption.

I believe that Blake would have held the system to be traditional, or, as he would have thought of it, timelessly existing—an ideal toward the expression of which every poem strives. The existence of the system, as Blake expressed his understanding of it in the later prophecies, provides an ideal against which poems may be judged. Blake's prophetic books were meant as a mythic corpus of language in which the symbolic conventions proper to the system were properly set down. The important difference between Blake's corpus and "gram-

[1] *Blake's Innocence and Experience* (London, Toronto, and New York, 1928), p. 26.

From *Texas Studies in Literature and Language*, II (Spring 1960), 18–37; edited by Philip H. Graham and published by the University of Texas Press. Reprinted with revisions by the author, by permission of the journal.

mars" of poetic myth, such as Robert Graves's *White Goddess*, is that Blake's is a body of metaphor while Graves's is a reductive explanation of it. Swinburne's belief that Blake's prophecies were a "drugged and adulterated compound" of several myths is only a quarter-truth based upon a misunderstanding of why Blake drew upon widely separated mythologies in expressing the system.

My argument, then, though William of Occam might not have found it properly honed, is to hold that the system lies deep in the substratum of the early poems, or, to put it another way, that each early poem strives to become part of the timeless system that Blake would have called simply "vision"—something not merely *before* but *beyond* philosophy. I hold also that the system is quite naturally more difficult to apprehend in the early poems because it is sometimes expressed in fragments and sometimes, when the poems are most successful, in microcosm—in greatly compressed form.

It is clear, I think, from examining Blake's comments on other poets and his illustrations to the works of others that he evaluated all other poets on the basis of their ability to approach complete expression of the system. Blake's illustrations are often, perhaps always, attempts to correct certain "failures" of symbolic treatment in the works of poets he admired. Blake shows Dante's hell, for example, to be a delusory state from which man *may* be redeemed. Sometimes the illustrations correct a popular but, to Blake, partially misguided interpretation. Such is the case with the Job illustrations. In any case, Blake always seems to reveal the meaning of these works in terms of symbolic conventions as he understands them.

To suppose that Blake's own mythic corpus as it is later expressed in the prophecies will help to reveal the deepest symbolic content of his earlier lyrics is not only logically deducible from the view that one attempt at expression of a "system" will help explain another; it is also solidly supported by Blake's own theory of art. From his attack on Locke's denial of innate ideas to his formulation of the principle of the archetype in poetry, his theory enforces it at every point. For example, in his marginal comments on Sir Joshua Reynolds' *Discourses* Blake attacked Reynolds for holding the Lockean view: "Reynolds Thinks that Man Learns all that he knows. I say on the Contrary that Man Brings All that he has or can have Into the World with him. Man is Born Like a Garden ready Planted & Sown. This World is too poor to produce one Seed." [2] Blake's attitude toward the nature of reality would deny not only our conventional views of time but also the possibility that something can be created from nothing.

The symbols of poetry, according to Blake, come from the *real* world, the permanent timeless world of eternity: "There Exist in that Eternal World the Permanent Realities of Every Thing which we see reflected in this Vegetable Glass of Nature." [3] The real world is a world of spirits, but, says Blake, "A Spirit and a Vision are not, as the modern philosophy supposes, a cloudy vapour, or a nothing: they are organized and minutely articulated beyond all that the mortal and perishing nature can produce." [4] For Blake, the greatest art is the minutely articulated vision of the real world, which if clearly seen would reveal itself as the vision of an apocalyptic resolution of all things into the form of "contraries." This real world he thought any man capable of perceiving if he were to look *through* instead of *with* the eyes: "I question not my Corporeal or Vegetative Eye any more than I would Question a Window concerning a Sight. I look thro'

---

[2] *The Complete Writings of William Blake* (Geoffrey Keynes, editor; London and New York, 1957), p. 471. With the exception of the transcription of "The Tyger," all quotations from Blake's works in this essay are from this edition, hereafter referred to as *K*.

[3] "A Vision of the Last Judgment," *K*605.

[4] "A Descriptive Catalogue," *K*576.

it & not with it." [5] Northrop Frye has re-
marked that no matter how many eyes we
have we still have only a single mind and
that for Blake the eye is a lens and perception a mental act.[6] Furthermore, each minute perception *through* the eye is a vortex of experience which carries with it, in
microcosm, the totality of experience. Imagination requires minute discrimination:
"He who does not imagine in stronger and
better lineaments, and in stronger and better light than his perishing and mortal eye
can see, does not imagine at all." [7]

Implicit in Blake's theory of art is the
idea that there is a final and perfect form
which all art seeks to approximate. The
duty of the artist is to recreate out of the
materials of the fallen world a work of art
embodying the "central form" of the real
world. This is the reason for Blake's assumption that there is a universal system. A
work of art may be judged by the extent to
which it has succeeded in recreating this
reality in terms which man may comprehend *through* the senses, in terms not de-
based by the veil of material delusion.

Objects seen *through* the eye form the
"minute particulars" of this system. They
are vortexes, points of experience which
expand back through the mind to infinity.
Or, more exactly, they are infinite eternity
(spatially and temporally free) contracted
to minute particulars in the act of perception: "the world in a grain of sand." The
delusion we call the material world is a
congeries of multiple images broken from
an essential unity where all things are infinitely expanded and therefore one:

> My Eyes more & more
> Like a Sea without shore
> Continue Expanding,

[5] "A Vision of the Last Judgment," K617. Also:

> "We are led to Believe a Lie
> When we see not Thro' the Eye."
> —"Auguries of Innocence," K433.

Elsewhere Blake distinguishes between the "in-
ward" and "outward" eye (K817).
[6] *Fearful Symmetry* (Princeton, 1947), p. 19.
[7] "A Descriptive Catalogue," K576.

> The Heavens commanding,
> Till the Jewels of Light,
> Heavenly Men beaming bright,
> Appear'd as One Man.[8]

In eternity the lion lies down with the
lamb: we *see* them particular but *know*
them as parts of the whole. Many of the
"Proverbs of Hell" in Blake's *Marriage of
Heaven and Hell* illustrate this point. For
example: "Let man wear the fell of the lion,
woman the fleece of the sheep." [9] Men and
women, in Cabalistic and in Blakean
thought, are fragments of an eternal unity.
All things are aspects of God himself, or
eternity:

> The pride of the peacock is the glory of God.
> The lust of the goat is the bounty of God.
> The wrath of the lion is the wisdom of God.[10]

Man, also, is a microcosm of God and,
therefore, God himself or a reflection of
God in particular terms. What Blake calls
the "human form divine" is man's eternal
form—or God. Man, if he knows how to
interpret his perceptions, is capable of seeing *sub specie aeternitatis* by practicing
the observation of "minute particulars."
Blake denies dualism as a necessary condition of human experience, particularly the
dualism of universality-concretion. Duality
creates negations, not contraries.

Taken together, the ideas that there is a
single timeless reality, that time is itself an
illusion at least insofar as we think we
know it, and that man has innate ideas
when he enters the fallen world suggest
that Blake, looking back on his early shorter poems, would not have been surprised
at his genius. Instead he would have held
that failure to anticipate the "system"
would have been failure as a poet. He
would have held that by definition any true
poem is a creation *pars pro toto* of the single system which it is the business of art
constantly to recreate. He would have
judged his early poems on their power to

[8] Letter to Butts, K805.   [9] K151.
[10] K151.

discriminate particularly aspects of eternity.

Readers have generally assumed that "The Tyger" is one of Blake's two or three greatest lyrics. For this reason, it is interesting to see that "The Tyger" most fully and particularly assimilates the whole of Blake's great system.[11] If we take as our criterion Blake's own view of what a poem should be, we discover that we have not overrated it. This leads us to suspect two things: that Blake's own standard is a reasonable one, at least insofar as the kind of poetry he wrote is concerned; and that an interpretation of Blake's shorter poems in the light of other and usually later expressions of the system is not only allowable but also perhaps imperative, if we are to understand what these poems really are. The meaning of "The Tyger" has remained a source of endless speculation; commentaries upon it have been general, fragmentary, or specialized. The excellent general approach to Blake of Frye, for example, puts us in a position to understand the poem but does not treat it in any detail. The interesting commentary of David V. Erdman, on the other hand, is limited by his special concern with Blake's politics.[12]

Here it is in the form which perhaps satisfied its author—the form in which Blake engraved it: [13]

[11] In the last chapter of his recent book, *The Piper and the Bard* (Detroit, 1959), pp. 277–287, published after this essay was completed, Robert F. Gleckner discusses parallels between "The Tyger" and *The Four Zoas*. He reaches some conclusions similar to my own, but he approaches them from an opposite direction, being interested primarily in how "The Tyger" as a song of experience throws light upon the later poem. My own discussion is a considerable development of some ideas originally presented in *Blake and Yeats: The Contrary Vision* (Ithaca, 1955), pp. 236–240.
[12] *Blake: Prophet Against Empire* (Princeton, 1954), particularly pp. 178–181.
[13] Blake's punctuation was inconsistent, particularly in his use of commas and periods, colons and semicolons. This inconsistency is made even more confusing (if that is possible) by his tendency to write commas that look like periods and

Tyger Tyger. burning bright, [.]
In the forests of the night: [;]
What immortal hand or eye. [,]
Could frame thy fearful symmetry?

In what distant deeps or skies.
Burnt the fire of thine eyes?
On what wings dare he aspire?
What the hand, dare seize the fire?

And what shoulder, & what art,
Could twist the sinews of thy heart?
And when thy heart began to beat,
What dread hand? & what dread feet?

What the hammer? what the chain,
In what furnace was thy brain?
What the anvil? what dread grasp, [.]
Dare its deadly terrors clasp?

When the stars threw down their spears
And water'd heaven with their tears: [;]
Did he smile his work to see?
Did he who made the Lamb make thee?

Tyger Tyger burning bright,
In the forests of the night; [:]
What immortal hand or eye, [.]
Dare frame thy fearful symmetry?

"The Tyger" is a poem of rather simple form, clearly and cleanly proportioned, all of its statements contributing to a single, sustained, dramatic gesture. Read aloud, it is powerful enough to move many listeners (small children, for example) without their having much understanding of the poem beyond its literal expression of a dramatic situation. But Blake warns us that there is a great gulf between simplicity and insipid-

semicolons that look like colons. This problem is well illustrated by the plate from *Songs of Experience* on which "The School Boy" is engraved (reproduced in Northrop Frye's Modern Library selection of Blake). In the word "nip'd" of line one, stanza five, the apostrophe looks like a period, though in "strip'd" of line three it is clearly an apostrophe. I have chosen to reproduce Blake's punctuation as best I can without being swayed by a desire for consistency. Possible alternative readings appear in the brackets. No two Blake scholars have agreed on the correct transcription; it is clear that subtleties of interpretation cannot often be based upon Blake's punctuation.

ity. The total force of the poem comes not only from its immediate rhetorical power but also from its symbolical structure.

Blake's images, at first sensuous, are to continued inspection symbolic. Things which burn, even tigers perhaps, are either purifying something or being purified. In the dark of night, in a forest, a tiger's eyes would seem to burn. The tiger's striped body suggests this same conflagration. In any case, Blake is trying to establish a kind of brilliance about his image, a brilliance which he associates not surprisingly with the apocalyptic figure of his minor prophecies, Orc:

But terrible Orc, when he beheld the morning in
    the east,
Shot from the heights of Enitharmon,
And in the vineyards of red France appear'd the
    light of his fury.[14]

There are many examples of the same imagery throughout the prophecies. Another visual image which Blake may be suggesting here is consistent with what we shall see in the nature of the tiger itself. In many religious paintings (and in Blake's own work, the popularly mistitled "Glad Day," [15] for example) the central figure seems to be emerging from or surrounded by a vast light: figuratively he "burns." Visually the fire image suggests immediate violence; traditionally it suggests some sort of purgatorial revelation.

The forests of the poem represent those famous mythological areas inhabited by blatant beasts, lost knights, and various spiritual wanderers and travellers. These forests *belong* to the night: Blake clearly invites us to read his line symbolically. For Blake, night suggests the delusion of material substance and the absence of the kind of light which surrounds revelation. There is a violent contrast between light and darkness, between the tiger and its surroundings, and the reader recognizes that the forest and the night are to be thought

14 "Europe," K244-245.
15 See Erdman, p. 6, for an explanation of how it came to be so titled.

of in a derogatory way. The tiger, on the other hand, is presented ambiguously. In spite of its natural viciousness, it seems to suggest also clarity and energy. If the reader has had prolonged experience with poetry and mythology, other associations will sharpen these ideas. He will perhaps associate the "forests of the night" with the traditional dark night or dark journey of the soul through the dens of demons and beasts. The tiger's brightness may suggest the force which the sun so often symbolizes in mythology. If the reader has read Dante, he may associate the forests with Dante's descent from the dark wood into the underworld; if he has read Goethe, he may notice a striking symbolic relationship between Blake's imagery and the imagery of enclosure—the forest, the study, the cave, the circle—in *Faust*. Finally, if he has read Blake's own body of work, he will know that since the Fall of Man was a fall into a material world, he may associate the night with matter. In forests in the darkness men are trapped in an enclosure similar to Plato's cave, hobbled by the growing rubbish of materialism, blocked off from light by material substance. Men stand in forests surrounded by webs of leaves, limbs, vines, and bracken (Blake's illustrations provide ample evidence for such a symbolic interpretation of fallen life). Blake's prophecies work toward a similar expression of this idea in expanded form. In *The Book of Urizen*, Urizen, the arch-materialist of Blake's myth, traps himself in webbed enclosures similar to jungles. In *The Four Zoas* he sits in his "web of deceitful religion." The forest is also a symbol of the natural cycle of growth and decay in the fallen, natural world. It therefore represents not only spatial but also temporal enclosure. In his later prophecies Blake refers to the fallen world in its material, spatial form as the "mundane shell." Its opacity prevents man from seeing through to eternity. The time-form of the fallen world Blake calls the "circle of destiny," the world falsely seen in the spirit of materialistic determinism. The stars, which enter our poem in stanza five, are a part of the concave surface of the mundane shell where man is trapped, and their movements represent the delusory, mechanical aspects of time. This shell is also a kind of egg, holding an embryo capable eventually of breaking the shell and leaping into real life free of the cycles of time and the enclosures of space.

In *The Four Zoas*, night symbolizes the history of the fallen world—its time-form, the circle of destiny. The archetypal man of Blake's prophetic books, Albion, a primordial giant symbolizing the human world, succumbs to sleep at the time of the fall and awakens only at the last judgment. In an early scheme for *The Four Zoas* Blake divided the history of the fallen world into nine "nights," each a historical cycle; and he subtitled his poem "The Death and Judgment of the Ancient Man, A Dream in Nine Nights." The fallen world is therefore a nightmare in the mind of Albion, who is afflicted by materialist delusions: for the materialist, the tiger appears out of darkness, a nightmarish figure, bright and violent, perhaps the vehicle of that terrible judgment he has been taught to believe in. What the tiger is to the visionary, the poem is about to tell us, but in a subtler way.

Now all of the symbolic relationships that I have suggested may not be apparent to a cursory reading *in vacuo*. As the reader acquaints himself with, first, the poem's clearly symbolic diction, the symbolical and allegorical tradition in western poetry, and finally Blake's own symbolical world, the poem gathers force. It is true that the reader is, to a certain degree, reading back and away from the poem into the world from which it has come, but even this is consistent with Blake's own view of the world: Man creates the world by the process of imagination; reading back and away from the poem is also reading back and *into* one's own mind. In one sense, at least, Blake wrote poems which the reader himself creates.

A reading of Blake's early drafts of "The Tyger" in the Rossetti MS reveals a rather important metamorphosis of the attitude of the speaker of the poem. Certain phrases from these drafts, later deleted, suggest that the speaker's attitude as Blake first conceived it was more clearly one of failure to understand and consequent fear of the tiger.[16] For example:

> What dread hand and what dread feet?
> Could fetch it from the furnace deep
> And in thy horrid ribs dare steep
> In the well of sanguine woe.

The hellish imagery of these lines (Blake contended, after all, that hell was a kind of delusion), the reference to horrid ribs and deadly terrors, both of which strongly suggest that the tiger is a product of a *real* hell and a *real* deathliness—several of these images are eliminated from the poem so that the balance between fear and admiration is made less precarious. It is still possible to read the final draft and find overtones which suggest that the speaker *might* be a figure living in the fallen world and deluded into thinking that his world is the real world—someone like Urizen as he appears in *The Four Zoas*, particularly in Night Seven (a), where he meets Orc:

> But Urizen silent descended to the Caves of Orc
> & saw
> A Cavern'd Universe of flaming fire.[17]

There is still in the final draft the assertion that the tiger may come from "distant deeps." To such a person the tiger is hor-

---

[16] The interpretive conclusions of Martin K. Nurmi's "Blake's Revisions of 'The Tyger'," *PMLA*, LXXI, 4 (September 1956), pp. 669–685 are not, I think, inconsistent with the view expressed here, though they differ in emphasis. He writes: "Blake [can portray] the tiger's symmetry as containing a really fearful component because he can see clearly and fully at this point the place of the tiger in the divine plan." From my point of view it would be better to say that Blake can portray the tiger's symmetry as having visionary beauty for this reason.

[17] "The Four Zoas," *K320*.

rific. It does not conform to established law, fails to fit into the established world picture, and is therefore evil. It is the corporeal eye of such a person that is described in *The Marriage of Heaven and Hell:* "The roaring of lions, the howling of wolves, the raging of the stormy sea, and the destructive sword, are portions of eternity, too great for the eye of man." [18]

But I think it is clear that there is also another speaker of the poem who presents us with an alternative reading, a speaker whose attitude casts an ironic perspective upon the words as they are spoken by our Urizenic questioner. This speaker knows the answers to his questions and is really forming them rhetorically. This means ultimately that the speaker is a visionary, a "mental traveller" who sees the world in its proper perspective. Careful examination shows that the questions he asks imply certain answers, and that from them we learn not only what the tiger is but also who his maker is.

The question of stanza one involves the speaker's assumption that the "hand or eye" forms the tiger. The hand is the shaping force of the blacksmith. The "eye" image, which as we have seen occurs elsewhere in Blake in the same sense, suggests the shaping spirit of imagination. If we take the maker of the tiger to be God (provisionally, for this is not the whole story), the appearance of "eye" in this context means that God's method of creation is supernatural and that what He creates is not material. For Blake there is a clear distinction between the material, lidded or "outward" eye (an image like that of the "mundane shell") and the immortal, visionary eye which the artist sees *through* instead of *with*. The one raises a wall against true perception. The other opens a door: "If the doors of perception were cleansed every thing would appear to man as it is, infinite." [19] Erdman has pointed out that the eye appears as a visionary image in Blake's illustrations and drawings. [20] In *Jerusalem*, Albion sleeps through history with eyes closed; his moments of vision and assertions of new life occur when he opens his real eyes and creates thereby the real world, not the nightmarish apparent one:

> Upon the Rock, he open'd his eyelids in pain,
>   in pain he mov'd
> His stony members, he saw England. Ah!
>   shall the Dead live again? [21]

"Eye" suggests also the cycles of history named by God in *The Four Zoas* and *Jerusalem*. In those prophecies, history is divided into seven periods or "eyes of God," as Blake calls them. Each of these is a wheel containing within it the microcosm of all history, each wheel the same play with different players; or perhaps better, each the same group of players acting a slightly different but archetypal drama: "as one age falls, another rises, different to mortal sight, but to immortals only the same . . . Accident ever varies, Substance can never suffer change nor decay." [22] Thus each "eye of God" is an intuition of the full scope of the historic process, and the eighth eye will act as the culmination of this process. This view of history and reality is consistent with Blake's argument that reality lies within "minute particulars," if only each particular is observed *through* the eye. Thus each eye of God is figuratively the "world in a grain of sand," or better, the grain of sand in which the world exists. The tiger as a creation of the imaginative eye of God and a symbol of that imaginative power is microcosmically implicit in each cycle, immanent and imminent. To the tiger's more complex relation to the culmination of history or the "eighth eye of God," I shall return shortly.

The tiger-maker is, as I have already suggested, not God simply defined. He is a false god or true God depending upon the speaker's perspective. Urizen would consid-

---

[18] *K*151.
[19] "The Marriage of Heaven and Hell," *K*154.
[20] P. 313. The source is Ezekiel.
[21] *K*742.
[22] "A Descriptive Catalogue," *K*567.

er the maker of the tiger a false god, a devil
—that is why Blake often sides with "the
devil's party," as he seems to do in *The
Marriage of Heaven and Hell,* showing that
"angels" are representatives of passive reason and thus lieutenants of Urizen to be
associated with the stars, while "devils"
are truly creative: "Active Evil is better
than Passive Good." [23] Urizen's god is really the false god. Therefore, if the questions of the poem are taken as spoken by
the materialist they imply that the creator
of the tiger is some kind of interloper, a
breaker of order. Icarus and Prometheus,
the mythological personages of whom there
are definite overtones in stanza two, were
both interlopers. Both defined the order of
things (the material order, Blake would
say) and both were punished for it. Icarus
aspired to the sun and was flung down into the sea. Prometheus stole fire (the persistent image of Blake's poem) from the
Gods, brought it to man, and was chained
to a rock for his transgression.[24] There is
a parallel to this in Blake's own work,
where Orc, Blake's first major apocalyptic
figure, is also chained to a rock so that he
too may be punished and controlled. According to Urizen, then, the creator of the
tiger, a threatening figure like Orc, or perhaps Blake's ultimate hero Los, must be
some lawbreaker sent by the forces of the
devil himself. Part of Orc's serpent nature
is that imposed upon him by the deluded
imaginations of Urizen.

But the visionary, asking the same questions rhetorically, sees these same interlopers not as evil creatures but as heroes.
They have embarked on the inevitable journey any hero must make in order to meet
the forces of materialism and to do battle
with them. Icarus' ascent on wings attached
to him by wax suggests a terrible misjudg-
ment of the consequences of approach to
the fire of heaven, but Prometheus' descent
sets the stage for the more important final
battle to come, the loss of Aeschylus' *Prometheus Unbound* being an irony of history. Prometheus' gift of fire to man symbolizes hope of eventual apocalypse, a
cleansing of all material things in purgatorial flame. His act is therefore related
closely to the image Blake draws of a burning tiger threatening to consume the forests with fire. The "seizing" of fire is also
the typical act of a blacksmith preparing
to forge some object. In stanzas three and
four, furthermore, the speaker assumes that
the creator of the tiger is a blacksmith or
at least someone who has done a blacksmith's job. This particular smith is not
only the strongest of creatures but also the
greatest of artists. He is not only a Prometheus but also a Hephaestus; and we recall that the blacksmith Hephaestus was also hurled from heaven by Zeus, that he was
the Greek god of fire, and that his name
was used by Greek and Roman poets as a
synonym for "fire."

From the perspective of Urizen again,
the questions of stanzas three and four imply that the blacksmith is some devil-maker.
If we take the blacksmith as an archetype
of the artist, then we see that from this perspective the artist is a creator of illusions
and that the poet, in Sir Philip Sidney's
terms, "lyeth," but for evil reasons, not for
greater good. Urizen would ban him from
the republic for reasons somewhat different from Plato's—because he is a fabrica-
tor and a dangerous revolutionary who pre-
tends to see a world other than the material
one. In his annotations to Bacon's *Essays,*
Blake objects to the idea of the poet's lying in order to give pleasure. Only someone who sees *with* the corporeal eye would
for a moment be so naïve as to say that
the poet lies: "What Bacon calls Lies is
Truth itself." [25] Blake's blacksmith-artist
Los works steadily with anvil and forge,
hand and eye; the wonders of his labors
are his creations of form out of miasma.
His actions illustrate the principle of *outline* in Blake's aesthetic. According to

---

[23] Annotations to Lavater's *Aphorisms,* K77.
[24] Robert O. Bowen, *Explicator* VII, 8 (June 1949), Item 62, first mentioned these overtones.
[25] K397.

Blake, when error is given proper outline it ceases to be error, for in its true form it has lost the power to delude. If, then, we begin to suspect that the creator of the tiger is, in Blake's terms, Urizen's nemesis Los, we shall not be far wrong.

But this is not the whole story either. Stanza five is perhaps the most difficult in the poem. No interpretation of it that I have seen seems adequate. The most elaborate recent one is by Kathleen Raine in an essay which proposes to find the answer to the poem's question (Who made the tiger?) in Blake's alchemical and occult reading.[26] She points to a quotation from Reuchlin's *de Arte Cabbalistica*, which is mentioned twice by Robert Fludd in his *Mosaicall Philosophy* and once by Thomas Vaughn in his *Lumen de Lumine*, "both books well-known to Blake." The quotation is: "There is not an herb here below but he hath a star in heaven above; the star strikes him with her beams and says to him: Grow." Miss Raine construes the action of the stars in throwing down their "spears" (beams) as making possible the creation or "growth" of the tiger and the fallen world. By a somewhat devious process of reasoning, Miss Raine concludes that the Elohim (whom she associates with Urizen), as distinct from God, created the tiger, because in Blake's sources the Elohim created the fallen world. Therefore, she argues, "the answer is beyond all possible doubt, No"; God, who created the lamb, did not create the tiger.

I can only say that I totally disagree with the conclusion and the method used to arrive at it. Miss Raine has perhaps discovered a valuable source for Blake's star imagery, but she has completely ignored what Blake has done with the imagery in assimilating it to the poem. In the first place, if we accept the source, Blake has substituted "spears" for "beams," and it is difficult to assume that he did this merely to find a rime for "tears." "Spears"

brings a suggestion of war into the poem. "Stars" in Blake's symbolism are always associated with Urizen and materialism. As warriors they seem to represent his own legions, who have lost the battle against the creator of the tiger and in the course of this loss have actually helped to create what they most feared—the wrath of righteousness. I believe that further examination of Blake's imagery here will sustain this view. In Blake's symbolism the stars represent the movement of a delusory scientific time and the concave, inner surface of the mundane egg which is the fallen world. The image is particularly apt because the stars are ineffectual in daylight; they are apparent only at night or during fallen history. To Urizen the act of the stars in throwing down their spears would suggest that creation of the material world—the end of the "wars of Eden" leading to the fall. Stars are traditionally angelic intelligences, but Blake uses both angels and stars ironically as forces of reaction. The action of the stars here represents a fall in the war in heaven during which the "demonic" orders, represented by the tiger, were created. An important analogy to this act occurs in the Preludium to *Europe* where the earth female characterizes herself as an upside-down tree, the inverted delusory fallen Sephirotic tree of the Cabala, and the stars that appear to be rising are in fact the fallen angels and false gods, while the falling stars are the rising gods. This topsy-turviness is typical of Blake's fallen world and accounts for Urizen's loss of direction in *The Four Zoas*.

Several commentators upon this poem (most recently F. W. Bateson) [27] have pointed out that the stars also throw down their spears in Night V of *The Four Zoas*. In this passage Urizen is speaking of past events:

"I well remember, for I heard the mild & holy voice
"Saying, 'O light, spring up & shine,' & I sprang up from the deep.

[26] "Who Made the Tyger?", *Encounter* II, 6 (June 1954), pp. 43–50.

[27] *Selected Poems of William Blake* (New York, 1957), pp. 117–119.

"He gave to me a silver scepter, & crown'd me
    with a golden crown,
"& said, 'Go forth & guide my Son who wanders
    on the ocean.'
"I went not forth: I hid myself in black clouds
    of my wrath;
"I call'd the stars around my feet in the night of
    councils dark;
"The stars threw down their spears & fled naked
    away.
"We fell. I seiz'd thee, dark Urthona." [28]

This passage tells of a fall (obviously based
on Milton's account of the Fall of the
Angels, says Bateson) similar to that in
The Book of Urizen, but here it is told not
objectively but from Urizen's point of
view. Here, too, we have a rather different
Urizen, with more self-awareness than formerly. He seems at least partially aware of
the reasons for and the pathos of his fall.
The stars are, in any case, the legions of
Urizen now fallen into the upside-down
material world of his own mental construction, a world created when Albion fell
asleep:

But now the Starry Heavens are fled from the
    mighty limbs of Albion.[29]

They now compose the "starry floor" or
the limit of the fall referred to in "Introduction" to *Songs of Experience*. Urizen's
error is to think that they are rising points
of light while the energetic light of the
demonic orders seems to him destined for
some awful abyss. The stars are trapped,
then, in the world delusion which Urizen
next proposes to explore:

"I will arise, Explore these dens, & find that deep
    pulsation
"That shakes my cavern with strong shudders;
    perhaps this is the night
"Of Prophecy, & Luvah hath burst his way from
    Enitharmon." [30]

Urizen's song ends with his proposing to
organize his domain—the materialist
world. It is unlikely that in the stubborn-

ness of his own revolt Urizen (if we may
conjecture) would fully understand the
weeping of the stars. He might consider it
an expression of pity for those hurt in the
havoc wrought by what to him was a necessary war in behalf of progress. But it is
more likely that the tears are really tears of
chagrin and fear reminiscent of the allegory in Blake's *America*, in which the soldiers of the king of England, also associated with Urizen, throw down their arms
to flee the vision of revolt, Orc.[31] Urizen
would not understand the chagrin of the
stars at their woeful upside-down enclosure
in the "starry floor" of circular zodiacal
movement—for him this would constitute
the brilliant new order:

In sevens & tens & fifties, hundreds, thousands,
    number'd all
According to their various powers, subordinate to
    Urizen
And to his sons in their degrees & to his beauteous
    daughters,
Travelling in silent majesty along their order'd
    ways
In right lined paths outmeasur'd by proportions
    of number, weight,
And measure, mathematic motion wondrous along
    the deep.[32]

These lines are from a section of *The Four
Zoas* in which we see Urizen's ordered
world as Urizen may first have seen it in
the flush of creative pride.

From the point of view of the visionary
the action of the stars is something more
profound. Erdman makes a suggestion
worthy of mention: "The climax of the
forging of stanza four of 'The Tyger' is a
mighty hammering which drives out the
impurities in a shower of sparks, like the
falling stars children call angels' tears. At
this point in 'The Tyger' Blake employs the
symbols which in his political writing sig-

[28] *K*310–311.   [29] "Milton," *K*486.
[30] *K*311.

[31] See Erdman, pp. 178–179; also Mark Schorer,
William Blake: The Politics of Vision (New
York, 1946), p. 251: "When the stars throw down
their spears and weep, they are soldiers abandon-
ing their arms in contrition and readiness for
peace."
[32] "The Four Zoas," *K*287.

nify the day of repentance when the king's 'starry hosts' shall 'throw down . . . sword and musket.' " [33] For the visionary the image of these lines is visual and particular, leading toward an intuition of apocalypse when, with the tiger formed, the sparks hurled, and heaven itself cleansed by pity and (perhaps, ironically) by fear, total resolution can be foreseen. The imagery of the stanza, rather than deriving its meaning from a single source, seems to me to describe an ambiguous event. If Miss Raine's hint is useful, it is to suggest that the hurling down of the spears of light at the time of the creation of the tiger is one of those typically ambiguous Blakean acts in which progression comes out of its own opposite. Thus the capitulation of the stars, in contributing to the "growth" of the fallen world, helps to bring about its apocalyptic destruction, just as Los's "hand or eye" brings form out of miasma and completes a divine plan which seems to have begun in total degradation. The visionary understands the paradox of progress and therefore is able to "keep the divine vision in time of trouble." The falling of the stars into the "starry floor" of the heavens is combined, then, with an image of pity, for they fall into this position in the form of tears, where they are a constant reminder of God's mercy in creating a lower limit for the fall.

There is a further qualification to be made. For Blake, there are true and false tears, true and false pity. For someone like Los, the true pity is to hold in check any immediate or sentimental expression of that emotion, just as Orc in Book VII of *The Four Zoas* "contemns" the pity of Urizen.[34] If Los were to pity Urizen before he had given him his true form, he would harm the whole of creation in the long run. Los, as artist, must purge himself even

of apparent pity in order to be capable of its higher form. The violent tiger itself is Blake's symbol for the denial of false pity. Urizen was fooled by the stars; they pitied themselves. The kind of pity of which Urizen is capable in his fallen state is itself error. In *Milton,* Blake speaks of Satan as having no "science of wrath, but only of pity." One contrary is necessary to the creativity of the other. Only Los combines the contraries.

In the fallen world even the apocalypse seems to have an ambiguous form. In total resolution the purgation by flame which is the tiger and the baptism by tears which is the weeping of the stars lead out of the fallen world into the new in the traditional rituals of rebirth. The perfect balance of eternity is achieved, and the tiger lies down with the lamb, an image to which Blake turns in other lyrics.

If by now we do not have a fairly clear idea of who created the tiger and what the tiger is, the prophetic books can tell us more. Early in the poem the word "dare" is dramatically substituted for the word "could" of stanza one. Physical strength to create the tiger is evidently not the only necessity—there must be *will*; the figurative journey is both physically and spiritually difficult. In the prophecies the tenacious spirit is Los, who wipes "the sweat from his red brow" and confronts those miasmal, hovering, indefinite creatures to whom he must give a form. It is Los, then, who howls in anguish, bestows no false pity, and holds to his task:

I know that Albion has divided me, and that thou,
   O my Spectre
Hast just cause to be irritated; but look stedfastly
   upon me;
Comfort thyself in my strength; the time will
   arrive
When all Albion's injuries shall cease.[35]

If we return for a moment to a point already made about Blake's theory of vision, we recall that he found the visionary at

---

[33] Erdman, p. 180. Ralph D. Eberly, *Explicator* VIII, 2 (November 1949), p. 12, has also associated the spears with a shower of sparks from the forge of a heavenly smithy.
[34] *K322.*

[35] "Jerusalem," *K626.*

least latent in every man. Every man is a *Los* or at least has a *Los*. When in *Milton* Blake finds his own prophetic inspiration, it is Los who appears to him as a burning spiritual form:

. . . Los descended to me:
And Los behind me stood, a terrible flaming Sun, just close
Behind my back. I turned round in terror, and behold!
Los stood in that fierce glowing fire, & he also stoop'd down
And bound my sandals on in Udan-Adan; trembling I stood
Exceedingly with fear & terror, standing in the Vale
Of Lambeth; but he kissed me and wish'd me health,
And I became One Man with him arising in my strength.
'Twas too late now to recede. Los had enter'd into my soul:
His terrors now possess'd me whole! I arose in fury & strength.[36]

Since the power of vision is the power of artistic creation in a non-material world, the power of God is the power of man, and each man is a kind of artist. It is no surprise to see that Blake takes the next step and asserts that man is a microcosm of God, God is the spiritual body of communal man.

In *Jerusalem*, when the seven eyes of God are named, it is said that "they nam'd the Eighth: he came not, he hid in Albion's Forests." [37] For fallen man, such a creature is truly horrendous, hidden gleaming like an eye—like a tiger—in darkness, an image of the judgment he fears. Fallen man sees with "a little narrow orb clos'd up & dark / Scarcely beholding the great light." [38] Such an eye Blake implies cannot "judge of the stars" and can therefore certainly not "measure the sunny rays." [39] For

such an eye, tigers and lions are not human forms but those "dishumaniz'd men" [40] seen by Urizen in his travels. Their spiritual reality is covered over by a material excrescence:

. . . A Rock, a Cloud, a Mountain,
Were not now Vocal as in Climes of happy Eternity
Where the lamb replies to the infant voice, & the lion to the man of years
Giving them sweet instructions; where the Cloud, the River, & the Field
Talk with the husbandman and shepherd.[41]

But for the visionary, the tiger illuminated is the tiger creating out of the forest the light of day in one vast apocalyptic conflagration similar to the awakening of Albion in *Jerusalem:*

. . . Albion rose
In anger, the wrath of God breaking, bright flaming on all sides around
His awful limbs; into the Heavens he walked, clothed in flames.[42]

The leap of the tiger in the forest, inevitable to the eye of the visionary, is equivalent to the purgative fire which sweeps all before it, the eighth eye of God rending the veil of materialism. The tiger is thus an image of man's own hopes—the God in man, but also something created by the artist in man on the anvil of inspiration. It is a "fearful" image because, in the "forests of the night," false pity is misdirected. The artist who chooses to capture the miasmal mist of error and from it create significant form must not succumb to the temptations of right reason: "The tygers of wrath are wiser than the horses of instruction." [43] To do so would be suddenly to succumb to the Urizenic view of what the tiger represents. Blake, himself, knew the

---

[36] *K*505.
[37] *K*686.
[38] "Milton," *K*484.
[39] *K*485. Compare the angel in *The Marriage of Heaven and Hell*, whose fear makes him see Hell in the form of a gigantic serpent with a forehead

colored like that of a tiger, while Blake finds himself sitting beside a bank listening to a harpist. For the political implications of the passage see Erdman, p. 165.
[40] "The Four Zoas," *K*314.
[41] "The Four Zoas," *K*315.
[42] *K*742.
[43] "The Marriage of Heaven and Hell," *K*152.

temptation to treat the tiger as an obsessive, evil demon:

I am under the direction of Messengers from Heaven, Daily & Nightly; but the nature of such things is not, as some suppose, without trouble or care. Temptations are on the right hand & left; behind, the sea of time & space roars & follows swiftly: he who keeps not right onward is lost, & if our footsteps slide in clay, how can we do otherwise than fear & tremble? [44]

And even Los is capable of momentary delusion during which the negative hatred of the spectre appears similar to the tiger's wrath:

While Los spoke the terrible Spectre fell shudd'ring before him,
Watching his time with glowing eyes to leap upon his prey.[45]

But in certain visionary circumstances wrath and pity merge in a single imaginative act. The totality of the man of imagination, expressed in the image of the four Zoas and their eyes, is combined with the seven lamps, the seven spirits, and the seven seals of *Revelation* in Blake's description of his pictorial Vision of the Last Judgment: "The whole upper part of the Design is a view of Heaven opened: around the Throne of Christ [in a cloud which rolls away are the] Four Living Creatures filled with Eyes, attended by Seven Angels with the Seven Vials of the wrath of God." [46] Blake clearly associates these seven angels and vials with his own seven historical cycles culminating in the total eighth.

The eighth eye or total man is the "Four Living Creatures." Even in his fallen state the prophetic power in this man is capable of being raised above his own sleeping form so that he may see God's wrath and its sevenfold cyclical expression in history as a form of spiritual recreation and therefore proper pity. This is the case with Milton:

The Seven Angels of the Presence wept over Milton's Shadow.
As when a man dreams he reflects not that his body sleeps,
Else he would wake, so seem'd he entering his Shadow: but
With him the Spirits of the Seven Angels of the Presence
Entering, they gave him still perceptions of his Sleeping Body
Which now arose and walk'd with them in Eden, as an Eighth
Image Divine tho' darken'd and tho' walking as one walks
In sleep, and the Seven comforted and supported him.[47]

To "dare frame" the tiger's "fearful symmetry" is to "keep right onward," to hold the visionary attitude. It is also to confront the tiger with assurance. To be tempted and to succumb is to become the materialist and to find oneself staring, as it were, into a mirror at one's own spectre, without realizing that one sees there the reflection of a brute self. Nature's "vegetable glass" shows Urizen only his own image. Not knowing that he sees himself, he chases that image through the world, failing ever to subdue it. The "wild beast" which Blake calls the "spectre" in "My Spectre around me . . ." is an intimation of the divided state of fallen man. If it is horrific, its existence, like that of the tiger, indicates man's condition if he cares to or can read the sign. In the conclusion of *Visions of the Daughters of Albion*, Oothoon, a free spirit condemned as a harlot by the man she has loved, lists a "glowing tyger" as one of the creatures of the night which can be blotted out by the "mild beams" of the sun—beams which bring expansion to the "eye of pity." [48] Having come this far, Oothoon needs only to see a little farther through the eye and into the tiger's fire to understand that the blotting out of the horrific glowing tiger in the greater light of the sun is similar to the disappearance of the sun in the light of

[44] Letter to Butts, *K*812–813.
[45] "Jerusalem," *K*627.
[46] "A Vision of the Last Judgment," *K*444.
[47] "Milton," *K*496.   [48] *K*195.

the glory of God, which is described to us in *Revelation*. In the apocalypse the tiger's fire returns to the light of which it is a fallen intimation. To the visionary, the tiger symbolizes the primal spiritual energy which may bring form out of chaos and unite man with that part of his own being which he has allowed somehow to sleep-walk into the dreadful forests of material darkness. In *Europe*, Blake speaks of materialist "thought" as the cause of such a retreat from reality:

Thought chang'd the infinite to a serpent, that which pitieth
To a devouring flame; and man fled from its face and hid in forests of night.[49]

The tiger is formed on the anvil of inspiration which is the eye of man and God, but it is also a symbol of the very same eye which created it, for Blake believed that men are what they behold, that the outer and inner worlds are really one: "To the Eyes of the Man of Imagination, Nature is Imagination itself. As a Man is, So he Sees. As the Eye is formed, such are its Powers."[50] Several times in the prophetic

[49] *K241.*   [50] Letter to Trusler, *K793.*

books Blake announces that a character has "become what he beheld." The manner in which one beholds the tiger is all important to its and one's own spiritual nature. As guardian of the forest, so to speak, it may opaquely repel, or it may indicate the existence somewhere nearby of the passage toward vision. Man has the power to create his world, for that world is really himself, caught in the vortex where the spirit takes on perceivable form.

"The Tyger" is concerned with both the unprolific or distorting and the truly creative process in spiritual life. The latter is a process equivalent to the process of creation in art. Creation in art is for Blake the renewal of visionary truth. From the point of view of the visionary, the tiger, fearful as he may be, is created form, error solidified and metamorphosed into a vision of the last judgment. He is, therefore, a creature to be confronted and contemplated not with undiluted fear but with that strange gaiety suggested by the visionary intensity of the poem itself—a gaiety which can find a place in the divine plan for both the tears and spears of the stars, for both Los and Urizen, and for both the tiger and the lamb.

John E. Grant

The Art and Argument of "The Tyger"

BLAKE's "The Tyger" is both the most famous of his poems and one of the most enigmatic. Critical statements about the poem abound, yet there has never really been an attempt to deal with this work as a whole. It is noteworthy also that no version of the poem, apart from facsimile texts, published in a collection of Blake's writings gives an accurate transcription of the author's punctuation. The reader is referred to Mr. Adams' judicious text on page 53 for a conservative transcription, while the reproduction of Blake's illuminated page below will facilitate study of the design. The attempt within a single essay to interpret every aspect of this complex work of art is certain to fail because a complete discussion of the relevant problems would require at least a monograph, but one may at least try to take a stand on all the major issues.

There is certainly no consensus about the general meaning of the poem. Martin K. Nurmi, in his valuable study of the manuscript revisions and of the probable movements of Blake's mind as he composed the poem, asserts that the poem is "a complex but essentially positive statement affirming the dread tiger's divinity, and not a probing of good and evil, as it has sometimes been interpreted," and he cites a number of distinguished Blakeans as supporting this view against Damon and a lesser array of other critics.[1] It is my contention, however, that it is impossible to convert the mighty questions of the poem into any-thing that can properly be called affirmation. As I see it, the poem is not a vehicle for positive thinking, but a study in perplexity and metaphysical rebelliousness, though in so far as it is a work of art, it is of course the result of positive action on the part of the poet.

The reader should be aware that there is in fact a third force among the interpreters of "The Tyger" which prefers to follow the rhetoric of the questions rather than to translate them into rhetorical questions. Both Kazin and Basler, who are concerned with expounding unorthodox or secular aspects of Blake's imagination, insist on the primacy of the questions.[2] And recently, though his general view of Blake is quite different from theirs, Northrop Frye has expressed a similar opinion while registering a strong protest in behalf of the common reader:

> Scholars will assert that the question in "The Tyger," "Did he who made the lamb make thee?" is to be answered with a confident yes or no: yes if Blake is believed to be a pantheist, no if he is believed to be a Gnostic. Most of those who love the poem are content to leave it a question, and they are right.[3]

[1] "Blake's Revisions of *The Tyger*," *PMLA*, LXXI (September 1956), 670.

[2] Alfred Kazin, "Introduction" to *The Portable Blake* (New York, 1946), p. 43; and Roy P. Basler, *Sex, Symbolism and Psychology in Literature* (New Brunswick, 1948), p. 21. As a matter of fact, Joseph Wicksteed, *Blake's Innocence and Experience: A Study of the Songs and Manuscripts* (London, 1928), could also be considered a member of this school; see p. 94.

[3] Northrop Frye, "Blake After Two Centuries," *University of Toronto Quarterly*, XXVII (October 1957), p. 12.

First printed in *Texas Studies in Literature and Language*, II (Spring 1960), 38–60; edited by Philip H. Graham, published by the University of Texas Press; reprinted here in a revised version.

There can be no thought that the third force has loved the poem better than the more determinate Blakeans, to be sure, but in this respect they have loved it more wisely. Of course, a systematic interpretation of the poem can hardly rest content with the assertion that a question is a question. But the significance of the rhetoric cannot be explained apart from a consideration of other problems.

Consider the illustration which accompanies the poem. Few qualified critics have had the temerity to study the poem in the context of its design, though the picture of the Tyger has invited those who know it casually either to treat this work of England's greatest painter as a bungle or to use it as a point of departure for demonstrating the dichotomy between poetry and painting,[4] a position which can hardly be supported by anything else Blake did.

Nothing, either in the illustration or in the poem, is likely to strike the impartial reader as being obviously affirmative, except perhaps for the question about the creator: "Did he smile his work to see?" Almost all the other actions described in the poem might be interpreted to be the work of an energetic god hostile to man, though such a being has no exact counterpart in Blake's developed system. Very relevant to the question of the ethical status of the Tyger is the intimate relationship indicated between creator and creature. Several critics have observed that in the heat of creation the creator is scarcely distinguished from his creature and therefore the ethical implications of either affect the other.

I consider an identification of the speaker in the poem to be the most crucial problem for interpretation because unless we understand his character we are unable to evaluate what he sees and says. It should be clear that he is not the omniscient Bard of the "Introduction" to *Songs of Experi-* ence "who Present, Past, and Future sees," because he has too many questions. Nowhere in the poem is he able to provide even such enigmatic answers to his questions as are possible for the speaker of "The Fly." As will become more evident, the speaker's questions sometimes express outrage comparable to that felt by Earth in "Earth's Answer." This awestruck voice in Experience is that of an average but also imaginative man who is almost overwhelmed by the mysterious prodigy he sees as a Tyger. In Blake's prophetic terminology, he belongs to the class of men called the "Redeemed," as opposed to the Urizenic "Elect" (as argued by Mr. Adams), or the prophetic "Reprobate" (as assumed by most other interpreters). But we cannot quite suppose that the speaker has stumbled upon the Tyger in the midst of the forests of the night, because under those circumstances he would be much too busy to ask questions about the beast. The vision of the Tyger has some of the hair-raising quality of Eliphaz's vision in Job, but a more instructive analogy is provided by the conjured rough beast of Yeats's "The Second Coming," for the conception of the general situation is influenced by Blake's poem, though it also sharply diverges from it. Observe that Blake's speaker is an ardent questioner about the origins of his beast in view, whereas Yeats's is more reflective about the spectacle, its implications, and its identity. The questions of Blake's speaker are more radical and likewise more emotional; in this state of mind he can never reach the philosophic (or theosophic) understanding potentially accessible to the Yeatsian visionary.[5] It will become more clear later that what Blake's speaker sees

---

[4] See René Wellek and Austin Warren, *Theory of Literature* (New York, 1949), p. 128, who speak of the "grotesque little animal" depicted as though it were entirely irrelevant to the poem.

[5] Mr. Adams hears another voice, that of the Blakean visionary who knows the answers, behind the bemused and baffled questioner. Few Blakeans would deny that Blake himself knew the answers, but I see no evidence that such a speaker is actually "in" the poem. He can be found in other *Songs of Experience*, but a poem as great as "The Tyger" ought to be granted its own autonomy.

and reacts to is a compound of truth and error which produces mystery. For the reader who achieves prophetic perspective, the primary focus of interest in the poem is on the speaker as *subject* and on the Tyger as *percept*, rather than as *object*.

The conception of the speaker as a member of the Redeemed class, filled with frustration, obsessed with fears and doubts, and resistant to the neat answers of Urizenic theology, does much to justify a discussion of various ambiguities contained within the mighty lines of the poem. The reader may become wearied with tracing the nuances of doubt because Blake's own ideas are usually precise and definite. But in "The Tyger," as in such poems as "Earth's Answer," "The Little Vagabond," or the opening stanzas of "A Little Boy Lost," the speaker is not Blake. Nevertheless, in these cases the speaker is treated with sympathy and patient understanding. After having learned much of what Blake knew, a number of Blake scholars have displayed a very un-Blakean impatience with those of Blake's characters who have not achieved comparable illumination, though Blake himself had great sympathy for those like Tom Paine who were finally on the side of the "devils," no matter how much doubt and error they spread.

If we follow the poem through, interpreting it word for word and bearing Blake's heavy punctuation and powerful measured cadence, we should be able to establish a basic reading against which to test any general interpretation. Since such a reading has never really been attempted before,[6] I shall mention a number of quite obvious things.[7] The speaker begins by ad-dressing the Tyger, and in the heavy alliteration and primarily trochaic beat of his words the beast is envisioned as burning in the darkness of nocturnal forests.[8] Flame is a clear symbol for passion [9] and is set off by the blackness of the nocturnal forests. Forests per se are sinister symbols in Blake, corresponding to Dante's *selva oscura*, for they stand for the merely or triumphantly vegetable world he elsewhere calls the "stems of vegetation" at the bottom of the state of generation. A beast whose natural home is in such a place would therefore likewise be ominous. The contrast between fire and night, of course, corresponds to the contrast of yellow and black stripes ringing the Tyger itself.

As a paraphrase for the question Blake's speaker puts to the Tyger about its origins, "What immortal made you?" is totally inadequate. Part of the force in the questioning of the first stanza derives from the fact that the fourth line is iambic. The movement from trochaic to iambic in the third line corresponds to the shift from

---

[6] The nearest approach to this kind of study, except for Mr. Adams' accompanying essay, is contained in Stanley Gardner, *Infinity on the Anvil* (Oxford, 1954), pp. 123–130. But even Gardner is more concerned with the resonances of the major symbols than in the poem as a developing whole.

[7] A complete rhetorical analysis should be coordinated with a prosodic one and both should be combined with a semantic study. Among the things one would wish most to note is the subtle and brilliant use of the words "In" and "What" especially in the initial position of the lines which follow their first introduction in lines 2 and 3. But the coordination of this material would make this essay too complicated.

[8] "Nocturnal forests" does not, indeed, properly render the overtones of "forests of the night," though it is better than the other annotational suggestion, "forests at night," given by F. W. Bateson in his edition, *Selected Poems of William Blake* (London, 1957), p. 118. (Hereafter called Bateson.) These paraphrases give priority to the forests, whereas the poem has it the other way around. We get closer to the spirit of Blake's image by recalling that Miltonic void that is "the realm of Chaos and Old Night."

[9] A friend draws my attention to the adverb "bright," a word with primarily favorable overtones. But if the Tyger is partly admired for its brightness, it is seen by this speaker only as a bonfire, not as a forest fire that will burn up the forests of error in the apocalypse. Only a Reprobate could see it in this way. For the forest fire image, see David V. Erdman, *Blake: Prophet Against Empire* (Princeton, 1954), p. 181, where Jeremiah 21: 12–14 is cited.

vision to question.[10] With this in mind we can better paraphrase the import of the question itself as follows: "What immortal organ could produce (by hand) or even conceive (with the eye), shape, or limit your fearful or terrifying balance or proportion?" The grammatical possibilities are: "How in the world did he have either the ability or the courage, etc., to do it?" or "Why did he presume against the Tyger's nature—or transgress against man —to do so?" And "frame" means to form, contrive, or limit (like a picture or a prison). Idealism so pervades Blake's thought that every incarnate thing can be considered to be in a trap. Most readings seem to assume that the first alternatives for "could" and "frame" are the only relevant ones, but nothing in the poem necessitates such restricted interpretations. The speaker is too bemused to attain certainty.

Stanza two inquires first into the source of the material cause of the beast and then into the antecedent circumstances of its efficient cause or maker. We oversimplify the first question if we take it to ask whether the fire in the Tyger's eyes came from hell ("deeps") or heaven ("skies"), but this is better than Bateson's suggestion that the "deeps" are "perhaps volcanoes rather than oceans." [11] Neither of Bateson's equivalents is at all satisfactory, because the reader knows by this time that a metaphysical creature like the Tyger could never have had a merely physical place of origin. Observe, however, that "deeps or skies" does not imply traditional metaphysics and it has the exact combination of definiteness and suggestive vagueness which characterizes both the question and the questioner. The merely conceptual translation "hell or heaven" obscures the real significance implied by the question, namely, that the speaker *doesn't know*. It is also necessary to observe that the poem has moved from a concern with the creator's eye in the first stanza to that of the Tyger here, thus beginning to link the two.

The exact implication of the last two lines of the second stanza is even harder to spell out. "Did the creator go under his own power (wings) or that of another?" or "What remarkable wings would enable him—to aspire?" "Aspire" seems to mean "soar," "mount," or "tower" as in "The Sunflower" (though there a goal is indicated) to some vaguely understood place up in the "skies" where the creator could get the fire of the Tyger's eyes. But if we follow Blake's punctuation, "aspire" means aspiration for its own sake and thus it would indicate ambitious pride, a state of mind very objectionable to the orthodox, though not in the same sense to Blake. And the word "dare" can be taken to reinforce the suggestion of a dubious audacity, though it may simply imply courage. The parallel structure of the fourth line also maintains this dual ambiguity; it asks "What kind of hand would have the courage or presumption to seize (i.e., grasp decisively, or steal) the fire (which is shown in the Tyger's eyes)." It should also be observed that "dare" is probably the present subjunctive tense of the verb, a fact which tends to bring these presumably past events into the imagination's present focus as the questioner meditates on them.

The sinister overtones of the creator's actions have been scarcely regarded by criticism based on the supposition that Blake is the speaker, but there is nothing in the poem which rules them out. Since "All Religions are One," it is useful to observe parallels to the action of the poem in myth. Bateson recalls Prometheus, the fire bringer—and (co-)maker of man—who stole fire from heaven.[12] A creative blacksmith reminds us of Hephaestus. Both had trouble with Zeus, a fact which becomes relevant to "The Tyger" when we begin to ask

[10] The meter of this line is remarkable, for it seems (to me, and to at least one other reader) to start out trochaic and melt into iambic. This correlates with a tendency on the reader's part to read "What" as exclamatory until he discovers in line four that it is interrogative.

[11] P. 118.

[12] P. 118.

why the creator would have to "aspire," above himself. From this point of view, the creative fiats of the Deity of Genesis can hardly be what the speaker is referring to. Aspiring on wings, indeed, recalls Satan's journey out of Hellfire in *Paradise Lost*.

A passage from *The Marriage of Heaven and Hell* is particularly relevant here:

> It indeed appear'd to Reason as if Desire was cast out; but the Devil's account is, that the Messiah fell, & formed a heaven of what he stole from the Abyss . . . the Jehovah of the Bible being no other than he who dwells in flaming fire. Know that after Christ's death, he became Jehovah.[13]

The convoluted ironies of *The Marriage* make any brief interpretation of this passage both provisional and oversimplified. But what this passage implies, when juxtaposed with the second stanza of "The Tyger," is that the fire of the Tyger's eye came initially from the deeps of hell: that the Messiah creator stole it from the "Abyss." The trouble is that the "history" of the creation asserted in *The Marriage* passage is only polemical half-truth, for true energy is not devilish, except in the very ironic sense in which Blake uses the word in that work, but *prophetic*. But in "The Tyger" it is clear that the questioner is not able to make such subtle distinctions or to indulge in such complex rational speculations, because he is wholly engaged in his awesome vision. He does not know whether the creation is a good or a bad thing, though he suspects both, but he does know that the Tyger was not created to improve his lot in the world, and he feels a holy dread as he meditates on the divine power which went into its creation.

It is more important for the critic to be able to define the attitude and feelings of the questioner toward his vision of the Tyger and his intimations of the creator than to use "The Tyger" as an occasion to dilate on the status of the creation in

Blake's developed thought. Nevertheless, there are at least three things to be gained by doing so. We can, first of all, more clearly understand what to make of the specific questions which the speaker asks; secondly, we can evaluate the significance of certain analogies to "The Tyger" which other critics have suggested; thirdly, the problem provides an occasion for characterizing the difference between the lyrics and the prophecies, for there is still a good deal of confusion on this point.

Very few major symbols or symbolic acts in Blake's system are treated as unequivocally bad, but Blake usually chooses to regard the creation in its malign aspect. "I think the Creator of this World must be a very Cruel Being." [14] Generally speaking, the creation and the fall are two aspects of the same thing; at best the creation is a measure to stop the gap in Eternity caused by the fall. Thus Adam and Satan are the human forms of the limits of contraction and opacity made to save the Divine Humanity from dropping into something worse, oblivion or "Non-Ens." Therefore, when Wicksteed said that the proper illustration for "The Tyger" would be the picture called "The Ancient of Days," which appears in one form as the frontispiece to *Europe*, he must have forgotten the sinister implications of the painting of the creator with his compass, because he appears to think of the creation of the Tyger as being for the best.[15] Also any scene of the creation in Blake must suggest the great picture of "Elohim Creating Adam," as Bateson recognizes.[16] But, in spite of their grandeur, the first painting presents at best a dubious benefit, while the presence of the serpent in the second assures that no unmixed blessing is depicted.

Actually, an adept of Blake's system has no great difficulty in identifying traces, not

---

[13] Geoffrey Keynes, ed., *The Complete Writings of William Blake* (London, 1957), p. 150. (Hereafter referred to as Keynes.)

[14] Keynes, p. 617.

[15] *Blake's Innocence and Experience*, p. 193. Cf. Northrop Frye, *Fearful Symmetry* (Princeton, 1947), especially p. 433.

[16] P. 118.

only of Prometheus, Hephaestus, Satan, and Elohim, but also of the distinctively Blakean characters Urizen, Orc, and Los,[17] in the vision of creation conjured up by the questions of the speaker in "The Tyger." From Blake's point of view such a conglomeration is intellectually unintelligible, which is why he was concerned in the prophecies to distinguish these "states of being." But if we look around us, we see that imaginative average men are capable of experiencing the doubts and confusions of the speaker in "The Tyger." Moreover, even the inspired reader must retain emphatic powers great enough to be capable of feeling them too *as though* they were his own. The incompatibilities in the questioner's vision are intellectually muddled, but they paradoxically represent a *discordia concors* because they are imaginatively and existentially real and therefore moving. The prophecies, "allegories addressed to the intellectual powers," are rarely confused in this way; therefore they can provide a basis for judging the lyrics which primarily engage the emotions. The intellectual structure of prophecies enables them satisfyingly to contain visions of Experience despite the fundamental incoherence of that state.

With the dramatic situation so defined, we may resume a detailed commentary with the third stanza—in the faith that the character of the speaker in this masterpiece is so crucial as to deserve the most thorough attention. In this stanza the focus is on the making of the Tyger's heart. The dual subject of the first question, "shoulder" and "art," should be recognized as a modulation of the organs mentioned in line three

of stanza one, "hand or eye," but there is a progression in the process of creation indicated here. First we should notice that instead of the option, "or," there is the conjunction "&." Furthermore, the shift from "hand" to "shoulder" suggests how much more *force* is necessary, while the change from "eye" to "art" implies the need for more practical activity in this stage of the design of the beast. Now the Tyger is coming off the drawing boards and is about to live. In this context the word "could" is less ambiguously a reference to ability than it was in the first stanza, while the word "twist" along with "shoulder" begins to suggest the image of a blacksmith which becomes manifest in the next stanza. The fact that the very heart of the Tyger is said to have "sinews" suggests a beast made for violence rather than compassion. The reader is able to feel the etymology of "sinews," which emphasizes the binding rather than the connecting function, and thus the heart, the organ of pity, is bound by twisted cords in its very make-up. It is necessarily a Tyger of wrath.[18]

In the third line the Tyger comes to life. Then occurs one of the famous cruxes in the poem, for the syntax of the fourth line is incomplete despite Blake's two question marks. Everybody knows that Blake originally wrote next "Could fetch it from the furnace deep." But on a formal level such a continuation is impossible because either the stanza would be too long or the sentence would run on into the next stanza. Neither effect was what Blake wanted. Among the other things, either possibility would disturb the effect of precise stage-by-stage progression which the final poem creates. And, of course, explicitly to locate the source of the Tyger's heart in the deep furnace of hell woud be to betray the bril-

---

[17] Los, the redemptive blacksmith, might seem to be the primary analogue to the blacksmith in the poem. But—and it is essential to understand this point—what we have in the poem is a speaker who does not know Los, who does not recognize the Los latent within himself, and who therefore speculates about evil in the universe from premises that are partly true and partly erroneous. In the prophecies, Los does not make the Tyger, it should be noted.

[18] The fact that Blake elsewhere condemns pity and praises wrath does not invalidate for this poem the more common attitudes toward these emotions. For Blake each emotion is good and each is incomplete without its opposite, but all the speaker sees is the organic source of wrath, and he is justifiably frightened.

liant indeterminacy of origin established in the "deeps or skies" of the second stanza. The revisions indicate that it took Blake himself some time to realize that the speaker in the poem could not know as much as the Bard should know.

There are two emendations for the printed version of this line, "What dread hand? & what dread feet?", which have some authority: Malkin's "forged thy dread feet," which has been praised by some critics, and Blake's own "Formd thy dread feet," written in ink in one copy of the *Songs*.[19] One objection to "forged" is that it too explicitly anticipates the blacksmith who is revealed in the next stanza. But Blake's own emendation, especially because it is capitalized, deserves some consideration even though it was an afterthought. It is important to understand that Blake's plates were not easy to change, so that the whole plate might have had to be redone if a major emendation were to be neatly integrated into the text. As it is, Blake incompletely obliterated the engraved text and simply penned in the change. Note that he capitalized this word, thus making it the only word in the poem, except "Tyger" or "Lamb," which is capitalized when it is not the first in a line. Blake capitalized for emphasis with great freedom in other places, but it is unlikely that he would have wished to call attention to the Tyger's feet. On the other hand, it is easy to suppose that the capitalized "Formd" indicates exasperation. It may be that some stickler complained to him and that Blake thus said, in effect, "There now, does that make you happy?" [20]

Whatever the circumstances of the emendation, there are several things to be observed about the printed wording. In the unpunctuated second draft, which omits stanzas two and four, Blake allowed the first draft of this stanza to stand unchanged, though the line in question is even more obviously syntactically incomplete in this version than in the final one. It is true, however, that by straining one can integrate this line into its stanza in one of two ways: either, "What dread hand and what dread feet twisted your heart after it began to beat?" or, by changing Blake's question marks to exclamation points, "What dread hands and feet appeared on the Tyger as it came alive!" But it is obvious that neither of these will really do; each reading is feeble in its own way. We should note that both the hand and the feet were those of the creator in the original version, while the feet belong to the Tyger in the Blakean emendation. But the Tyger's "feet" (not its "paws," or "claws") are not so remarkable as to deserve special attention. Adam's feet of clay are the last part of him to be formed by the creator in "Elohim Creating Adam," [21] but such attention to the Tyger's feet in this poem would be almost as bad as the "ankle" and "knee" of the creator which wandered into Blake's vision during the first draft. As a matter of fact, the loose syntax of Blake's printed text is the kind of thing one encounters frequently in his prophecies. It is a distinctive part of his art and idiom which usually justifies itself in context. This device is not to be confused with the indefinite in art which Blake hated; generally it expresses mutuality or indeterminacy and a proper reading will recognize this to be a rhetorical device, not the result of carelessness. In "The Tyger" we should observe that the indeterminate syntax intimately relates the creator and his creature. Any sharp division would constitute a "cloven fiction," like the assertion that a good God can create evil, and the questioner is too imaginative to rest content with this kind of fallacy. The mutual-

19 See Nurmi, "Revisions," pp. 678–679.
20 Bateson, p. 118, correctly judges that the emendation does not help, but his reasoning is obscure to me and he conflates the two emendations.

21 Feet are, of course, important symbols in the prophecies, but a discussion of other uses here would add little to our understanding of this poem.

ity of the creator and the Tyger is like that implied in Yeats's famous question, "How can we tell the dancer from the dance?"

There is one further point to be made concerning the line. Even if we should accept the emendation, weak as it is, the *dread* hand, at least, belongs to the creator. In any case, both creator and creature inspire dread, and a dreadful creator is Nobodaddy, Urizen, or Satan because dread is not a Christian religious emotion as Blake conceives of Christianity. It is true that Blake had no use for creeping Jesus, but from Blake's point of view "Christ the tiger" is the creation of the Church of Caesar and a little old man.

In stanza four, the already living Tyger is completed by the addition of his brain. A prosaic account would merely assume that the questioner has shifted his attention from the Tyger's heart to its brain, but the imaginative reader recognizes that creation has reached a climax. The meter suggests that now the creator has caught the full rhythm of his work, and the questions come thick and fast as the speaker conjures up the movement of creation by his questions. In this stanza suggestions of the previous stanzas, like "fire" and "shoulder," are more manifestly combined with the "hammer" and the "anvil," thus presenting the image of a smith in his smithy. Notice too that the *what the* formula of stanza two, line four, here recurs in lines one and three. But the sense is slightly different in each case. "What the hammer?" refers to a shaping instrument; i.e., "What kind of tool could hammer out this archetypal Tyger?" But "what the chain" has different connotations, and part of the evidence is that Blake did not choose to put a question mark after the phrase as Keynes does in his text. A chain, after all, is not a shaping instrument, though it is a limiting one. The chain is one of Blake's primary symbols for tyranny; it is an instrument which keeps the fallen world from rising, and it has the famous "mind-forg'd manacles"

hanging from it.[22] Those in chains are usually portrayed sympathetically by Blake, to be sure, but on idealist premises "mind-forg'd manacles" mean *both* the compliance of the victim and the scheming of the tyrant. The rhyme of "chain" and "brain" in this stanza, together with the fact that there is no full stop at the end of the first line, links the two inevitably together.

In the second line of stanza four, the questioner in effect gives the fire of previous stanzas a more definite place of origin, a furnace. Briefly we can say that the furnace is another ambivalent symbol which is usually presented in its malign aspect in the earlier work. It represents the natural body which imprisons, limits, and therefore torments the energy characteristic of life.[23] In its benign aspect, however, the tormenting fire is seen to be the energy itself. There is nothing basically peculiar in Blake's ambivalent fire: the three fires of the three regions in Dante give us a clear example of how the significance of the symbol may be modified by its context. But we saw earlier how the source of the Tyger's heart in the first draft was the infernal "furnace *deep*." Even though Blake suppressed this because it is discordant with the state of mind of his speaker, the reader probably feels the infernal associations of "furnace" in the completed poem more strongly than any heavenly ones. Part of the reason for this is that the "sinews" of the heart in stanza three correspond to the association of "chain" and "brain" here, thus suggesting that the Tyger's creation is netted in the iron web of materialism, which is Blake's version of evil. In any case we should at least feel a kind of imaginative hiatus be-

---

[22] As mentioned before, almost every symbol of evil may be seen as potentially redemptive. The great painting of Michael binding the Dragon Satan is a case in point. The illustration of Los's smithy on plate 6 of *Jerusalem* shows the bellows bound down by a chain. However, the binding of Orc by Los in the earlier prophecies is more ambiguous.

[23] Cf. Frye, *Fearful Symmetry*, especially p. 288.

tween the organic and the inorganic in this stanza. It is horrifying, as well as awesome, to think of an animate thing being hammered into shape in a smithy.

The last two lines of the stanza bear out these implications. The "anvil" of the third line is the other half of the shaping instrument, along with the "hammer" of the first line. They, as it were, spatially bracket the chain-brain forged between them. Then the "dread grasp" of the creator, the act of his "dread hand" of stanza three, line four, "*dares*"—as he dared to aspire and seize the fire in stanza two, lines three and four —to "clasp" (again a bracketing) the "*deadly terrors*" of the Tyger's brain. The expression "deadly terrors" can hardly be explained away as a mere periphrasis for energy. The feeling of the final question in this stanza is not—as it was in the first stanza—that the creator was presumptuous or audacious; it is that the relationship between creator and creature is one of irresistible force and immovable object. The Tyger appears to be a Frankenstein's monster, and the speaker suspects that its creator must also be quite monstrous to retain control of it.

The fifth stanza represents a distinct shift of thought. The very fact that none of these lines contains a heavy caesura, as do at least some lines in all the other stanzas, helps to communicate a sense of release and relief after the labor of the preceding stanzas. Nevertheless, this is the most difficult stanza in the poem, and thus it demands the most careful attention. Notice first of all that the stanza breaks into halves according to Blake's punctuation (as opposed to Keynes's comma), which places a colon after the second line. Blake's punctuation makes interpretation slightly more open-ended than the simpler climactic order indicated by the punctuation of his editors. But before we can attempt to interpret the *meaning* of the action described in the stanza, we must have before us several *possibilities* of action that are grammatically implied by Blake's words.

It is noteworthy that Blake has no mark of punctuation after the first line of the stanza:

> When the stars threw down their spears
> And water'd heaven with their tears:
> Did he smile his work to see?
> Did he who made the Lamb make thee?

Thus the defeat of the stars and their apparent repentance [24] is conceived of as being a single action. Blake's colon does make it possible, however, that "his work" in line three refers to the defeat of the stars by the creator. But the preceding stanzas have devoted so much attention to the creator's work in making the Tyger that the reader probably supposes him to be smiling at the finished beast. Or we can combine the two and read the lines as though the Tyger were created earlier and that later the beast defeated the stars, causing the creator to smile his approval. A fourth possibility would be not to try to work out any causal relationship between the two events, but simply to suppose that the stars capitulated when the creator smiled with satisfaction at his created Tyger.

This is one of the cruxes in the poem where it is most essential to recognize that the poem asks questions rather than makes assertions. Here the state of mind of the awestruck questioner is such, as indicated by his ambiguous questions, that he does not know whether there is a definite relationship between the two events and, for all the reader can tell from what the ques-

[24] The word "water'd" indicates that something is involved more efficacious than mere sorrow, but one can hardly expect the speaker to trace the Blakean sequence from the "sorrows [that] bring forth" repentance, to pity, mercy, and forgiveness. This psychological sequence corresponds to the metaphysical transformation of the "Gates of Wrath" into the "Gates of Paradise." Was heaven too dry before it was irrigated by the tears of the stars? This metaphor would befit Shaw more than it does Blake, but it corresponds well enough to what Blake felt about the arid law of the Decalogue that ruled the world before the Advent. Furthermore, the speaker is uneasily aware that this law still rules this world, a fact that filled Blake with indignation.

tioner says, he may never be able to decide.

Mr. Nurmi has drawn our attention to the fact that in the early drafts Blake entertained the possibility that the creator "laughed" to see his work, a wording which would suggest a joyous occasion.[25] But he does not discuss the contrary fact (though he properly transcribes it) that Blake also considered "Dare" instead of "Did" as the first word for both of the last two lines of this stanza. One clear implication of the "Dare" wording is that the creator had his nerve to do so. How dare he smile (or laugh, for that matter) to see the Tyger (or, less likely, the defeat of the stars) that he made, and how dare he who made the Lamb make the Tyger? This phrasing tends to make the creator seem insolent as well as tyrannical, rather than courageous. But Blake did not want his speaker to be so violently rebellious, and therefore he settled for the more neutral repeated "Did," which also makes the tense of the questions a more definite past.

As for the famous question about the Lamb and the Tyger, the grammatical possibilities are roughly these: "Did he who made the Lamb (first?) next make the Tyger, or was the creation of both simultaneous with the defeat of the stars?" Or the question may be a relatively independent afterthought, a speculation which arises from all the previous implications of the poem: "How could the same creator make both the Lamb and the Tyger (and if he could, where is the justice of heaven)?" For Blakean scholars who have supposed that Blake is asking the question, the answer is obviously *yes*, though a few recent interpreters have thought the answer to be as obviously *no*. The poetic answer, I must assert again, is that for the speaker the question is a question. In this connection, one should observe that the form of the question in the third line suggests that of

line four, thus making it appear as a kind of afterthought, although it cannot be decided on a purely rhetorical level whether the last question is less important than the first, even more important, or of equal importance.

But while from certain points of view the question is not central to the primary concerns of the poem, it represents the climax of the poem for many readers. The whole stanza is a kind of glorious digression from the primary point of attention in the poem, the creation of the Tyger, and introduces a number of new ideas, but the line in question is only the final leap in a series. According to narrowly formalist standards, the sudden increase in scope provided by the stanza makes it a technical excrescence, but from an imaginative point of view it assures the triumph of the poem. On the other hand, symbolic foreshadowing such as that traced by Gardner [26] is not enough to guarantee specific poetic excellence. It is a cause, but not a sufficient cause.

If the ambiguities of the stanza have been traced with some completeness, we must next consider the complex problem of interpreting it in relation to Blake's whole symbolic system. Nurmi makes a concise statement about the assumptions behind the first two lines:

In Blake's work in general, stars and heavens symbolize the rigidly categorical restrictions imposed upon man by laws derived from abstract reason, and the weeping of stars symbolizes at the cosmic level an apocalyptic melting or breaking down of these barriers separating man from his own humanity, a return of man from the "forests of night." [27]

This is an accurate account of Blake's symbolism and thought, and yet there are several problems which arise when we try to apply it directly to "The Tyger." If the defeat of the stars is invariably a part of the final apocalypse, why is it treated in the *past* tense in this stanza of "The Tyger"?

---

[25] Gardner, *Infinity on the Anvil*, pp. 129–130, gives a particularly effective explanation of the poetic superiority of the final wording.

[26] *Infinity on the Anvil*, p. 128.
[27] "Revisions," p. 672.

The apocalypse must be an event in the future, or at best the present, from the perspective available to this questioner. Man does not return from the forests of night until the Last Judgment is at hand. If the defeat of the stars is a stage of the apocalypse, then the questioner must be asking his questions from "Eden" or Eternity after Doomsday. But no questions would be necessary in the day of revelation and, furthermore, it is necessary to recall that the Tyger is *at present* still in the forests of the night, which is why he is so awesome. As Nurmi notes in another pasage,[28] the Tygers themselves return *from* the forests as part of the apocalypse in Night Nine of *The Four Zoas*. Can the questioner have mistakenly sighted the apocalypse as Enitharmon did in *Europe*?[29] This too is clearly unsatisfactory. Another hypothesis is required.[30]

[28] P. 674.
[29] See Nurmi, "Revisions," p. 682 n, and Keynes, pp. 243–244.
[30] It may be objected that my attempt to distinguish sharply among the three cardinal points of the Christian conception of history, Creation, Advent, and Judgment, is un-Blakean because the apocalypse is an everyday occurrence for Blake: "Whenever any Individual Rejects Error & Embraces Truth, a Last Judgment passes upon that Individual" (Keynes, p. 613). This is too large a problem to be treated extensively, but it is too important to be passed by without comment. Blake's own visionary abilities have led some critics to confound *a* Last Judgment with *The* Last Judgment and thus to trivialize the conception so that "Last Judgment" becomes poetic diction for a mere change of mind. But the vision of consolidated evil and energy perceived by the speaker in "The Tyger" is not equivalent even to *a* Last Judgment because the speaker has not rejected error. The phrasing "*When* the stars threw down their spears" implies no awareness on the speaker's part of the present possibility of this vision, but rather the speaker's mind wanders lost in some notion of an indefinite past-ness of the event. The hypothesis I put forward, following Wicksteed, is in itself too definite to mirror the speaker's state of mind exactly, but one can suppose the speaker believes that the tremendous events attendant on the Incarnation took place "a long time ago in another country" as he has been told. From Blake's point of view, documentary "history" and "geography," which claim that the

This hypothesis appears in Wicksteed's reading of the stanza, though it must be said that his excited prose tends to obscure the point almost as much as it reveals its meaning. For Wicksteed the stanza deals with the Incarnation:

The stars are the broken and scattered lights of eternity which night itself cannot quench, but which melt into dawn with the dewy return of day. They symbolise the hard cold realm of Reason and War before compassion came with Christ . . . But the tears symbolise generation and birth and are connected with the entrance of the Deity into earth's watery vale by his incarnation in the Virgin's womb.

Are the Lamb and the Tyger alike the offspring of that Divine event? Does God smile equally upon the two? Are both expressions of His very mind and being? There is some meaning even deeper than that, I think, in Blake's question. It does not merely mean, "Did God make both?" It means to ask whether when the morning breaks upon the forests of the night, we shall then see that in making the Lamb God *had* made the Tyger—in making the Tyger, *had* made the Lamb?[31]

The stanza, then, refers not to the end of time,[32] but to the *center* of it in the Chris-

———

Incarnation took place at one time and place in the past, are equally vague because the metaphysical character of the event is obscured by statistics. As for the Last Judgment, the Redeemed fear it because they have been taught by the Elect that it is to be a Day of Wrath. The image of a spectrous future darkens the present until everything seems obscure and fearsome "in the forests of the night."
[31] *Blake's Innocence and Experience*, p. 198.
[32] There is, of course, a persistent attempt to connect this stanza with the War in Heaven in *Paradise Lost* and thus to the beginning of Christian history. See Bateson, p. 118. Actually such an interpretation is impossible for a number of reasons, one being that we hear nothing of weeping rebel angels in Milton's authoritative account, because they are frustrated rather than repentant. If they had repented, there would have been no need for the bleak aeons that followed man's loss of paradise; indeed, there would be no mere man, the result of creation, at all. Moreover, neither the Lamb nor the Tyger in the poem is simply the animal made during the general creation at the dawn of history. These metaphysical creatures appear only at a later phase of

tian idea of history, which Blake accepted, as always, with qualifications. Two poems of Milton which Blake illustrated are particularly relevant here: "On the Morning of Christ's Nativity" and *Paradise Regained*. At the Advent, the night of time in the fallen world begins to turn toward the dewy morning which will follow the bloodred apocalypse of dawn. Both the Lamb and the Tyger will have their parts in this apocalypse, but their natures cannot be harmonized until after Armageddon during the Millennium.

So detailed a commentary on the stanza can only be made from the perspective offered by the later prophecies. But the ability to recognize the differences as well as the similarities between the various phases of Blake's work is also important for criticism; consequently, some other apparent analogies should be evaluated. On Plate 91 of *Jerusalem*, for example, a battle takes place between Los and his Spectre in which Los "reads the Stars" while "forming Leviathan / And Behemoth,"[33] which are Blake's final reinterpretation of the Tyger symbol. These beasts in turn consolidate into Antichrist, the epitome of Error. The final *question* of the fifth stanza of "The Tyger" thus eventually becomes translated into the assertion that Los made the way for the Lamb while his Spectre abetted the progress of Antichrist.

But the analytic assertions of *Jerusalem* can only paraphrase, and thus somewhat distort, the mighty questions of "The Tyger." Antichrist is a makeshift conglomeration of error and the "rejected corse of death," Conrad's "flabby devil," while the Tyger is fiery energy bound and limited by the fallen world, Melville's Moby Dick. If he who made the Lamb also made the Tyger, it is because the two beasts are con-

traries. On one hand, Antichrist, the epitome of error and negation, is transcended and cast out, while the Tyger, as Nurmi says, is redeemable.[34] "For every thing that lives is Holy," concludes the final chorus of *The Marriage of Heaven and Hell*. But everything that lives in the fallen world, lives in error, and if it lives in the forests of the night, it lives by the law of the jungle. If the creator smiles because he sees that in the end the Tyger will leave the forest along with man, a man may feel justified in asking why it is his lot now to be cast among savage beasts. This question cannot be removed from "The Tyger," and, in spite of assertions to the contrary, it was one of the questions which continued to concern Blake throughout his life.

The only variation in wording between the last stanza of "The Tyger" and the first is the shift from "Could" in line four to "Dare" in the final line. This change has been widely noticed and frequently explained. My foregoing discussion, however, should prepare the reader to feel the overtones of "Dare" in the final line as an expression of indignity. Together with the accumulation of questions which lead up to the smile of the creator and the reference to the Lamb, the word seems to indicate that outrage as well as fear is implied in the line. "Dare" may still indicate courage on the part of the creator, but since the speaker continues to the end of the poem preoccupied by a vision of the forests of the night, having more promise than evidence that day will dawn, he must be more struck by the Tyger's fearful aspect than by its symmetry. Awe or wonder may characterize the reaction of the reader to the spectacle, but horror predominates in the speaker's mood. On the other hand, the symmetry of the poem which ends in a manner so like its beginning ought also to impress the reader. The fact that in the last stanza the poem comes full cycle, with its speaker having achieved only one word more of insight than he possessed at the

---

history when the providential course of events begins to manifest itself. Insofar as the events at the creation of the second Adam resemble those at the creation of the first, however, the images of the two events coincide.

[33] Keynes, p. 738.

[34] "Revisions," p. 674.

outset—and this in spite of the wide perspective taken in during the whole poem— should serve to relate this poem to such later poems as "The Mental Traveller" which study the tragic "Orc" cycle of life in a more analytic manner. Events at the end of *Jerusalem,* Blake's last prophecy, also come full cycle, but that poem is a cycle to end all cycles, and the events are there brought to an epic resolution.[35]

II. THE ILLUSTRATION

No account of the meaning of "The Tyger" can pretend to completeness unless it contains a study of the details of Blake's illustration. Yet only two critics have made any serious effort to deal with the total meaning of the design. Wicksteed, who can be a most painstaking and valuable exegete of Blake's pictorial symbolism, says merely:

We know that he had never seen a tiger in the forests, and one would almost say, if one judged by the illustration, that he had never seen one, where they were in those days kept, at the Tower. As one looks at the quaint creature in the design, one almost wishes that Blake had chosen to paint its purely spiritual form as he painted the ghost of a flea. But he had tried to portray the smile of the Deity on its lips, and to show the ultimate "humanity divine" of Nature's most terrific beast—unless it is best to regard the whole design as a mask, deriding those who expect upon a mortal page the picture of the Deity at work.[36]

---

[35] See Appendix, below.
[36] *Blake's Innocence and Experience,* p. 193. Blake's final vision of the Tyger is probably best communicated by the Blake Trust facsimile (London, 1955) of copy Z (1826), which depicts a distinctly heavier and possibly older Tyger than that shown in earlier versions such as copy O (about 1800), here reproduced by courtesy of the Harvard College Library. Among other differences to be noted is the fact that in the later version the Tyger's mouth is agape (though it is not smiling), which gives the beast a more formidable (if slightly more fatuous) appearance than in earlier versions. For those interested in recovering Blake's exact punctuation, it is noteworthy that there is a distinct comma after the first word "Tyger" in line 21 of this version.

Wicksteed's reading of the poem itself, however, shows no influence of these observations. More integrated are the remarks of Erdman:

"The Tyger" raises the cosmic question: How can the tiger of experience and the lamb of innocence be grasped as the contraries of a single "fearful symmetry"? The answer, suggested in the question form, is that the very process of the creation of the tiger brings about the condition of freedom in which his enemies (his prey) become his friends, as angels become devils in *The Marriage.* The tiger in Blake's illustration of this poem is notoriously lacking in ferocity, and critics have sometimes concluded that Blake was unable to "seize the fire" required to draw a fearful tiger. He could at least have tried, but he is showing us the final tiger, who has attained the state of organized innocence as have the adjacent lions and tigers of "The Little Girl Lost" and "The Little Girl Found" who demonstrated that "wolvish howl" and "lion's growl" and "tygers wild" are not to be feared. Blake had no difficulty drawing a fearful were-wolf . . . or for that matter a fearful *flea.* But his tiger is not even baring its fangs.[37]

What Wicksteed and Erdman certainly establish is that the depicted Tyger is no accident and that it deliberately does not exist on the same level as the Tyger envisioned in the poem. Wicksteed's initial suggestions are not very convincing, however; the Tyger's mouth is not smiling, in fact its lined face suggests worry, and there is certainly nothing depicted which resembles the enigmatic smile the creator may have smiled, according to the poem.[38]

---

[37] *Blake: Prophet Against Empire,* pp. 179–180.
[38] At least there is no trace of a smile in the British Museum Small version he reproduces on p. 192c. Like Blake's other designs, the "Tyger" plate varies considerably from one version to another because Blake seems to have approached the problem freshly each time he painted it in water colors. The standard bibliographical study of the *Songs* is contained in Geoffrey Keynes and Edwin Wolf 2nd, *William Blake's Illuminated Books: A Census* (New York, 1953), especially pp. 50–69; their letter designations of the twenty-six known original copies supersede the earlier codes of Sampson and Keynes. I have examined four original versions of the "Tyger" plate: cop-

As for the Tyger's depicting the "humanity divine," strictly speaking, the Tyger would have to be even more heroic, as well as human, than the one suggested by the *poem* in order to reflect the Edenic state; possibly Wicksteed had in mind something like Erdman's organized innocence, however. Wicksteed's final suggestion, that the illustration is an obscure joke on the read-

er, will be considered below. Just as it was important to identify the speaker of the poem, however, it is also necessary to account for the visionary perspective of the painter of the picture. The most fruitful hypothesis, since the effect of the design is deliberate, is that the painter is prophetic, or Reprobate, in a partially satirical mood. Doubtless it is easier to say "Blake," but that is really too vague to characterize the pictorial critique of the Redeemed speaker of the poem.

Erdman's attempt to see the Tyger as an expression of organized innocence, on the other hand, had more initially to recommend it, and his reference to "The Little Girl Found" does give us a valuable perspective on the Tyger design. There is, for

ies I (Weidner), K (Pierpont Morgan), O (Harvard), and P (formerly Emerson). The photographic reproduction in Wicksteed is evidently from copy T, a color-printed page which differs considerably in character from the engraved versions. Except for Wicksteed's reproduction, the most accessible version is the Albion-United Book Guild facsimile (1947), evidently of copy O. More accurate is the photographic reproduction in Keynes and Wolf, plate 2, p. 53a, of copy P.

example, a more powerful (though possibly less formidable) looking tyger depicted on the first page of "The Little Girl Found." It should be observed, however, that this beast stands in darkness under a dead tree whose limbs become entangled in a serpentine vegetation growing up in the left margin. And on the second page of the poem a baby is depicted riding an animal which is possibly a tyger minus its stripes ("Among tygers wild"), though it is probably a lioness. On this page, however, the tree in the right margin is a double-entwined living tree—expressing the union of love—which does *not* overarch the figures of animals and children. In the left margin there is a delicate tree entwined with a vine. Here the lioness with the rider is going in the same direction as the Tyger, but it is significantly looking back to the right toward the vital Tree of Life.[39] There is no doubt that the situation depicted on this second page is "organized innocence," [40] but I suggest that the term should be applied to Blake's pictorial symbolism only when there is a rider on the beast. Thus even the Tyger on the first page of "The Little Girl Found" is a tyger of experience, as the sinister vegetable setting makes

clear. Some further ramifications of the organized innocence symbolism will be examined below. But I wish to make still more clear the basis of my disagreement with Mr. Erdman's general interpretation of "The Tyger." His assertion that the creation of the Tyger in itself can bring about a condition of freedom in which enemies become friends seems to oversimplify Blake's conception of history.[41] As I suggested earlier, this is the *final* result of the action implied by the fifth stanza of the poem, but what the poem itself is primarily concerned with is the condition *prior to* the reversal. The Tyger and the Lamb do not lie down together in the forests of the night.

One picture ought to be worth a thousand words in these matters, but if we have studied Blake carefully, and also his interpreters, we are aware that people see what they want to see and sometimes nothing else. The only way, therefore, to be certain that the design is being properly interpreted is for the critic to enumerate every potentially significant detail whether he can account for every detail or not. The hypothesis is that every design is totally intelligible. The Tyger is going toward the left with its left front foot forward and its left hind foot pushing. Thus it is in exactly the opposite position to the Lamb in the foreground of the *Song of Innocence*. Wicksteed's brilliant theory about the general meaning of right and left in Blake's pictorial symbolism has been challenged by several recent critics, but it would be hard to deny that contraries are being depicted by this device. We have commented previously on the lined and rather worried (or possibly pathetic) look on the Tyger's face. In the left margin in front of the Tyger is an indefinite object which is evidently a seven- or eight-pronged bush. One stem

[39] In the Blake Trust facsimile of copy Z, the mild Tyger depicted on the first page has stripes hardly more distinct than the thin lines on the ostensible lioness shown on the second page.

[40] For an explanation of the term, see Erdman, *Blake: Prophet Against Empire*, pp. 105–107, 115–118. Robert T. Gleckner, *The Piper and the Bard: A Study of William Blake* (Detroit, 1959), p. 46 and *passim*, effectively discusses a related concept which he usually calls "higher innocence." The main difference between the two ideas seems to be that "organized innocence" represents an innocence that retains its identity even in the fallen world by actually employing devices of experience for its own ends (and thus might almost be called "organized experience"), whereas "higher innocence" is innocence glorified as a result of learning through experience, and thus it is practically identical with what Blake in the prophecies means by "Eden." The two terms can also be related to Los and Urthona respectively. Actually Blake never quite uses either of these terms, though both are helpful in explaining what he sometimes means by innocence.

[41] In saying this, I do not intend to challenge Mr. Erdman's unequaled grasp of how Blake responded to *contemporary* history, but only to suggest that "The Tyger" is more obliquely related to the American and French Revolutions than are the prophecies.

goes up the left side of the page and ties in on the loop of the *T* of "The" in the title of the poem. This should be compared with the above-mentioned serpentine stem in the left margin of the first illustration of "The Little Girl Found." Underneath the loop a bird flies to the left. The title of the poem occupies the top of the page. In the right margin is the large mottled and striped tree which leans slightly to the left at the top of the page and curves down until it spreads out at its base and blends with the hindquarters of the Tyger. Three dead branches extend from the tree: two shoots from the top branch bracket the last three letters of the title and the third underlines the last two words of the first stanza, thus setting it off from the second stanza. The second branch has only one distinct shoot which crosses the entire page in most copies, thus splitting the text of the poem in half. The bottom branch also has three distinct stems, two of which are short. The first short one points to the word "make" in the last line of the fifth stanza; the second underlines primarily "made the Lamb" of that line and functions as a separation between the last two stanzas; the lower short stem points to the word "eye" in the last stanza. Two more devices in the design should also be mentioned. The tails on the letter *y* of the word "thy" in the fourth and last lines of the poem are very prominent, especially the latter one which points to the Tyger's head. Note that the letter has no such flamboyant tail in such a word as "deadly" in stanza four. The tails on the letter are even more exuberant in the word "symmetry" in the final line. The first has a triple serpentine squiggle which underlines the last three letters of "fearful" and corresponds to the torso of the beast, while the final *y* points to its hindquarters. The three areas of the Tyger which are thus picked out correspond to the head, heart, and loins that assume considerable importance in Blake's symbolic system.[42] As a

[42] For unmistakable evidence that even the shapes of letters may be meaningful in Blake's

partial summary of the total effect of the design, note that the depicted Tyger is first framed by a band of color beneath the poem, and that then the stanzas themselves, together with the shoots, especially the one that bisects the poem, successively box in the animal from above. An examination of the intermingled lines of the branches and title at the top of the page will confirm the fact that this is a deliberate effect.

This enumeration of the "minute particulars" of the design should by itself indicate the kind of meaning which this symbolic picture communicates. Though the colors in some versions of the design lighten the effect, the symbolic function of the lines is to communicate tyranny and repression. As in the first page of "The Little Girl Found," the huge dead tree is the tree of mystery, which Blake identified with the Biblical tree of knowledge of good and evil, and its twigs circumscribe the text of the poem itself. The fact that the tree is distinctly striped in some versions shows that it is the vegetable equivalent of the Tyger. This Tree of Death epitomizes the fallen or "vegetable" world; it represents the forests of the night which begin at the lower limit of the state Blake elsewhere calls Generation, where spiritual energy is imprisoned and almost dissipated in conflicting cross-purposes. It is no accident that the Tyger's loins are set against this tree so as, in the color-printed copy T version, to be almost indistinguishable from it. All the weary

work see, for example, plate 17 of *The Marriage of Heaven and Hell: Reproduced in Facsimile with a Note by Max Plowman* (London, 1927). The penultimate word "twisted" has a triple squiggle on the letter *d*. It is true that there are flamboyant tails on the Y's in some of the other *Songs* which do not seem to have any semantic significance. But it appears that Blake often used exuberant calligraphic devices as a kind of italic. He was opportunistic rather than consistent in his use of such devices, however; where possible he would try to add a shade of meaning, but he also understood the limits of such pictorial fancy. At any rate, the tails on the *y*'s in the final line of "The Tyger" are rather different from any others in the *Songs*.

and distinctly unheroic features of the bedraggled little Tyger are consistent with the doubtless modern folklore notion that only old decrepit tigers are dangerous. I might add that the Tyger looks as though he has not had his dinner of Lamb recently, which is as likely to make him weak as to make him ferocious.

There is a sense too in which the illustration is a joke, but it is a joke (*pace* Mr. Wicksteed) not so much on "those who expect upon a mortal page the picture of the Deity at work" as it is on the awestruck questioner,[43] on the Tyger, and perhaps on the creator himself. "Did he smile his work to see?" Is this the best that fallen world can show? When immortal energy is hammered into merely mortal form, what else can appear but a parody of eternal vitality? Note how these questions emerge from the contrapuntal irony contained in the relation between the last line of the poem and the depicted shabby beast. "Dare" appears over the toothless muzzle of the Tyger; "frame" over its limited head and brain; "thy" over the shoulder, but, as said, the long-tailed *y* points again to the head; "fearful" over the unimpressive torso; and "symmetry" (along with the blackest question mark in the poem)

[43] See Mr. Frye's discussion (p. 47, above) of *America*, plate 9, concerning the deliberate incongruity between the perception of Orc by Albion's Urizenic Angel as told in the text and the serene innocence of the children depicted with the ram in Beulah. Cf. also the fourth "Memorable Fancy" of *The Marriage*. The page in *America* is a symbolic modulation of the second page of "The Little Girl Found," as the figure of the sleeping girl proves, but it depicts innocence, rather than "organized innocence," where vehicular energy of terrific beasts is involved. If one combined the *America* design with the "Tyger" design, he would achieve organized innocence, as I point out in the last paragraph of this essay. But the relation between text and design in the page of *America* is more polarized than the subtler contrasts of the "Tyger" page. The text in the latter contains the honest doubts of a Redeemed character, whereas Albion's Angel is the spokesman for error that must be cast out. The prophetic artist painting the "Tyger" design shows that Behemoth is only a poor pussy cat at which it is foolish to be frightened.

over that part of the loins which emerges from the overwhelming background of the tree. Perhaps the final meaning of the serpentine squiggle on the first *y* of the word is that the depicted beast is in fact a travesty of symmetry, and it certainly corresponds to the episode in *The Marriage of Heaven and Hell* where the fearful aspect of the Tyger is identified with the serpentine Leviathan.

If we now study the details at the top of the page, from which the depicted Tyger is successively cut off, we see that the maze of serpentine branches and letters has only one exit, the winding one between the two words of the title. This is the final confirmation that the Tyger is closed in from above, tied down to this fallen world, framed. Indeed, the gratuitous loop on the tail of the letter *y* in the title may remind us that the name of the beast is pronounced as though it were spelled "Tie/ger"! But what of the tiny bird winging its way to the left under the serpentine vegetation? Surely it is mentioned in the "Proverbs of Hell": "When thou seest an Eagle, thou seest a portion of Genius; lift up thy head!" or in the motto to the first "Memorable Fancy" which precedes the "Proverbs":

How do you know but ev'ry Bird that cuts the airy way,
Is an immense world of delight, clos'd by your senses five? [44]

The bird in "The Tyger" plate has entered into the fallen world, but it is still far from the Tyger. In *Milton* this bird will be the lark who flies to the gate of heaven to bring back news of the Apocalypse when Eternity will again embrace the productions of time. Here the bird expresses the tiny portion of the Tyger's genius which is least circumscribed, least imprisoned in the forests of the night. The fact that the Tyger's head, as opposed to his loins, is outlined against the light, shows that the dawn may after all not be far off and that the Tyger will soon cast off the rags of its fallen state and

[44] *The Marriage of Heaven and Hell*, Keynes, pp. 152, 150.

reassume the lineaments of its original glory.[45] Thus all three times, Creation, Advent, and Apocalypse, are suggested in this mammoth little poem-design, and the whole spectrum of attitudes from heroic to mock-heroic, vision to question, is contained within its scope.

We can say with more certainty now that the depicted Tyger represents, not organized innocence, but experience about to be organized when, on the great day, this beast leaps from the jungle. If we wish to see an animal version of the resulting state, we must turn to plate 15 of *The Marriage of Heaven and Hell,* where a drunken eagle carries off a smiling serpent in what is the best emblem in the book for its title. The mutual ecstasy is more complete than in the illustrations of organized innocence in *America* and *The Book of Thel,*[46] because the vehicular power is provided by the rider, not by the mount. If the "devils" have usurped the energy, it is because the "angels" have deserted their own nature. The balance will be restored on Judgment Day. But the illustration to "The Tyger" primarily depicts the divorce of heaven and hell, the split between the Eagle and the Tyger, which is the most important fact about the world we live and die in.

APPENDIX

BLAKE'S SYMBOLISM IN "THE TYGER"

There is much in this lengthy commentary on the poem, particularly that on the fifth stanza, which will probably strike the

[45] This is particularly evident in copy Z, where the Tyger's head and left front leg are outlined in pink. But the perspective achieved in the illustration is both more optimistic and more comprehensive—more *prophetic*—than that attained by the speaker of the poem. Note also that the peculiar division at the top of the Tree of Death, which increases the number of branches to four in the version of the page in copy O, is an optimistic detail. Such a transformation of the sinister "sexual" threefold into the visionary "human" fourfold signifies that the apocalypse is at hand. But this detail is not clearly depicted in other versions I have seen.

[46] See *America,* plate 11 (both the upper and lower illustrations), *The Book of Thel,* plate 6, and Erdman, p. 107.

common reader of "The Tyger" as being an intrusion from what is often called "Blake's private symbolism." But there are really no arbitrary personal symbols in "The Tyger." The most that one finds are consistent interpolations and variations on traditional Christian symbolism. Consider the Tyger itself. This Far Eastern beast is not found in Biblical symbolism, but other great carnivorous cats do figure there. The Tyger is, as it were, halfway between the unavoidably majestic, or at least violent, lion, and the inevitably fraudulent leopard. The characters of these beasts are defined in The Revelation of St. John 5:5 and 13:2 respectively. Mr. Nurmi correctly links the Tyger with the Leviathan of the fourth "Memorable Fancy" in *The Marriage of Heaven and Hell* by means of this second reference, but neglects to analyze St. John's complex symbol.[47] The leopard is manifestly fraudulent to the visionary because it has usurped the incongruous feet of a bear and the mouth of a lion—with which it speaks blasphemies. Moreover any resemblance between Blake's Tyger and this beast weakens Nurmi's case for a positive Tyger. Certinly Blake's painting of the aquatic avatar of this beast (Rev. 13:1) is no less scathing than St. John's description.

Northrop Frye once pointed out to me that the ambivalent character of the Tyger, its simultaneous strength and weakness, resembles Blake's conception of the Covering Cherub (which is based, in turn, on Ezekiel 28:13–19), and it should now be evident how the description of the beast embodies the contrary natures of the lion and the leopard described in the Apocalypse. It is also worth noting, in connection with the question "Did he who made the Lamb make thee?" that immediately after Christ has been identified as "the Lion of the tribe of Judah" in Revelation 5:5, He is revealed as the slain Lamb in Revelation 5:6, thus fulfilling the spirit of Isaiah's prophecy. But all attempts to identify Blake's Tyger as "Christ the tiger" conflate the lion and the Tyger and thus distort Blake's poem. Even

[47] "Revisions," p. 671 n.

the "Proverbs of Hell" do not really equate
the two beasts. To be sure, "The tygers of
wrath are wiser than the horses of instruction," that is, wiser than Swift's Houyhnhnms, but not than the "eternal horses." But
"The wrath of the lion is the wisdom of
God," [48] an unqualified assertion.

Blake's well-known association of stars
with reason, on the other hand, may be an
arbitrary sign, though it too is based on
natural symbolism. But the stars in "The
Tyger" function less in their tropological
sense as reason than in their anagogical
sense as angels—rebel angels. The stars as
allegorical light—"for those poor souls who
dwell in night"—also have a redemptive
function in Blake in so far as they preserve
some of eternity's light as indicated in the
quotation from Wicksteed above. Both the
good and the evil potentialities of stars are

[48] Keynes, pp. 152, 151.

clearly recognized by St. John in the same
chapter of Revelation where the woman
clothed in the sun who has a crown of
twelve stars (12:1) is opposed by the dragon whose tail drew a third part of the stars
of heaven down to earth (12:4). Many of
the other major peculiarities in Blake's system can be explained as similar interpolations from various public texts like the
Apocalypse rather than from hermetic ones
that also derive from St. John, like Boehme
and Swedenborg.

In this study I have tried to explain almost all of Blake's symbolism on a literary
or archetypal basis. But I believe that a
complementary historical perspective is necessary to achieve a complete understanding
of Blake's symbols. Mr. Paul Miner's as yet
unpublished essay on the historical bases
for the symbol of the Tyger should do
much to redress the balance.

Mark Van Doren

On "The Little Black Boy"

My mother bore me in the southern wild,
And I am black, but O! my soul is white;
White as an angel is the English child,
But I am black, as if bereav'd of light.

My mother taught me underneath a tree, 5
And sitting down before the heat of day,
She took me in her lap and kissed me,
And, pointing to the east, began to say:

"Look on the rising sun: there God does live,
And gives his light, and gives his heat away; 10
And flowers and trees and beasts and men receive
Comfort in morning, joy in the noonday.

"And we are put on earth a little space,
That we may learn to bear the beams of love;
And these black bodies and this sunburnt face
Is but a cloud, and like a shady grove. 16

"For when our souls have learn'd the heat to bear,
The cloud will vanish; we shall hear his voice,
Saying: 'Come out from the grove, my love & care,
And round my golden tent like lambs rejoice.'"

Thus did my mother say and kissed me; 21
And thus I say to little English boy.
When I from black and he from white cloud free,
And round the tent of God like lambs we joy,

I'll shade him from the heat, till he can bear 25
To lean in joy upon our father's knee;
And then I'll stand and stroke his silver hair,
And be like him, and he will then love me.

It is difficult to imagine a poem that would sound more childlike than this. It would also be difficult to find one that was more complicated and profound. Blake's little black boy, as if he were speaking a piece, delivers with effortless delight an idea such as Dante would have loved and did indeed manipulate in certain cantos of his *Divine Comedy*. The child keeps going a singsong stanza of his own invention, seldom varying the rhythm he takes for granted as perfect for his purpose. Only in lines 11 and 12 does he take advantage of the infinite variety offered by iambic pentameter to anyone who chooses to play with the possibilities. And those lines are truly remarkable, not only for the series named in the first but even more for the reversed beat of the second—trochaic or dactylic, according as one's ear decides, but certainly not iambic.

Comfort in morning, joy in the noonday.

The accents leap at the reader, certifying the comfort and joy the sense of the words asserts. The series in line 11:

And *flowers* and *trees* and *beasts* and *men*

is emphatic to the limit of emphasis, and suggests a thousand other items in addition to the four there is room to list. The monosyllables force themselves upon our attention as monosyllables do in every line of the poem. Seven lines are entirely monosyllabic—fewer than we suppose when the poem is done, for the effect has been constant. The child, looking steadily at us, has spoken as if there were no long words in the language. These at any rate would do for him, and to each of them he has given its full value, as if everything depended on his speaking the piece right. But we have no suspicion that it is not his piece. He knows very well what he is saying. Child

Reprinted from Mark Van Doren's *Introduction to Poetry* (New York, 1951) by permission of Holt, Rinehart and Winston, Inc.

though he is, he is master of an idea. His
voice is the voice of authority, as that of
any philosopher is who has completed his
thought. Really completed it, so that he
can put it into words of one syllable.

The boy's idea is everywhere in the poem,
but it is most directly stated in two monosyllabic lines (14 and 17) containing the
word "bear." The little black boy's mother
told him one hot day, as they sat in the
shade of a southern tree, that the souls of
men endure with difficulty the beams of
their Father's love, which like the beams of
the sun can burn and destroy as well as
nourish with everlasting life. God's love,
beating fiercely on a soul unprepared to
sustain it, would bestow neither the comfort nor the joy that flowers and trees and
beasts and men receive at noonday from
the risen sun. Even then the bodies of men
search out shadowy places, and benefit by
clouds; for the heat of the sun itself is hard
to bear. As nevertheless we learn to bear it,
so in a parallel fashion our souls learn to
bear the heat of love, which if we were ex-
posed to it all at once would be as fearsome a thing as Dante found it in his *Para-
diso*, where stage by stage he was disciplined to endure it and its accompanying
light.

The parallel is not perfectly drawn, any
more than Donne's parable of the sun [in
"A Lecture upon the Shadow"], or Yeats's
of the moon [in "The Cat and the Moon"],
could be pushed to its ultimate detail. Ideas
are not finally physical, and phenomena
cannot prove them. But this does not dis-
qualify the attempt, which in Blake's case
yields more than simple proof. For his real
interest is not so much in the parallel as
in the fact that there are black people and
white people, and in his desire to persuade
us that they are equals under the skin. The
skin of either is but a cloud—in the one
case black, in the other case white—which
protects the wearer until the day when no
protection shall be needed; then both, having cast off their clouds, their skins, will be
able to go where God is. The idea produces

more complications, once Blake has translated it into terms of sun and shade, than
the poem can take care of. The poem does
not lose by this, but that is because Blake
never lets us linger over the difficulties.

The boy begins by saying that he was
born under the southern sun and therefore
is black; but his soul is white—as white as
the body of an English child, who because
of his exterior is not misunderstood as
black children are. I look, says the boy
(line 4), as if I had no light at all, as if I
had no soul; but my soul is inside of me
as the soul of the English child is inside
of him, and mine is as white as his. My
mother explained this to me once, and made
me understand a certain advantage there is
in being outwardly black. She took me on
her lap, kissed me, and pointed to the east
where the sun rises. There God lives, she
said, and sends forth His light and heat,
and all things enjoy them. But we could not
enjoy them as we do if we were not pro-
tected from their full strength. God for the
time being has given us a cloud to cover
us; it is like the shade of a grove; it is our
color, which we shall continue to need until He decides that we have learned how to
bear His love direct. Then He will call us
out of our grove and we shall play like
lambs around His golden tent. My mother
told me this, the black boy says (line 21),
and kissed me again.

And now I say to the little English boy,
who does not know what I know, that he
wears his own protective cloud—white,
rather than black, but it is certainly a
cloud. He has not learned this yet; he is
deceived by its whiteness, which he identifies with the soul's whiteness. But there
is no connection, any more than there is a
connection between my white soul and my
black body. The English boy doubts that I
have a soul; he does not love me. But
when our two souls are free of their respective clouds, and we stand around God's
golden tent of which my mother spoke, I
will shade him a little longer, until he has
made up for his lack of discipline under

the sun. Then we shall be equal lovers and friends, and I shall stroke his white hair; there will be no difference between us, and he will love me as even now I love him.

What are the difficulties we face if we insist upon understanding all this literally and logically? In the mother's tale is God the sun—no more, no less? And if He is nothing but the sun, is it merely our distance from Him on earth that accustoms us to His beams? Supposing this to be so, how shall we be prepared for the sudden change when that distance disappears? And what heat will the English boy still feel in heaven—unless we have been right in assuming what the poem does not say, namely that the English boy has benefited from his white cloud less than he would have benefited from a black one? And is this a matter of his not having understood that there was a cloud? But a cloud is a cloud, and protects us whether or not we know it does. Also, does the northern child keep his silver hair—which has no connection with his soul—at the knees of God? And has the black boy the same complexion there? Is that why the two souls will love each other? Or are their bodies to survive, and the black boy's to become like the white boy's?

There are even more questions our paraphrase might arouse. For it is from the paraphrase, not the poem, that perplexities emerge. The poem itself is always simple, like the voice of the child who speaks it; and like his soul that speaks through it. For he has a conviction with which we cannot argue, since it is born of the very love that is his subject. His love of the English boy is more important than any proof he is advancing of their equality. Equality cannot be defended; it can only be felt, and the little black boy knows everything about how it feels. It is what reduces his sentences to the utmost simplicity—as when in line 22 he leaves out "the" before "little," and as when in the next line he omits any form of the verb *to be* after the pronouns. Above all it is what makes the last two lines so inexplicably moving. The stroke of a hand smooths every syllable and leaves it pure of everything except its own innocent intention; and the monosyllables in the closing line—like those in the seventh line of Herbert's "The Flower"—are invincible to any unbeliever. To anyone, that is, who before he read the poem had not known how equality feels. He still might have arguments against it, but he could not use them here. They would have no more effect on the little black boy's faith than the little black boy's argument, in so far as he has one, needs to have on anybody. The real poem, the poem we hear as we read, has left the body of argument as far behind it as the souls of the twin boys will leave their flesh when they become twin lambs that rejoice. It is all, of course, for the benefit of "little English boy," who had not known till now how much love was waiting for him in the southern wild.[1]

[1] The reader interested in a full study of Blake's ideas on slavery should consult David V. Erdman's "Blake's Vision of Slavery," *Journal of the Warburg and Courtauld Institute*, XV (1952), 242–252, or the same author's *Blake: Prophet Against Empire* (Princeton, 1954), especially pp. 211–224.—Ed.

John H. Sutherland

Blake's "Mental Traveller"

DIFFERENT critics have offered startlingly different interpretations of Blake's "Mental Traveller." The poem tells the fairly simple story of one cycle in an apparently end-less·series. The characters in it are obvious-ly symbolical, and most of the different readings of the poem have depended on a number of quite different identifications of them. Thus one may read the poem as an account of the path of the mystic (with Foster Damon); as a sun myth combined with an account of the Incarnation, plus a galaxy of other things esoteric (with Ellis and Yeats); as the story of "an Explorer of mental phaenomena" and the develop-ment of a new idea (with W. M. Rossetti); as the presentation of a version of the Orc cycle (with Mona Wilson or with Northrop Frye); or one may throw up one's hands (as Bernard Blackstone did recently) and say that *The Mental Traveller is an ex-tremely cryptic poem in quatrains: as to its meaning, one reader's guess seems as good as another's.*" [1]

When one considers that the foregoing list by no means exhausts the variety of sug-

[1] See S. Foster Damon, *William Blake, His Phi-losophy and Symbols* (Boston and New York, 1924), pp. 129–132; Edwin John Ellis and Wil-liam Butler Yeats, *The Works of William Blake* (London, 1893), II, 34–36; Mona Wilson,. *The Life of William Blake* (London, 1932), pp. 156–157 (this includes a long quotation from W. M. Rossetti); Northrop Frye, *Fearful Symmetry* (Princeton University Press, 1947), pp. 227–229; Bernard Blackstone, *English Blake* (Cambridge University Press, 1949), p. 131. The present paper uses, as its most helpful starting point, the excel-lent analysis in Professor Frye's *Fearful Sym-metry*.

gested readings of the poem, it seems quite clear that there would be little point in merely adding one more possible interpre-tation. What is needed is an approach which can provide more evidence for the positive identification of symbols. If this is too much to hope for—since a poem is not a mathematical formula—one can at least reaffirm one's faith that the poet did mean something quite definite, and pursue that definite meaning as far as possible.

There are two important methods which can be used in an explication of this sort. One of these has been widely and success-fully used on Blake's prophetic works, but has not yet worked as well on this poem as on others: it is to search out parallel fig-ures and situations in Blake's other poems, and thus relate the poem in question to the great myth which Blake created. The other method, although commonly used in the reading of the work of other poets, has not been applied to Blake's poems as systemati-cally as it might be. It is to pay very close, literal attention to background, situation, and point of view in the poem, in the hopes that establishing these things will make the nature and significance of the central fig-ures stand out more clearly and certainly. The present paper uses both these meth-ods, but leans more heavily on the second. It is, frankly, an attempt to present a com-plete reading of the poem, and to solve all the major difficulties connected with it. Such an arrogant effort probably does not even deserve success, but the method of at-tack may, in any event, help to further clar-ify the nature of the puzzle.

From *ELH (A Journal of English Literary History)*, XXII (1955), 136–147. Reprinted by permis-sion of the author and the journal.

One key to the structure of the world as Blake saw it—which is also a necessary key to the background and structure of "The Mental Traveller"—is to be found in the major prophetic book *Milton*. There Blake makes an admirably plain statement about matters which are often thought to be beyond hope of human comprehension:

The nature of infinity is this: That every thing has its
Own Vortex, and when once a traveller thro' Eternity
Has pass'd that Vortex, he perceives it roll backward behind
His path, into a globe itself infolding like a sun
Or like a moon, or like a universe of starry majesty,
While he keeps onward in his wondrous journey on the earth. . . .[2]

Blake's system seems to have had many affinities with Berkeleian idealism: it presupposed that the only reality is psychological reality, and that the materialism of physicists, chemists, and astronomers is error and self-deception. His theory of vortexes is an amusing, and surprisingly neat, way of explaining figuratively the relationship of the temporal sense data perceived by the individual to the raw material of Eternity and infinity. The theory is thoroughly explained in Northrop Frye's *Fearful Symmetry*.[3] Briefly, it amounts to this: The fundamental pattern of visual awareness, as Blake thought of it, took the form of a cone opening into the observer's eyes and mind, and coming to its apex at the object perceived. Thus "every thing has its Own Vortex." An individual on a higher plane of awareness would, depending on his state, either realize that sense data only existed within himself (since, as Berkeley pointed out, the existence of objects depends entirely on their apprehension by a conscious mind), or else would see things as much smaller and more manageable than they appear to the fallen senses of those of us who seem to be at the mercy of the material world.

Such an individual, passing from a higher plane of awareness into the fallen world of the senses, would pass (as it were) *through* objects of apprehension like the sun, moon, and stars. Moving on, down toward Earth, he would pass from the objects into the cones, or vortexes, of the objects. When he looked back, he would see the material of Eternity—contracted to fit his fallen sense organs—roll out behind him like marbles. Instead of seeing something infinitely greater, he would see the globes, balls, and flickers that most people agree to see in the sky at night. Instead of realizing that he, as a perceiving mind, comprehended all matter, he would think of the material world as composed of many frightening things much bigger than himself.

Since fundamental reality was human reality, a mental traveller of this sort could, in one sense, travel without ever leaving this earth. And by this earth Blake did not mean the large, round planet of the astronomers: he meant—in terms of each individual—that the part of the world which was bounded by the limits of one man's apprehension was not only his Earth, but also his Universe:

The Sky is an immortal Tent built by the Sons of Los:
And every Space that a Man views around his dwelling-place
Standing on his own roof or in his garden on a mount
Of twenty-five cubits in height, such space is his Universe:
And on its verge the Sun rises & sets, the Clouds bow
To meet the flat Earth & the Sea in such an order'd Space:
The Starry heavens reach no further, but here bend and set
On all sides, & the two Poles turn on their valves of gold;
. . . .
Such are the Spaces called Earth & such its dimension.

[2] *Poetry and Prose of William Blake,* ed. Geoffrey Keynes (London, 1948), p. 392.
[3] P. 350 *et passim.*

As to that false appearance which appears to the reasoner
As of a Globe rolling thro' Voidness, it is a delusion of Ulro.[4]

This seems, at first consideration, to be a very primitive world, since it is limited by the boundaries of one man's senses. However, Blake did not think of it as limited, since he set no limits to the glories which might be apprehended by the senses. To think of the world as Blake did was to deny the validity of that which is seen by the materialistic reasoner; and to deny that was to affirm a belief in much more which might be seen, but which was hidden from the self-deluded reasoner. Each man (each in his own world) could be, like Blake, a mental traveller. Each man was, whether or not he desired it, a traveller through eternity:

Thus is the earth one infinite plane, and not as apparent
To the weak traveller confin'd beneath the moony shade.
Thus is the heaven a vortex pass'd already, and the earth
A vortex not yet pass'd by the traveller thro' Eternity.[5]

One more point should be mentioned. Between Earth and Eternity (or Eden) was another place, a sort of half-way spot which Blake called Beulah. Blake thought of Beulah as a gentle, shadowy place inhabited by women and children, and connected with ideas of birth and growth. Like Earth, it was a merciful release for those who were unable to face the wonders of Eternity; however, the inhabitants of Beulah were much closer to the vision of Eternity than to the limitations of Earth:

There is a place where Contrarieties are equally True:
This place is called Beulah. It is a pleasant lovely Shadow
Where no dispute can come, Because of those who Sleep.

. . . .

4 Keynes edn., p. 413.   5 Ibid., p. 392.

Beulah is evermore Created around Eternity, appearing
To the Inhabitants of Eden around them on all sides.
But Beulah to its Inhabitants appears within each district
As the beloved Infant in his mother's bosom round incircled
With arms of love & pity & sweet compassion. But to
The Sons of Eden the moony habitations of Beulah
Are from Great Eternity a mild & pleasant Rest.

. . . .

And the Shadows of Beulah terminate in rocky Albion.[6]

With this much of the stage set, a close examination of "The Mental Traveller" can be attempted. Enough has been said to make it possible to establish background and point of view in the poem. It is hoped that the precise nature of the background will become clearer as the discussion progresses.

The first stanza sets the scene where over half the story takes place. It also establishes the point of view, since it identifies the poet Blake as the mental traveller who sees and reports all that happens. He says:

I travel'd thro' a Land of Men,
A Land of Men & Women too,
And heard & saw such dreadful things
As cold Earth wanderers never knew.[7]

The last line of this stanza makes it clear that the stage is not Earth as seen by limited human beings. Later on in the poem a descent to the world of the senses indicates that what went before was on a much larger scale. To put an arbitrary name to it at the beginning, we might say that the stage is set somewhere in Eternity—evidence further on may enable us to be somewhat more specific when we come to it. The "Men & Women" who inhabit Eternity are risen, giant forms; they have a great deal

6 Ibid., pp. 415–416.
7 Ibid., pp. 110–113. All subsequent quotations from "The Mental Traveller" are taken from these pages.

more energy and significance than the "nonpeople" (as e. e. cummings would call them) that we see around us every day. Moreover, knowing Blake's other poems, it seems a safe guess to say that some of these figures must be archetypes, or eternal forms, of forces which manifest themselves in a different way on this earth.

The final stanza demonstrates that the whole poem is devoted to the account of a cyclical process. This has led a number of critics to look for parallels between the story of the male Babe and the so-called "Orc cycle." The parallels are genuine and instructive, particularly during the early part of the poem; however, the male Babe's experiences are more complex than Orc's simple rise, stagnation, and fall.

When read in the light of this comparison, the early stanzas offer little difficulty. The Orc-like male Babe (probably representing repressed principles of energy and creative power) is nailed to a rock, like Prometheus, while the "Woman Old" (probably representing Nature) tortures him, and "lives upon his shrieks & cries." The diet seems to agree with her, since "she grows young as he grows old."

In stanzas six and seven, the Babe, grown up, subdues the woman (now a young virgin), rapes her, and thus makes Nature, or Mother Earth, his ". . . dwelling place/ And Garden fruitful seventy fold." This is a symbolic statement of a universal historical truth. It has led to the male Babe being taken to represent a variety of different movements and ideas, since religions, philosophies, and civilizations—as well as individual men—have risen to subdue and cultivate the world that tyrannized them in their infancies. Similar symbolic relationships may be found in the stories of major gods of antiquity.[8] It seems obvious that identifying the male Babe as being akin to the Orc-principle satisfies the general truth of the allegory better than any more specific reading possibly could.

The Babe does not retain his youthful

vigor very long. The eighth stanza refers to him as an "aged Shadow . . ./ Wand'ring round an Earthly Cot." This "Cot," or cottage, is described as being filled with "gems & gold/ Which he by industry had got."

The "aged Shadow," as has been pointed out before, has much in common with the figure which Blake elsewhere calls Urizen.[9] Orc, the youthful, archetypal spirit of revolt, after having achieved his minimum goals, all too naturally hardens into the conservative spirit of order and oppression. As the Jehovah-like Urizen, the spirit hurts and destroys just because he wishes to preserve things without change.

All this takes place in terms of particular scenes and circumstances, as observed by Blake, the mental traveller. The aged Shadow is in Eternity still, but is becoming more and more bound and limited to the physical world. The symbol of this is the "Earthly Cot," which seems to be either the Earth, or else another planet like the Earth. (Such worlds of the fallen senses are, to a mental traveller, no more than cottages— temporary dwelling places of the soul.)

The "gems & gold" with which the aged Shadow filled the Earth are explained in stanza nine. They are "the gems of the Human Soul"—which is to say that they are made up of various manifestations of human suffering. "The martyr's groan & the lover's sigh" to which Blake refers in this stanza can be compared with these famous lines from "The Grey Monk":

For a Tear is an Intellectual Thing,
And a Sigh is the Sword of an Angel King,
And the bitter groan of the Martyr's woe
Is an Arrow from the Almightie's Bow.[10]

Tyrants (both earthly and archetypal) delight in human suffering. Blake didn't like either tyrants or suffering, but he recognized their inevitable place in the organization of a fallen world.

In "The Mental Traveller," Blake is intensely, and ironically, aware of the value

[8] Frye, p. 228.

[9] Cf. *ibid.*, p. 229.   [10] Keynes edn., p. 118.

of suffering to the tyrant: "They [groans and sighs] are his meat, they are his drink." Blake is purposely ironic as he records the aged Shadow's generosity with this kind of riches: "He feeds the Beggar & the Poor." His door is "for ever open" to those who are vulnerable to human pain. Moreover, this is a give-and-take arrangement. The groans and sighs seem to be deliberately conceived as ambivalent: they are produced by poor, oppressed mortals for the delectation of the tyrant Shadow, and they are distributed as food (or in lieu of food) to the poor and oppressed by the Shadow.

This is the normal end of the Orc cycle. The next step would be the breakdown of the static and corrupt establishment, a falling back into a period of gestation, and then the rebirth of the young spirit to repeat the process. However, as a mental traveller with creative vision, Blake did not see man as inexorably caught by such a pagan nightmare. Stanza eleven records what can happen if people in the cottage (i.e., on earth) find, to the aged Shadow's grief, some way of exercising their creative powers:

His [the Shadow's] grief is their eternal joy;
They make the roofs & walls [heaven and earth]
    to ring;
Till from the fire on the hearth
A little Female Babe does spring.

The Female Babe springs from fire— symbolically the source of energy and inspiration. She is described in stanza twelve as being "all of solid fire/ And gems & gold"—so awe-inspiring that no one dares to touch her. The aged Shadow (in stanza thirteen called the "aged Host") fears and hates this splendid product of man's creative powers. He feeds on man's grief; it makes perfect sense that the creative imagination, which can free man from grief, is the source of his grief. In terms of the ideas symbolized, the exact, mechanical, and limiting principles in the universe must have something to limit in order to exist at all. Thus, when applied to man, they exist, lit-

erally, because of man's grief. When men find their way through to some source of creative energy, they free themselves and bring grief to that power which previously had oppressed them.

In stanza thirteen, the Female Babe is presented as an archetypal spirit closely akin to a muse. She is described as coming "to the Man she loves" (the artist, and perhaps the mystic and the saint); together, the man and the Female Babe drive out "the aged Host,/ A Beggar at another's door." (Here "the Man she loves" seems to be primarily the human individual, who can, through creative inspiration, free himself from the dead hand of Urizen; however, it may also refer to mankind as a whole, since the fate of the aged Host after he loses his kingdom is described in symbolic terms which can apply at any level. He could be losing control of one man and one man's world; he could also be losing control of the whole planet, as mankind now knows it through its fallen senses.)

Once Urizen has been driven out, he tries, more and more desperately, to find some person or thing to impose himself on. He finally wins a "Maiden":

And to allay his freezing Age
The Poor Man takes her in his arms;
The Cottage fades before his sight,
The Garden & its lovely Charms.

The maiden seems to represent materialism and the world of the fallen senses. The aged Shadow, now appropriately called the "Poor Man," embraces materialism as a last resort, and very naturally falls out of the world of archetypes in Eternity into the limited world which is the lowest common denominator of sensory apprehension. There is nothing said here of vortexes, in the sense Blake used the term when explaining the nature of infinity in *Milton*; however, it is quite clear that the aged Shadow has passed through the vortexes of the material world and now sees things from a point of view similar to that of a person on this earth. In Eternity, Earth was but a cottage, and its inhabitants were all together. To the fallen senses, Earth seems a vast ball, and its inhabitants appear to be separated by great distances:

> The Guests are scatter'd thro' the land,
> For the Eye altering alters all;
> The Senses roll themselves in fear
> And the flat Earth becomes a Ball;
>
> The stars, sun, Moon, all shrink away,
> A desart vast without a bound,
> And nothing left to eat or drink,
> And a dark desart all around.

Although Blake does not say so directly anywhere in the poem, it seems likely that the maiden the cast-out aged Host turns to is a frustrated female Babe, grown older without finding "the Man she loves." Just as it was natural for the male Babe, Orc, to cease to represent energy and revolt, so it is natural for a female Babe—once a muse —to degenerate into a coquette and sensualist. It is noteworthy that sensuality and the artifices of physical and emotional love have an entirely different effect on her than they do on the aged Shadow. His part is to pursue the fleeting pleasure of simple indulgence, and this, very naturally, makes an infant of him. Her part is to lead him through "Labyrinths of wayward Love" by means of "various arts of Love & Hate." Just as naturally, this makes an old woman of her.

There is violence and inaccuracy in the giving of abstract equivalents for these figures at any of the stages of their development. However, if one allows for that, it seems illuminating to consider the direct proportion here suggested: the female Babe is to the Maiden (who becomes the weeping Woman Old), as the male Babe is to the bleeding youth (who becomes the aged Host). This is to say: creative imagination is to sexual love (which ages into the cruelty of "Mother" Nature), as creative energy is to physical construction (which ages into the conservative principle of tyranny and repression).

The principal weakness of this propor-

tion is that it suggests static balance while Blake is talking about cyclical flux. The relationship of the two figures in the poem follows the general line of the relationship in the proportion, but it is dynamic, and constantly shifting, as is necessary for the continuation of their cyclical existence. Near the end of the poem, the conservative principle reverts again to infancy as it is betrayed and teased in the world of the senses. The cycle is completed when "he becomes a wayward Babe,/ And she a weeping Woman Old." At the same time they return from out the fallen world into Eternity as "The Sun & Stars are nearer roll'd." (Note that most of these relationships are supported directly by the text of the poem. The hypothetical connection between the female Babe and the Maiden only adds detail to the structure.)

The return to Eternity does not involve physical travelling—it is brought about by an improvement in the sense organs. In *The Marriage of Heaven and Hell* Blake explains the process this way:

> If the doors of perception were cleansed every thing would appear to man as it is, infinite.
>
> For man has closed himself up, till he sees all things thro' narrow chinks of his cavern.[11]

In "The Mental Traveller," the improvement in apprehension seems to come at least partly because of the improvement in environment. Paradoxically, although the fall seems to have been partially due to fear ("The Senses roll themselves in fear,/ And the flat Earth becomes a Ball"), the planting of the desert is also partly due to fear ("Like the wild Stag she flees away,/ Her fear plants many a thicket wild."). Those thickets which are not due to fear are the result of a kind of love which is very closely related to fear: ". . . the wide desart planted o'er/ With Labyrinths of wayward Love,/ Where roam the Lion, Wolf & Boar." Thus, that which helped cause the fall from Eternity is an indirect cause of the temporary regaining of Eternity.

11 Keynes edn., p. 187.

These thickets of passion are very like those described in greater detail in some of the *Songs of Experience* ("A Poison Tree," "The Garden of Love," "My Pretty Rose-Tree"). They are far from being happy products, but they are—like the jungle—symbols of simple fertility. As such, they are a necessary background to the development of love, and to the growth of cities and civilization. Love and civilization represented creative achievement to Blake; he thought of them as important stages on the road to seeing things (at least partially) in their eternal forms. Thus, at the very time that the thickets of love have made a Babe of the aged Host, and a Woman Old of the Maiden, they have made an environment in which "many a Lover wanders," and which helps bring about the return to Eternity.

Immediately after the return, Blake describes the background this way:

> The trees bring forth sweet Extacy
> To all who in the desert roam;
> Till many a City there is Built,
> And many a pleasant Shepherd's home.

When taken in conjunction with details of the thickets of love, this stanza seems to suggest more precisely the part of Eternity involved than do the earlier sections of the poem. Beulah, the land of generation, has much in common with this place. It is in Eternity, but on the edges of Eternity, from which it is easy to fall into the material world. It is a seed place, whose inhabitants are preoccupied with sex, love, and growth. Thus one of the things the poem seems to be saying is that the Platonic ladder of love is inadequate: that the cycle here described touches, as its high point, the three-fold vision of Beulah, and then swings back inevitably into the thralldom of the material world.

Men may be subject to the terms of this cycle, or they may win free of them. The poem has nothing to do with the question of human reincarnation, and Blake is only indirectly concerned with ways in which man may find Eternity. Although stanza thirteen suggests, as we have seen, that a man may unite with a female Babe to drive out the aged Shadow, the poem is really about the dynamic relationships of eternal principles, and hardly about men at all.

At the end of the poem, these principles seem to be doomed to an everlasting repetition of the cycle we have traced. In finding its way back to the edges of Eternity, the male principle is inexorably reduced to hopeless infancy, and thus becomes, again, the male Babe, whose "frowning form" is so terrible (because of the potentialities it represents) that all flee from it. The only one who dares touch it is the Maiden, who has again become "a Woman Old." She nails it to a rock again, as another cycle commences.

Martin K. Nurmi

On *The Marriage of Heaven and Hell*

I. BLAKE'S IDEA OF EXPANDED SENSE PERCEPTION

ONE of the best places to see Blake the philosophical poet at work is in *The Marriage of Heaven and Hell*. This work, though in prose and written to expound directly two tenets of the philosophy that is needed to save man, is just as imaginative, and in its way just as poetic, as anything Blake ever wrote. It displays on every page the man who chooses to create instead of reason and compare, but who nevertheless has something to say to the reasoners.

The analysis of *The Marriage* given in Part II of the original version of this study is rather detailed, on the Blakean grounds that "he who wishes to see . . . a perfect Whole,/Must see it in its Minute Particulars, Organiz'd" (p. 558).[1] But I wish to consider briefly here the two conceptions which form its main themes: the idea of expanded "spiritual sensation" and the doctrine of "contraries." These two conceptions can be seen most clearly, I believe, in relation to Blake's humanism.

Blake is probably the most extreme humanist of all time. When he says "God becomes as we are, that we may be as he is" (p. 148), he is not uttering a bit of vague piety; he means it quite literally. Man is not merely capable of divinity, but is, even in his fallen state, divine in essence. "The Eternal Body of Man," he wrote on his engraving of the Laocoon, "is The Imagina-

[1] *Poetry and Prose of William Blake*, ed. Geoffrey Keynes (London, 1948). All subsequent references to Blake's work will cite this edition.

tion that is God himself / The Divine Body / Jesus: we are his Members" (p. 580). To him the terms "human" and "divine" are, in fact, interchangeable, for in *The Everlasting Gospel* he has God tell Christ, "Thou art a Man, God is no more, / Thine own Humanity learn to Adore" (p. 136). And the Fall, as Blake conceived it, came about because man, in creating a false material philosophy, also failed to perceive the divinity of his own humanity and thus strove to create abstract gods that were somehow more than human. Or, as Luvah, one of the fallen "Zoas," ruefully remarks, "Attempting to be more than Man we become less" (p. 367). Man's restoration to Eden, consequently, was to occur when man's now divided natures, the warring Zoas of Blake's psychological myth, were reunited by true philosophy and religion in the vital harmony of the Human state.

The full measure of Blake's humanism, however, may best be taken from his conception that the ultimate order of the cosmos, when perceived by that synoptic vision which perceives the grand order of all things at once, takes on the real or eternal form of "One Man." And the identity of man and God is reinforced when we learn that the One Man is Christ:

Mutual in one another's love and wrath all renewing
We live as One Man; for contracting our infinite senses
We behold multitude, or expanding, we behold as one,

From Martin K. Nurmi's *Blake's Marriage of Heaven and Hell: A Critical Study*, Research Series III of the *Kent State University Bulletin*, XLV, 4 (April 1957), pp. 14–23, 28–29, 59–61. Reprinted, with changes and omissions, by permission of the author and Kent State University.

As One Man all the Universal Family, and that
 One Man
We call Jesus the Christ; and he in us, and we
 in him
Live in perfect harmony in Eden, the land of life,
Giving, receiving, and forgiving each other's tres-
 passes. (p. 479)

Carrying to its ultimate limit the "anthro-
pocentric conceit of romanticism," as Santayana called the Romantic metaphysic,[2]
Blake makes the moral nature of man not
only the center of the universe, but literally the universe itself.

This Christian-humanist cosmological
idea—or perhaps it would be more accurate to call it a grand archetype—is the
closest thing we have to a "first principle"
in Blake's thought. All of his ideas can be
related to it. Especially closely related to
it is his conception of spiritual sensation,
since only by spiritual sensation can we
know the human character of the cosmos.
Indeed, in the clearest explanation we have
of either of these ideas, found in the poem
in which he tried to explain four-fold vision
to his faithful but un-visionary patron,
Thomas Butts, Blake makes this relationship very clear by considering both ideas
together.

In the first part of the poem, which records a visionary experience on the sand
at Felpham, the sand appears merely as
"Jewels of Light." Then, as Blake's vision
becomes more intense and passes firmly into its "two-fold" state, the grains of sand
begin to display their human quality, and
appear as individual men:

> I each particle gaz'd,
> Astonish'd, Amazed;
> For each was a Man
> Human-form'd. (p. 846)

Now follows the theoretical basis for this
transformation. The ordinary apparent
identities of things are only phenomena of
perspective—or *analogous* to phenomena
of perspective, since the differences be-

tween the various orders of vision are not
spatial but psychic. We fail to recognize
the human nature of creation because we
look as if from a distance.

> "Each grain of Sand,
> Every Stone on the Land,
> Each rock & each hill,
> Each fountain & rill,
> Each herb & each tree,
> Mountain, hill, earth & sea,
> Cloud, Meteor & star,
> Are Men seen Afar." (pp. 846–847)

This two-fold level of perception is superior to the "single vision of the materialistic philosopher because it begins to show
the imaginative form of things. But it does
not yield a comprehensive view of the
world. To gain this we must pass through
an affective state, the "three-fold vision,"
in which objects undergo a transformation
because the perceiver undergoes one: He
begins to view all things in a state of delight somewhat akin to the sexual delight
with which man looks on woman.

> I stood in the streams
> Of Heaven's bright beams,
> And Saw Felpham sweet
> Beneath my bright feet
> In soft Female charms . . .
> (p. 847)

In this state he can begin to know directly
by perception that on Earth there are only
shadows, that the Real is elsewhere:

> My Shadow I knew
> And my wife's shadow too,
> And My Sister & Friend.
> We like Infants descend
> In our Shadows on Earth,
> Like a weak mortal birth.
> (p. 847)

Having passed through this state, the
perceiver is now ready to move on to the
highest, or "four-fold" vision, which enables him to see all of existence synoptical-
ly as one, as "One Man":

> My Eyes more and more
> Like a Sea without shore

[2] George Santayana, *Three Philosophical Poets*
(Cambridge, 1927), p. 208.

Continue Expanding,
The Heavens commanding,
Till the Jewels of Light,
Heavenly Men beaming bright,
Appear'd as One Man . . .

(p. 847)

And this One Man is the mild, forgiving Christ, who welcomes Blake to his fold, as one of those who have awakened from "Newton's sleep," or the single vision of materialism:

Soft he smil'd,
And I heard his voice Mild
Saying: "This is My Fold,
O thou Ram horn'd with gold,
Who awakest from Sleep
On the Sides of the Deep."

(p. 847)

When the vision is over and the Saviour's voice fades, Blake passes into that state of enriched "innocence" which he had portrayed in *Songs of Innocence*. Now all things have been permanently transformed, by his glimpse of the infinite, into objects of joy:

I remain'd as a Child;
All I ever had known
Before me bright Shone.

(p. 848)

A vision like this is not, in the usual sense of the word, otherworldly. The significance of Blake's four-fold vision does not lie merely in its enabling us to transcend the limited sphere of practical life, but in revealing the order and unity of life as a whole, so that even our practical life is transformed by the knowledge that "every thing that lives is Holy" (p. 193). When Blake was, in fact, accused by the materialistic Rev. Dr. Trusler of being "in the outer world, or the World of Spirits" (p. 836), he settled quite unequivocally the question of his other-worldliness: "I feel that a man may be happy in This World. And I know that This World is a World of Imagination & Vision. I see Everything I paint In This World. . . ." But one must see aright:

To the Eyes of a Miser a Guinea is far more beautiful than the Sun, & a bag worn with the use of Money has more beautiful proportions than a Vine filled with Grapes. The tree which moves some to tears of joy is in the Eyes of others only a Green thing which stands in the way. Some see Nature all Ridicule & Deformity, & by these I will not regulate my proportions; & some scarce see Nature at all. But to the Eyes of the Man of Imagination, Nature is Imagination itself. As a man is, so he sees. As the Eye is formed, such are its Powers. You certainly Mistake, when you say that the Visions of Fancy are not to be found in This World. To Me This World is all One continued Vision of Fancy or Imagination, & I feel Flatter'd when I am told so. (p. 835)

If everyone learned to see this way, however, "If the doors of perception were cleansed," as Blake writes in *The Marriage*, and everything appeared to man "as it is, infinite" (p. 187), there would not only be a general transformation of men's view of this world. There would also, as a consequence of this new view, be a literal transformation of this world itself, an apocalypse. Viewing this world as "One continued Vision or Fancy," and knowing that life is truly a divine—and human—unity in Christ, men would re-establish society on a new foundation, forming laws of freedom and love instead of repression, abolishing every kind of tyranny that prevents man from realizing his potentialities, and celebrating the divinity that is in every man.

Spiritual perception, therefore, is obviously not merely a superior kind of physical sense perception such as Locke conjectured spirits to possess, enabling them to see "secondary qualities" directly, as if with microscopic or X-ray vision.[3] Blake explicitly rejects as useless for his purpose any kind of improvement in perception like that afforded by the telescope or microscope, which merely "alter / The ratio of

[3] Secondary qualities are the imperceptible powers in objects; these qualities produce primary or perceptible qualities. Locke, *Essay Concerning Human Understanding*, Bk. II, ch. xxiii, sec. 13.

the Spectator's Organs, but leave Objects untouch'd" (p. 413). Spiritual perception transforms objects. And it does so imaginatively, making them into symbolic forms which reveal the significance of those objects to the life of man, and thus shows their "real" form. The real form of the sun to Blake, for instance, is not that of a "round disk of fire somewhat like a Guinea," but "an Innumerable company of the Heavenly host crying, 'Holy, Holy, Holy is the Lord God Almighty'" (p. 652).

There is no use in objecting, "But surely the sun *is* more like a guinea than like a chorus of angels." To ordinary perception, yes, it appears so. But even ordinary perception departs from the abstract ideal of a noumenal sun independent of perception, for ordinary perception too is imaginative, whether we like it or not. In fact, as Blake suggests in the second "Memorable Fancy" of *The Marriage* (p. 186), imagination is "the first principle" of human perception. Some imagination is necessary to any kind of perception, if only to synthesize discrete sense data into objects, synthesizing the brightness, warmth, roundness, etc. of the sun into the physical sun. (Modern psychology would agree, boggling only at the term imagination.) The chief difference between seeing the sun as a guinea and as a chorus of angels, Northrop Frye points out, is that the one requires only a limited amount of imagination, whereas the other requires a great deal. "The guinea-sun," writes Frye, "is a sensation assimilated to a general, impersonal, abstract idea. Blake can see it if he wants to, but when he sees the angels, he is not seeing more 'in' the sun but more of it." [4] He sees it, that is, not merely in relation to the growth of cabbages, but, to adapt Spinoza's famous phrase, *sub specie humanitatis*, under the aspect of a cosmic Humanity.

Such a way of seeing is philosophical, because it takes into account the order of all things and the nature of the Real. Spir-

[4] Northrop Frye, *Fearful Symmetry: A Study of William Blake* (Princeton, 1947), p. 21.

itual perception is most philosophical, of course, when it apprehends the cosmic order directly, as it does in Blake's vision on the sands at Felpham. But Blake has too much common sense to insist that one should always see with a four-fold eye: Spiritual perception is flexible. He does hold, nevertheless, that if man is going to realize his potentialities for beauty and joy, individually and socially, he must keep the larger order of things in mind. Man must do so even when using the practical vision needed for everyday life, so that even his ordinary actions are at least consistent with a Human conception of life in which every man participates in the divinity of Christ, and in which "every particle of dust breathes forth its joy" (p. 212). When man can do this, "the whole creation," as Blake predicts in *The Marriage*, "will be consumed and appear infinite and holy, whereas it now appears finite & corrupt" (p. 187). It will only *appear* so. To the visionary the creation appears infinite and holy now. But when all men learn to see aright, and act according to an expanded vision, life in "this" world will in fact become infinite and holy and man will return to Eden.

II. HIS DOCTRINES OF CONTRARIES

Spiritual perception will return man to Eden; the doctrine of contraries, the other main theme of *The Marriage*, explains what life will be like there. It will not be insipid. "How wide the Gulf and Unpassable," exclaims Blake in mirror writing on a title page in *Milton*, "between Simplicity & Insipidity" (p. 415). The simplicity of Eden is the simplicity of wisdom when combined with vision, or, in short, "innocence," in Blake's special meaning of the word. It also has a surpassing vigor: "As the breath of the Almighty such are the words of man to man / In the great Wars of Eternity" (p. 415). These mighty words are spoken in war, but it is a war that is a creative enterprise "in fury of Poetic Inspiration, / To build the Universe stupendous, Mental forms Creating" (p. 415), for the wars are "intellectual wars."

The theoretical basis for the dynamic creativeness of Edenic "Human" life is stated in essence in another distinction which appears on the same page of *Milton:* "Contraries are Positives / A Negation is not a Contrary" (p. 415). Or as Blake states it in *The Marriage,* "Without Contraries is no progression. Attraction and Repulsion, Reason and Energy, Love and Hate, are necessary to Human existence" (p. 181). That is, a Human world must be informed by opposed yet positive and complementary forces which, when allowed to interact without external restraint, impart to life a motion and a tension that make it creative.

Contraries have appeared in the speculations of many ages, in many forms, and Blake's conception has been rather loosely identified with the conceptions of many other thinkers. To see clearly what Blake had in mind, therefore, it might be well to make a few illustrative distinctions.

Blake is not a Hegelian. Though he uses the word "progression" in *The Marriage,* his contrary forces do not, like Hegel's "thesis" and "antithesis," constitute a world process of "becoming." Indeed, Blake's Human world, in which the contraries freely interact, is not one of becoming at all, for it is perfect; the only "progression" there is in it is that of continued creativeness. And, of course, Blake would have nothing to do with anything as abstractly systematic as Hegel's dialectic.[5]

Nor, on the other hand, does Blake's doctrine resemble that of Nicholas of Cusa (1401–1464), the skeptic who taught that the contraries of this world become identical in God. For though Blake's cosmos has

ultimately the form of One Man, or Christ, the contrary forces of life do not become in any sense identical in the cosmic man, but remain as oppositions which give the cosmos its Human vitality. Cusanus' purpose was to make God a mystery transcending human understanding; Blake's, to reveal as clearly as possible the vital and energetic nature of God, man, and all of creation. Christ, for instance, though forgiving was to Blake not merely gentle— not, that is, "Creeping Jesus . . . humble as a Lamb or an Ass" (p. 135), as he described the Christ of the orthodox religious. He believed that Christ was characterized by love but also by a fierce energy. And, citing Christ's words, "I came not to send peace but a sword" (Matt. x. 34), Blake argues in *The Marriage* that "Jesus Christ did not wish to unite but to separate" the contrary classes of men upon earth.

Finally, Blake's contraries are not like "Yin" and "Yang," the cosmological principles of Tsao Yen (3rd century B.C.). For "Yin" and "Yang" function alternatively somewhat as do the alternations of electrical waves, whereas Blake's contraries interact simultaneously.

Blake's contraries neither progress, disappear, nor alternate because they polarize human life. They are cosmic forces to be seen in every "individual." Not, however, as forces external to individuals, but as immanences. Tigers and horses are contraries, but that which makes them contraries is not separable from them, for their contrariety is in everything they are and do. Everything, moreover, has an eternal "identity" in the cosmic scheme as either active or passive contrary: tigers and horses, male and female, poets and philosophers, plowmen and harrowers. And active and passive contraries exist in "every Nation & every Family," in every "Species of Earth, Metal, Tree, Fish, Bird & Beast" (p. 407). The tension of opposition is in every fibre of Blake's world.

But this opposition is not mere opposi-

---

[5] The distinction between Blake and Hegel, and other matters relating to Blake's contraries, are treated in relentless detail in my dissertation, "Blake's Doctrine of Contraries: A Study in Visionary Metaphysics," unpubl. diss. (Minnesota, 1954).

tion, for "Contraries are Positives / A Negation is not a Contrary." The contraries of Blake's world are opposed but not in such a way that they hinder or deny each other, for such an opposition would produce only destruction, or a kind of cold war, or a state of trembling impotence. Rather, they act positively in opposed but complementary directions, and their opposition is like that between expansion and contraction, between the creative imagination and the ordering reason, or between idea and form. To use the key terms of *The Marriage*, the contraries are "energy" and "reason," by which Blake means the desire for creation and the desire for order. And by "reason" here he intends an ideal reason which strives to supply the form and order which raw energy lacks.

"Negations," on the other hand, are not "contraries," because they simply deny and seek to destroy each other, as the false reason of the materialistic rationalists seeks to destroy imagination by denying it any validity as a means to knowledge, and as a tyrannical king seeks to destroy liberty by oppression and war.

The distinction between contraries and negations, in Blake's opinion, is a crucial one for the salvation of man. For to see the qualities of things as vital, necessary contraries is to live in a Human world of vision and imagination, whereas to see them as negations is to live in the fallen world of materialism and repressive social, religious, and political laws, a world in which the contraries are distorted and given the crude normative designations "good" and "evil." In *Jerusalem* Blake describes symbolically how contraries become negations. The fallen sons of Albion

. . . take the Two Contraries which are call'd
    Qualities, with which
Every Substance is clothed: they name them Good
    & Evil
From them they make an Abstract, which is a
    Negation
Not only of the Substance from which it is de-
    rived,

A murderer of its own Body, but also a murderer
Of every Divine Member. . . . (p. 442)

That is, according to Blake, every individual contains the two contraries and is itself, in turn, "identified" as one of the contraries in the unity of the cosmic One Man, of whom "we are . . . Members" (p. 580). But materialistic thinkers, and especially those of his age, who are able to perceive things only with the corporeal eye further dimmed by rationalism, mistake the immanent contraries for separable Lockean "qualities." Moreover, acting in the repressive spirit of that narrow orthodoxy to which Blake believes materialism gives rise, these thinkers then apply to the contraries the normative moral designations "good" and "evil." This would be bad enough, but they go farther still, and "make an Abstract" of these normative "qualities" from the things in which these qualities really exist. Thus they cut even these distorted ghosts of the contraries off from substance and give them a spectral independence as moral and political laws, and even as gods. Such a god is "Nobodaddy" (i.e., nobody's father):

Why art thou silent & invisible,
Father of Jealousy?
Why dost thou hide thy self in clouds
From every searching Eye? (p. 93)

Why indeed? Simply because he does not exist.

The great task, therefore, is to reverse this process (which is described again in the third expository section of *The Marriage*), and restore the abstractions which the "religious" call Good and Evil to their true and original identities as contraries. Good and evil, as the religious understand them, do not exist, says Blake. Good is simply "the passive that obeys Reason. Evil is the active springing from Energy" (p. 181). In order that man can be truly happy in this world and realize to the fullest his divine potentialities for joy and wisdom, he must learn to see creation as a Human unity in Christ. And he must reject the divisive moral categories which now pit one half of creation against the other half in destructive conflict. Conflict there must be, but it must be the creative conflict of the contraries in "intellectual war."

Categories like good and evil may seem to have little to do with an ontological scheme of opposition which embraces even the nature of "Earth, Metal, Tree, Fish, Bird & Beast." And indeed they are quite irrelevant. That is part of Blake's point: The abstract thinkers have so mistaken the nature of the Real that they fail to recognize that everything that lives is imbued with the organic vitality of contrariety. When these thinkers do recognize opposition, it is always in normative moral terms which imply the need for one of the opposed forces to suppress the other as quickly as possible. But there is another aspect to this, which we must understand if we are to grasp the essential character of Blake's thought. His doctrine of contraries does offer a comprehensive theoretical explanation for the "dynamic organicism" with which the Romantics wished to invest their world.[6] In fact, Coleridge, the most theoretical of the Romantics, would have saved himself a great deal of philosophical groping had he known Blake. But though Blake was a philosophical poet on a grand scale, and though all of his conceptions must be viewed in the cosmological matrix of his thought, his real interest is man. Although the contraries are immanent in every minute particular of his world, his attention is not so much engaged by these minute particulars as it is by men. Men are the chief contraries—and the chief negations. The most important application of the doctrine of contraries, therefore, is the social one: The contraries Blake is most interested in are the two classes of men, the energetic creators and the rational organizers, or the "devils" and the "angels," as he calls them in *The Marriage*. Both classes are necessary, and both must strive positively and vigorously each in its own way if man is to live the Human life.

III. ON THE STRUCTURE OF "THE MARRIAGE"

Entirely Blake's own is the structure of *The Marriage*. One of the reasons, I think, why this work has been misunderstood lies in its unorthodox structure. For though it expounds philosophical conceptions, it does not do so in any of the modes usual for such a purpose. It is developed according to no traditional logical or rhetorical plan. More than anything else, the structure of *The Marriage* seems to resemble the A–B–A′ of the ternary form in music, in which a first theme and its development are followed by a second theme and its development, followed in turn by a return to the first section or a modification of it. If a little intermingling of themes be allowed, *The Marriage* could be thought of as a rich philosophical rondo. Indeed, even the mode of development employed by Blake here is closer to musical than to rhetorical modes. For he does not rely upon argument, but uses the discursive expository sections of the work as "variations" of his theme, as it were, alternating them with "memorable fancies" and the other symbolic sections. In general, the first or "A" section deals with the idea of contraries, the second or "B" section with spiritual perception, and the third or "A′" section with the contraries again. So that the ternary structure of the work may be kept in mind the three main sections of the explication have been labeled A, B, and A′.

The first or "A" part, comprised of the first expository section (p. 181), "The Voice of the Devil" (p. 182), and the second expository section (p. 182), states the theme of the doctrine of contraries and introduces as a sort of counter-subject Swedenborg, who is to be the symbol of the angels who do not perceive the necessity of the contraries to Human existence. The main theme is first stated in the first expository section. It is then developed by the dramatic commentary of the devil, who,

[6] Morse Peckham, "Toward a Theory of Romanticism," *PMLA*, LXVI (March 1951), 5–23.

preaching partisan doctrine, presents the arguments against the angels. In the second expository section, Blake develops further the idea of contraries by explaining how one half of existence came to try to restrain the other half: he gives the history of that restraint which obscures the contraries, and gives as well both the angels' and the devils' versions of the story.

The tone of the "A" part is rather drier than that of the rest of the work, since this part contains two expository sections and only "The Voice of the Devil" as a variation. The middle or "B" part, however, comprising the first memorable fancy (p. 183), the "Proverbs of Hell" (pp. 183–185), the third expository section (p. 185), the second memorable fancy (pp. 185–186), and the fourth expository section (pp. 186–187), relies more on symbolic development. The main theme of this part is enlarged sense perception, introduced dramatically but quite formally in the short first memorable fancy. It is developed contrapuntally, as it were, in the "Proverbs of Hell," with the general theme of energy, as it is seen by the devils. Thus the "Proverbs" are parallel in the structure of this part of the work to "The Voice of the Devil" in the first part. Now follows in the third expository section another history, this time of the growth of abstract systems through the corruption of the enlarged sense perceptions of the ancient poets. This history is also parallel to the history of restraint given in the first part, since it shows the role of abstraction in the development of restraint. Now the second memorable fancy develops the other side of the question by associating enlarged sense perception with excess and energy, in the lives of Isaiah and Ezekiel. Finally, the fourth expository section ends this part of the work in a prophetic tone by announcing that men's perceptions will be enlarged, and it also provides a kind of musical bridge passage in the figures of the cavern and printing, which are picked up in the third part of "A'" part.

The "A'" part is the richest part of *The Marriage*, comprising the third memorable fancy (p. 187), the fifth expository section (pp. 187–188), the fourth memorable fancy (pp. 188–190), the sentence "Opposition is true Friendship" (p. 190), the sixth expository section (pp. 190–191), and the climactic fifth memorable fancy (p. 191), besides the final aphorism (p. 191). In this part in general Blake returns to the doctrine of contraries and brings the work to a close by joining the angel and the devil. But he also keeps the idea of enlarged perception in mind.

The doctrine of contraries, together with the idea of enlarged sense perception, is reintroduced allegorically, in this part, in the very meaty third memorable fancy, which also shows how enlarged perception leads to the free interaction of the contraries and subsequently to the creativeness that is characteristic of Human life. In the fifth expository section, which follows, Blake employs demonstration to show that there are two classes of men and that they must remain contraries. Returning to Swedenborg, who had been a counter-subject in the "A" part of *The Marriage*, Blake then shows in the remarkable fourth memorable fancy the true character of the angelic metaphysics that endeavors through fear and monsters of the mind to prevent creative strife by suppressing imaginative energy in all spheres of life. And he follows this in the last expository section by a direct and serious attack on Swedenborg as one of the angels, which should be read against the background of the robust comedy of the preceding satirical memorable fancy as in part a transitional change of mood leading to the climactic and prophetic debate that brings *The Marriage* to a close. This debate, in which the two contraries embrace and become one in the person of the prophet Elijah, effects the apocalyptic resolution toward which *The Marriage* has moved throughout its last part and which was announced at the beginning of the work ("Now is the dominion of Edom, & the return of Adam into Paradise") and again at the end of the "B" part ("The cherub with his flaming sword is hereby commanded to leave his guard at tree of life"). By marrying the angels and devils of this world, it prophesies that Human life, which was allegorically portrayed in the "Printing house in Hell," will actually come to pass.

Though not, perhaps, at once. *The Marriage* moves, like Blake's great epics—and indeed his prophetic lyric "The Tyger"—toward an apocalyptic conclusion, but in the last part there sounds a slightly less positive note, in the shift back to ironic point of view in which anyone who embraces energy becomes a "devil." It reminds one of Beethoven's tempering the positive resolution of his song cycle, *An die Ferne Geliebte*, by a brief snatch of its plaintive first theme. Perhaps even in the exultant mood in which Blake wrote *The Marriage*, he was not quite sure that the oppositions of this world could in fact become the contraries of the mental war.

And, indeed, the great synthesis of *The Marriage* was not to be a final one. Blake found that the dialectics of his initial formulation of the doctrine of contraries, in which he would simply transform into

fruitful contraries all oppositions now splitting this world, could not bring about the Eden he envisaged for man. After his initial excitement at the possibilities suggested by such a synthesis had lessened somewhat, he no doubt saw that the intellectual battles of an Edenic mental war of art and science were not to be fought as long as corporeal wars were waged by "spectres" such as George III. Evidently something very like evil did after all have a real existence, though it was still not what the religious call evil. And accordingly we find Blake becoming more uncompromisingly apocalyptic, demanding a more radical revolution in the modes of thought and life. In the next statement of his doctrine of contraries, in the so-called "Lambeth Books," we find that he has sharply distinguished the oppositions of this world and those of the Human world into negations and contraries; or rather, that he has applied to the idea of opposites the distinction between the positive virtue of "act" and its negative "hindering," which he had set forth at the end of his annotations to Lavater in 1789. Not all of the angels are capable of becoming contraries, for some of them can never do anything but hinder. There is no place for them in Eden.

Karl Kiralis

Intellectual Symbolism in Blake's Later Prophetic Writings

FOR various reasons, some simple, some complex, the later writings of William Blake have remained generally unread since the time they were composed in the early part of the nineteenth century. *Vala* or *The Four Zoas, Milton,* and *Jerusalem* have often been summarily dismissed as having been written by a man not completely in control of his senses, if not actually insane, or they have been disclaimed on the grounds that they so approach chaos that they simply are not worth the necessary effort to decipher. The general academic pattern is to speak well of the *Songs of Innocence and of Experience,* and to say a kind word or two, perhaps, of *The Book of Thel* and *The Marriage of Heaven and Hell,* but to ignore, sometimes gracefully, the later writings, even though Blake himself considered them, and particularly *Jerusalem,* his best work. That this neglect is unnecessary, if not rather foolish, has been made clear by a number of contemporary Blake scholars. S. Foster Damon and Northrop Frye, particularly, have demonstrated that Blake is readable—though not by the dilettante, for "the Most Sublime Poetry," as Blake defined it, is "addressed to the Intellectual powers, while it is altogether hidden from the Corporeal Understanding" (Letter to Thomas Butts, July 6, 1803).

In the hope of showing that the prophetic books are not as difficult to read as many seem to believe, I present some precautions and suggestions in this essay for interpreting the symbolism of the works, and finally I attempt to justify Blake's creation of his own symbolism. Though my concentra-

tion is on the text of *Jerusalem,* the last and generally considered the most difficult of Blake's major prophetic books, the explanations apply to his other later writings. I am well aware that any attempt to explain and codify symbols is fraught with danger. The symbol must be experienced in its context for the total meaning and the full effect, and outside of their context Blake's later symbols have little if any meaning—hence the need to utilize much of the text in explanation. Like Rimbaud, Blake has sometimes "put down the inexpressible" and "reserved the rights of translation." Ideally one must be Blake's peer to appreciate his works fully, and even the peer would be bound by the words of this world of time and space in his attempt to communicate Blake's meaning. Nevertheless, even though his peer is yet to be found, the attempt must be made toward expressing the presently inexpressible. For my purposes here, fortunately, much of Blake's symbolism is not of the inexplicable type—in fact sometimes it is even allegorical [1]—though more often than not Blake succeeds in his determination to rouse his reader's mental faculties to act.

Excluding the pictorial symbolism, a huge subject in itself, the apparent plethora of symbols can be reduced to four categories: personal, geographical, British-myth-

[1] My present thinking would substitute for *allegorical* some term such as "ultramathematical abstraction" that is both personal and impersonal, since it is Blake's own rendering of archetypal myth. But a defense of this substitution would require another paper.

From *Criticism, A Quarterly for Literature and the Arts,* I (Summer 1959), 190–210. Reprinted, with revisions by the author, by permission of the journal.

ological, and Biblical. My concentration will be on the personal symbolism since it usually causes the most difficulty for the reader and provokes the greatest animosity from the adverse critics of the prophetic books. One of the basic assumptions of modern Blakean scholarship, that the personal symbolism is not completely subjective, has been pointed out most forcefully of late by Kathleen Raine ("Blake and the Tradition," *Encounter*, November, 1956) in her attack upon T. S. Eliot's famous claim that Blake is outside the tradition. Miss Raine places Blake in the tradition of "the perennial philosophy of absolute spiritual knowledge and its unchanging symbols," rather than in Eliot's provincially Catholic tradition. Of course S. Foster Damon also makes this point, but it is difficult to find any approach to Blake, including my own, that has not been suggested by Damon's early but still seminal book. Students of social history and the history of ideas have shown in other ways that Blake's symbolism is not totally subjective.

But Blakean scholarship is not the only evidence for such a contention. It is remarkable how much modern critical commentaries on the Bible often do to clarify Blake's Biblical allusions. Paradoxically, some of his symbols make more sense viewed in the perspective of our time than they did to most people of his own. His use of Bacon, Newton, and Locke as his infernal trinity is an obvious example. Now it is clear that Blake considered them arch-rationalists who serve to replace eternal reality with temporal illusion, but it is quite doubtful that his contemporaries knew what he was about.

I do not mean to suggest, as Miss Raine does in her article, that Blake's works would become quite clear once his many allusions are discovered, for, as valuable as the discovery and evaluation of sources is, Blake is much too prone to interpret and use his sources for the sake of his own vision. A similar danger lies in the purely personal or biographical approach. Some of the gross errors in Joseph Wicksteed's commentary on *Jerusalem* stem from his attempt to relate Blake's life too closely to his work. Margaret Rudd's recent attempt in *Organiz'd Innocence* (London, 1956) to interpret the major prophetic writings as a concealed or disguised document of Blake's own psychological drama—specifically concerning the imagined difficulties of his love and the real problem of public neglect of his works—seems basically in error. There is no denying that a knowledge of Blake's biography and even of its psychological explanation is often important in understanding occasional passages, but a sole employment of this knowledge is insufficient to explain a whole series of works.

The solution, of course, is to synthesize the various approaches. All useful external aids to the text—be they sources, historical perspective or contemporary background, biography, psychology, or whatever—should be focused upon the author's works, and most sharply upon a careful reading of the particular text in hand. Perhaps this statement is not too obvious in view of much misunderstanding of Blake, particularly with regard to his attitude toward reason. Many, including the recently popular Colin Wilson, consider him a supreme anti-rationalist. This belief may be disproved or at least shaken most easily by noting that in plate 98 of *Jerusalem* Blake places Bacon, Newton, and Locke, the rationalists he most often condemns, in Heaven by the side of Milton, Shakespeare, and Chaucer. Science thus must balance art; these three, therefore, balance our three greatest poets. This concept of the desirability of the balanced man or universe is repeated often in the concept of the four Zoas (reason, imagination, emotion, the senses) who are deserving of Heaven only when no single one of them is dominant and they are in complete harmony. The misinterpretation of the character and nature of Vala, whom I shall discuss presently, is a further illustration of the need to look carefully at the text.

Before considering the symbolism in some detail, the reader should be aware of the fact that sometimes even Blake's simplest words can be misinterpreted. "Creation," for example, does not mean the bringing of something out of nothing into existence for the first time, but rather the giving of a definite form to that something. "Death" does not mean annihilation, as Albion (or mankind) complains in plates 21 and 23 of *Jerusalem*, but simply a change from one state to another, as from innocence to experience; and "Eternal Death" means the cutting off of man from eternity, though not forever. These meanings are not so arbitrary as they may seem, for neither creation nor death, as we commonly interpret those words, is possible if eternity exists.

The text of *Jerusalem* reveals many definitions, indicating that when it was possible to define his symbols, Blake did so quite clearly. The definitions listed below are basic ones; their essential meaning is little modified though much clarified by their other definitions, as I shall show later with the characters of Jerusalem, Vala, Rahab, and Reuben. Their actions and reactions must also be considered. Of course literary common sense must always prevail in the search for interpretation of the symbols. It would be manifestly absurd to accept as true the speech of one attempting to deceive—Gwendolen, for example. The words of the fallen sons and daughters of Albion must also be carefully weighed. Though usually fallen, Albion and Vala appear in various states so that their beliefs must be judged accordingly. On the other hand, the thoughts and sentiments of Los, who kept the Divine Vision in time of trouble, and of Jerusalem, the heroine of this epic, can generally be accepted as true. The state of the speaker must be observed. In short, be guided by the context and beware of quotation marks. The definitions given below are those of Blake speaking directly and expecting to be believed.

The Spectre:
The Spectre is the Reasoning Power in Man, &
   when separated
From Imagination and closing itself as in steel
   in a Ratio
Of the Things of Memory, It thence frames Laws
   & Moralities
To destroy Imagination, the Divine Body, by
   Martyrdoms & Wars.   (74:10-13)[2]

Jerusalem:
Jerusalem is named Liberty among the sons of
   Albion.   (Plate 26)

Jerusalem and Vala:
Man is adjoin'd to Man by his Emanative portion
Who is Jerusalem in every individual Man, and
   her
Shadow is Vala, builded by the Reasoning power
   in Man.   (44:38-40)

Rahab:
. . . the System of Moral Virtue named Rahab.
          (39:10)

Hand, Reuben, and Merlin:
Hand stood between Reuben & Merlin, as the
   Reasoning Spectre
Stands between the Vegetative Man & his Immortal Imagination.   (36:23-24)

The meaning of some of the symbols, Los and Albion for example, is obvious with only a cursory reading. Los (cf. *Sol*) is the poet, the creative man, and Albion is both the universal and the individual man, the most extraordinary average man of English literature. The sons of Albion represent civilization and its cruelties; the daughters, its female principles.

These definitions and the ones that follow might mean more to the uninitiated reader of *Jerusalem* if he knew its basic "plot," which is revealed through the interaction of the symbolic characters. Very simply, man (or Albion) is dead to eternity because he has accepted various delusions as reality. Two of his basic false beliefs are in moral virtue or a strict moral code (Rahab), and in reason alone (the

[2] All references to *Jerusalem* will be identified in the text by plate number or by plate and line numbers separated by a colon.

spectre) as the guide to his life. The over-all delusion is Vala, who represents earthly standards of truth and beauty as opposed to the eternal ones of Jerusalem. Vala constantly struggles to preserve her illusion of reality and to keep Jerusalem subjugated. It is the self-imposed and difficult task of the poet (Los) to help man to eternity by ridding him of delusion throughout the course of mankind's history, to free him from the errors present in Judaism, deism, and even Christianity. Man gradually becomes aware of his various misconceptions by recognizing Vala-Rahab for what she is. Then once he has learned the lessons of liberty and forgiveness (Jerusalem), and of the primal innocence and beauty of the body and love (Erin), he becomes balanced fourfold (with reason in its proper place) and lives in eternity.[3]

Interpreting such a key symbol as Vala requires careful study of the text. Since she is variously defined by different characters, her whole role in the work must be considered to determine what she represents. She is identified with Nature by two of the sons of Albion—"Babylon the City of Vala, the Goddess Virgin-Mother. / She is our Mother! Nature!" (18:29–30)—but this is the fallen sons' conception of her and not, as some critics have assumed, the basic meaning. The fallen Albion seems to have the same misconception of Vala, for he asks her, "art thou not Babylon? / Art thou Nature, Mother of all?" (34:8–9) The most significant fact about Vala in *Jerusalem* is that she is in constant strife with Jerusalem, with whom she is often contrasted (e.g., 17, 18, 20, 60, 79). The temporarily "unfallen" children of Albion call Vala Jerusalem's Shadow (11) as does Blake himself (12, 31, 44). If we add to

these facts the direct statement categorically made by Blake, "Her name is Vala in Eternity: in Time her name is Rahab" (70:31), and note the fallen sons' crowning of "their Mother Vala," whom they named Rahab and gave "power over the Earth . . . to build beyond the Throne / Of God and the Lamb, to destroy the Lamb & usurp the Throne of God" (78:15–19), we begin to realize that *Nature* is not an adequate description of Vala. Since she is the eternal prototype of Rahab, we must recall that Rahab was clearly defined by Blake in plate 39 as "the System of Moral Virtue" or, by association with Babylon, as "the Rational Morality." Vala, then, as she appears on earth is the system of moral virtue or rational morality. She is fallen man's conception of Jerusalem, who represents eternal standards of truth and beauty, but actually she is Jerusalem's opposite, the earthly standards of truth and beauty.

Deluded by these earthly standards, most men think that a system of moral virtue brings about a maximum of liberty. They are unaware of the true meaning of Jerusalem, Vala's opposite. The maximum of liberty is obtained by the granting of mutual forgiveness, for it is inevitable that man will err with his freedom. As Blake states when Albion is momentarily "In Great Eternity": "This is Jerusalem in every Man, / A Tent & Tabernacle of Mutual Forgiveness, . . . / And Jerusalem is called Liberty among the Children of Albion" (54:3–5). To reduce the margin of error, man must not artificially bind himself with moral laws but rather become wise with the "Gifts of the Spirit" through the exercise of "the Divine Arts of Imagination." "Can you think at all & not pronounce heartily That to Labour in Knowledge is to Build up Jerusalem, and to Despise Knowledge is to Despise Jerusalem & her Builders" (77). Considering Vala as a code of earthly standards, we can appreciate Blake's association of her in plate 18 with Babylon, the traditional opposite of

---

[3] For a much fuller treatment of the "plot," see my "Theme and Structure of William Blake's *Jerusalem*," *ELH*, XXIII (1956), 127–143, reprinted as Part V of *The Divine Vision*, London, 1957.

Jerusalem, and her manifestation (as Rahab) in the covering cherub or the antichrist in plate 89. Of course Vala is also nature—man's conception of the natural world and its beauty—but this is only part of what she symbolizes. Her fight to preserve herself by continuing to delude man with her false beauty and with her veil of moral virtue, as she openly admits in plate 80, shows her also to be the personification of the female will, as Northrop Frye and Albert S. Roe (*Blake's Illustrations to the Divine Comedy*, 1953) have already well described her. The female will also acts through her component parts, the twelve daughters of Albion, especially in the persons of Tirzah (see especially 67–68) and Gwendolen (80–82).

For the most part in *Jerusalem*, Vala appears in her fallen state, but she, like Blake's other major figures, also manifests herself in Eden and Beulah. In Eden there would be no need to distinguish earthly truth and beauty from the eternal, for there Jerusalem and Vala are one. Jerusalem describes this state when she asks Vala:

Wherefore hast thou shut me into the winter of
  human life,
And clos'd up the sweet regions of youth and
  virgin innocence
Where we live forgetting error, not pondering on
  evil,
Among my lambs & brooks of water, among my
  warbling birds:
Where we delight in innocence before the face of
  the Lamb,
Going in and out before him in his love and sweet
  affection?   (20:5-10)

Jerusalem also depicts Vala in Beulah, the ideal married life or the rest from the Eden of imaginative life:

When Albion rent thy beautiful net of gold and
  silver twine,
Thou hadst woven it with art, thou hadst caught
  me in the bands
Of love, thou refusedst to let me go: Albion beheld thy beauty,

Beautiful thro' our Love's comeliness, beautiful
  thro' pity.
The Veil shone with thy brightness in the eyes of
  Albion
Because it inclos'd pity & love, because we lov'd
  one-another.
Albion lov'd thee: he rent thy Veil: he embrac'd
  thee: he lov'd thee!
Astonish'd at his beauty & perfection, thou for-
  gavest his furious love.
I redounded from Albion's bosom in my virgin
  loveliness:
The Lamb of God receiv'd me in his arms, he
  smil'd upon us:
He made me his Bride & Wife: he gave thee to
  Albion.
Then was a time of love, O why is it passed
  away!   (20:30-41)

Certainly this is a different Vala from the one who freely confesses to keeping Albion's body "embalm'd in moral laws / With spices of sweet odours of lovely jealous stupefaction" (80:27–28).

The minor characters present more difficulty than the major ones just considered. None of the figures, major or minor, can be fitted together as characters to form a plot; their symbolic meanings must be understood in order that their appearances make sense. In this way at least, the prophetic books resemble the modern symbolic novel, as William York Tyndall describes it (*The Literary Symbol*, 1955); that is, the reader cannot be expected to understand either characters or events in a particular sequence of time; rather, the "reflexive relationships" of the parts must be grasped.

A particularly irritating minor figure is Reuben, Biblically the eldest son of Jacob, dispossessed because he seduced his father's concubine, Bilhah, and the founder of the eldest of the Twelve Tribes. The only episode involving him which has any continuity at all takes place on plates 34 and 36, in which Los successively limits all his senses except his touch. After each limitation, which extends to all who behold Reuben, Los sends him over Jordan only to have him return every time. But beyond this nothing appears consecutive in his momentary appearances. . . . In summary[4] Blake seems to have associated the Tribe of Reuben with the Israelites' forty years of wanderings in the wilderness and the crossing over into the Promised Land. The most outstanding occurrence regarding Reuben in plates 34–36 is his continued return from the Promised Land. That is, the poet keeps sending him over Jordan, but he inevitably returns. It is natural to assume that he returned the fourth time also, even though his return is not mentioned specifically, as thereafter he wanders. What Blake must have had in mind here was the fact that Reuben as a "Vegetative Man" (36:23–24) was not ready for the Promised Land and so Blake interprets the Biblical Reuben's decision to remain on the east side of the Jordan. Los therefore was trying to force the hand of Providence, since Reuben was eventually to settle on the east bank and his descendants preferred to live there. In the second half of *Jerusalem*, Reuben is mentioned mainly as a suffering wanderer until Blake has Los complete his cycle by placing him in Canaan. Blake's interpretation of the Biblical Reuben then is comparatively simple, but obviously this is not the whole explanation of Blake's Reuben.

The logical inconsistency of time and space relationships here in the account of Reuben and elsewhere in *Jerusalem* is readily explained by the fact that Blake chose to ignore our earthly patterns for eternal ones; he creates space and time "according to the wonders Divine / Of Human Imagination" (98:31–32). Or as he says in plate 74, all events are present before him as he walks up and down in human history; in 15:8–9, "I see the Past, Present & Future existing all at once / Before me." Granting this much (and the reader must allow this freedom in the use of time and space or

give up reading the prophetic books, as well as some major modern novelists such as Joyce and Kafka and poets such as Pound and Eliot), the meaning of Blake's Reuben, other than the fact that he is ubiquitous, is still unexplained.

Blake's first definition—"the Vegetative Man"—is certainly correct; it simply needs to have its full meaning clarified by the events and the further definition. "The Vegetative Man" is dominated by the instincts of his own body without any important intervention of his head or heart. What mainly differentiates Blake's Reuben from the Biblical one is his unsuccessful sexual attempts and his suffering brought on by the female, Jerusalem excepted of course. Perhaps Blake chose the Biblical Reuben for the role of the frustrated male because of his punishment for seducing his father's concubine, and because of his association with the aphrodisiac mandrake, but that he is representative of male frustration seems clear. Further support of this claim beyond his ineffectual sexual attempts with Tirzah and Gwendolen would include his unlimited sense of touch and the appeal of his "awful beauty" to the daughters of Albion, who proceed to deceive him with moral virtue and send him off to war. The best that can be done for such a man in the temporal world is to place him in a happy earthly marriage, but even this remedy is apparently not altogether successful as is suggested by his further suffering inflicted by the self-righteous and the female, who often use the denial of sex as their major weapon. The eternal view of earthly marriage shows a happy one to be nearly impossible:

"Have you known the Judgment that is arisen
    among the
Zoas of Albion, where a Man dare hardly to
    embrace
His own wife for the terrors of Chastity that
    they call
By the name of Morality? their Daughters gov-
    ern all
In hidden deceit!"   (36:44-48)

---

[4] Students interested in detailed evidence for Mr. Kiralis' conclusions should consult the original version of this essay in *Criticism*, pp. 197–199.—Ed.

Other questions regarding non-Biblical references in Chapter I can now be answered. Los's limiting of Reuben's senses except touch is of course to call attention to sex, which utilizes our only unfallen sense. Also it may be that since man must fall to be redeemed, his delusion is made more comfortable and even acceptable. The obtuse man on the whole has a much greater sense of well-being and happiness than does the sensitive man. Regarding the fact that Los raged "Sixty Winters" to build his "Moon of Ulro" with great care, Ellis and Yeats suggest that the figure "sixty" is used because this was about Blake's age upon completing *Jerusalem* (Vol. II, p. 207; cf. *Jerusalem* 34:57), and since Blake was far from financially successful with his prophetic books, his labor had to be a labor of love (Moon) in this world (Ulro). The definition of Reuben as Merlin exploring the three states of this world—creation, redemption, and judgment—is more difficult to explain satisfactorily. Merlin is the first English prophet and so representative of man's "Immortal Imagination." If the quotation read "Reuben *could be* Merlin" rather than "Reuben *is* Merlin," then Northrop Frye's explanation of these lines ("Reuben purified of his selfhood would become a prophetic imagination") would be highly acceptable and desirable; for if Reuben, the totally vegetated man, has the potential for becoming a prophetic imagination, then certainly we all have. Another explanation might be that since Merlin was seduced and corrupted, if not destroyed, by Vivien (and since the syntax will permit it), Merlin is actually "the Vegetative Man's imagination." Even the vegetative man in his present existence is drawn to explore "the Three States of Ulro: Creation, Redemption, & Judgment." Though perhaps he is not consciously aware of this concern, this is his ideal being in this world, for in eternity these states do not exist.

Thus far the discussion essentially has been limited to personal symbols on which there is basic agreement, despite varied approaches, to illustrate that Blake's address to "the Intellectual Powers" can have an harmonious response. Since "Organs of Perception vary," this concord among critics is not always present. But rarely is there total discord. Erin is a good example, since interpretation here lies somewhere between dissonance and consonance. Ellis and Yeats define the "Spaces of Erin" as "the impulses of the Spiritual Eden." Damon has her representative of "the body." D. J. Sloss and J. P. R. Wallis (*The Prophetic Writings of William Blake,* 1926) suggest that Erin, "providentially regenerative," is an equivalent symbol with the daughters of Beulah in their ability to envision final truth. Frye equates the "Spaces of Erin" with "individual vision." Erdman contends that Erin, a symbol of hope, represents the political situation of Ireland during the second decade of the nineteenth century when liberty-loving Englishmen like Shelley and Byron spoke for its true liberation. Margoliouth notes that Blake emphasizes the Atlantic as a sea of error; hence Erin acts as a breakwater to keep out the full force of the error. Wicksteed considers Erin as "the elemental Innocence of Childhood."

My interpretation does not contradict the general idea of Erin, presented by these major critics, as something to do with the body yet innocent and spiritual, offering hope of salvation, a bulwark against error, and individual vision. The political allegory presented by Erdman is a specific application of this general sense. For me Erin has the most meaning as Blake's philosophy of love: the appreciation of the body in its primal beauty and love in its primal innocence like the relationship between Adam and Eve before their fall. In these terms we can appreciate her frequent pleasant association with the comparatively "unfallen" characters, particularly with the daughters of Beulah since they represent the ideal married life (11, 48–50, 86), and also with the sons and daughters of Los (11) and Los himself (9, 11, 12, 88). As Ireland she is connected with the "ungenerated" (i.e., "unfallen") sons of Jerusalem (71:50–53) and with Jerusalem herself, for "Ireland is her [Jerusalem's] holy place" (29:20). Now we can better understand why the fallen forces are hostile to her:

Albion's Twelve Sons surround the Forty-two Gates of Erin
In terrible armour, raging against the Lamb & against Jerusalem,
Surrounding them with armies to destroy the Lamb of God.
They took their Mother Vala and they crown'd her with gold;
They nam'd her Rahab & gave her power over the Earth,

. . . .

Even to the stars exalting her Throne, to build beyond the Throne
Of God and the Lamb, to destroy the Lamb & usurp the Throne of God,
Drawing their Ulro Voidness round the Four-fold Humanity.   (78:12-20)

Also more meaningful is her association with the passage on the need to be generated to consummate bliss on earth (86: 42 ff.), and more particularly her mention in Los's sex struggle (86–88) with Enitharmon, the "vegetated mortal wife of Los, / His emanation, yet his wife till the sleep of Death is past" (14:13–14), in which Enitharmon frankly attempts to ensnare Los with sex:

In the little lovely Allegoric Night of Albion's Daughters
Which stretch'd abroad, expanding east & west & north & south,
Thro' all the World of Erin & of Los & all their Children.   (88:31-33)

Her own words about herself in the climactic speech closing Chapter II also become more clear, as does in fact the whole speech (48–50):

"By Laws of Chastity & Abhorrence I am wither'd up:
  Striving to create a Heaven in which all shall be pure & holy

In their Own Selfhoods: in Natural Selfish Chastity to banish Pity
And dear Mutual Forgiveness, & to become One Great Satan
Inslav'd to the most powerful Selfhood. . . ."
                                        (49:26-30)

Later in the speech she contends that Luvah—love or true emotion—"is named Satan because he has entered that State," as she pleads that the individual be differentiated from his state.

In conjunction with other details found in *Jerusalem,* a look at Blake's other work substantiates my definition. As an artist, he early discovered the importance of the nude, and so was the first English painter to make the nude the basis of his art—a point not noted in his discussion of Blake by Sir Kenneth Clark (*The Nude, A Study in Ideal Form,* 1956). The fact that Ireland is the terminal western point in *Jerusalem* (34, 63, 67, 83, 89; Japan is usually the eastern) places Erin in the realm of the body in Blake's fourfold system of the directions. The first big problem Blake as a thinker solved to his own satisfaction, as we know from his early lyrics, is the essential innocence of love. Erin is therefore the first creation of Los's furnaces in *Jerusalem* (9, 11). (Her "spaces" represent the widespread implication of this new "individual vision" which leads to the building of Golgonooza, the city of art, in plate 12.) In Ulro, this world or the lowest depth of the fall of man, the "Sexual Machine, an Aged Virgin Form"—i.e., the church's code of chastity and modesty arising from the adoration of the Virgin Mary—is especially out of place in Erin's land (44:21–27), where sex and the body are essentially beautiful. This vision of primal beauty is an apt choice to summarize the ills of Ulro as Erin does at the end of Chapter II. The "remembrance of Sin" would be taken away at least in part if "Erin's lovely bow" were appreciated (50:18–30). Since the body and love are not considered innocent in Ulro, however, unconditional forgiveness is necessary to remove the sense of guilt (cf. 61). Finally near the end of the work (94:12–13) Erin is located at the heart of Los's creative processes (furnaces) in an "Immortal Tomb." There she guards the sleeping Albion and England, "a Female Shadow," just prior to their awakening when the female as "the jealous wife" admits to having slain Albion "In Dreams of Chastity & Moral Law."

The choice of Dinah as Erin's "youthful form," who struggles to "take a form of beauty / Rooted in Shechem" (74:52–54), is most readily appreciated if we turn with Blake to the Bible (Gen. xxxiv). Dinah was willingly seduced by Shechem, who was killed for his love of her. His deceitful murder serves to illustrate the tragedy of honest love in this world. Also, since the first Israelite legislation can be traced back to the city Shechem (Joshua viii, xxiv), Dinah's struggle "to take a form of beauty" against a moral code should be apparent, since the primal innocence of love and the body obviates the need for a codified morality.

There are a few character-symbols in *Jerusalem* which cannot be explained without going to other writings of Blake for clarification—Ocalythron, Elynittria, Antamon, and Oothoon, for example; but such characters as these are few and not basic to an understanding of *Jerusalem*. However, since "every Word & every Character" is "Human according to the Expansion or Contraction, the Translucence or / Opakeness of Nervous fibres" (98:35–37), even the following passage offers meaning. In a lengthy speech lamenting his physical desires, Los cries out:

"Oothoon!
Where hides my child? in Oxford hidest thou
    with Antamon?
In graceful hidings of error, in merciful deceit
Lest Hand the terrible destroy his Affection, thou
    hidest her;
In chaste appearances for sweet deceits of love
    & modesty."   (83:27-31)

Unless the reader realizes that Oothoon plays the role of Magdalen in *Visions of the Daughters of Albion* (1794) and that Antamon is often associated with sex (cf. Damon, p. 387, and *Europe*, lines 176–181), he may not appreciate that here Blake is talking of an illicit affair made necessary by the conventions of society. This affair is located in Oxford probably because Rosamond's Bower, suggested by the word "labyrinths" just before the passage quoted, was in Oxfordshire. Although earlier (78:1–10) Los had curbed the spectre sons of Albion (of which Hand is one) to prevent them from destroying "the Feminine Affections," the apparent inconsistency can be justified (outside of Blake's disregard for logical time and space relationships) if we realize that here is a different facet of the attack on morality, so very important in *Jerusalem*. The sons of Albion are rational forces of civilization with Hand often representing the self-righteous and purely rational man, who of course would have little place for affection, as Swift illustrated with the Houyhnhnms. But as shown here, the hostility of reason only causes the affection to go underground.

References to such very minor characters as those just discussed are few, and familiarity with them is not essential to an understanding of *Jerusalem*. Although with these references it was necessary to go to Blake's other works, and although with Erin it was helpful to look at the body of Blake's works, usually it is not necessary. As I have illustrated, most of the characters in Blake's personal mythology who appear in *Jerusalem* can be understood within the framework of the work itself. This is not to say that a knowledge of literature, especially of the Bible, is not helpful; and a knowledge of Blake's life and general philosophy is clearly no hindrance. However, if care is taken to be faithful to the context, to observe the state and point of view of the speaker, and to judge all the definitions, actions, and reactions of the symbolic characters studied, and if the reader genuinely exercises his "Intellectual powers," most of the personal symbolism will be explained by the work itself.

Much more could be said regarding Blake's personal symbols, but in order not to neglect entirely the other kinds of symbols present in the prophetic books, the unpracticed reader of the later Blake may be helped by some generalizations which may seem obvious to the Blakean. Even though the charges of obscurity are most often leveled at Blake's personal symbolism, actually his use of geography makes for the most deceptive set of symbols. Ellis' recognition of Blake's use of the four directions has proved very valuable. He noted that often north was synonymous with imagination, south with reason, west with the body or the senses, and east with emotion. Therefore Ireland is equated with the body, Scotland with imagination, Wales with reason, and England with emotion, if we take England to be east. So when we hear that during the flood of time and space, "Wales & Scotland alone sustain the fight!" (66:67), we may assume that this is Blake's way of saying that only imagination and reason are able to combat the purely material way of life. Unfortunately, this directional system does not always supply the answer. Frequently Blake seemed to ignore direction for the sake of political allegory. Often he used the names of cities, counties, mountains, rivers and the like mainly for the sake of local color. The basic difficulty is to determine whether he was using the geographical name for its connotation to his countrymen or to himself, for its direction, or because "All things Begin & End in Albion's Ancient Druid Rocky Shore," or as a combination of some or all of these possibilities. The context, of course, has to be the major guide. The reader must also be aware of the fact that sometimes the apparently obvious place references do not mean what he expects them to mean— somewhat as the simplest words noted earlier do not have their usual meanings. Tyburn, for example, normally thought of

as the place of the execution of criminals on the gallows, is given a favorable position in Blake's description of the gate of the poet (38:49–59), where Tyburn is coupled with Golgotha. The hangings of Tyburn are thus associated with the crucifixion of Jesus, who, we are forcefully made to recall, was also executed for his failure to conform to the law.

Blake's use of British mythology can be noted here only briefly. In addition to his debt to conventional sources such as Geoffrey of Monmouth and the patriotic myth developed by such works as Warner's *Albion's England*, Spenser's *Faerie Queene*, and Milton's *History of England*, he also made use of such contemporary "celtomaniacs" as Jacob Bryant, Richard Brothers, and many others now forgotten except by specialists. This school of British history was intent upon proving that Great Britain was the seat of all culture, religion, and civilization. Blake then was drawing on contemporary belief when, maintaining that all things begin and end in Britain, he made Britain the seat of the patriarchal religion and Albion the parent of the druids from whom the Jews descended (27). This belief may also partially explain why Britain is given an important role to play in the unfolding of the epic and why Britannia is the mother of the major figures, Jerusalem and Vala.

Of course it must not be forgotten that Blake drew upon these contemporary myths only insofar as they pertained to his own visions. He selected only those which he felt to be divinely inspired and then used them to prove the validity of his own visions of eternity. Blake's eclecticism with regard to these now obscure myths makes it nearly impossible to understand fully his British mythological characters; familiarity with the origin of these myths is not imperative to an understanding of the prophetic books, however.

Although Margoliouth has written many helpful "Notes" on the subject, Blake's use of the Bible has been most thoroughly

discussed and illustrated by Frye. Unless
the reader is extremely well versed in both
Old and New Testaments, he is strongly
advised to have the Bible, its concordance,
and its dictionary close at hand when reading the prophetic books. Often Blake utilizes
the literal meaning of a Hebrew word.
Knowing that Heshbon means "reasoning"
or "prudence," or Rephaim " disembodied
spirits," often helps one in clearing the
meaning of an otherwise difficult passage.
Not all of his Biblical symbolism is difficult: for example, his use of Eden as a
convenient way of calling to mind "the
time of love and innocence," his employment of the Twelve Tribes of Israel to
denote all the people of the earth, his
coupling of the forty years of wandering
with Reuben's wandering, or his representation of Babylon as the godless and purely
material city of reason. What offers difficulty, besides Blake's inevitable condensa-
tion of thought, is his intermingling of
Biblical characters and lands with contemporary or Blakean characters and lands.
Canaan, for example, is superimposed upon
England, and as such is the Biblical reflection of all things beginning and ending on
Albion's shore. As noted earlier, Los and
the daughters of Albion have much to do
with Reuben. Blake's imaginative use of
time and space and his intense compression
of knowledge are illustrated by the following quotation and its necessary explanation.
The poet's reason is trying to convince Los
of the futility of trying to help man, since
in the present state of the world

"Hand has peopled Babel & Nineveh: Hyle,
    Ashur & Aram:
  Coban's son is Nimrod: his son Cush is adjoin'd
    to Aram
  By the Daughter of Babel in a woven mantle of
    pestilence & war.
  They put forth their spectrous cloudy sails which
    drive their immense
  Constellations over the deadly deeps of indefi-
    nite Udan-Adan.
  Kox is the Father of Shem & Ham & Japheth,
    he is the Noah

Of the Flood of Udan-Adan; Hut'n is the
    Father of the Seven
From Enoch to Adam; Schofield is Adam who
    is New—
Created in Edom."   (7:18-26)

To explain this combination of Biblical
and personal symbols necessitates the use
of many of the principles reviewed in this
paper. The four locations (l.18) represent
the cardinal points of the compass: Babel,
south; Nineveh, north; Ashur, west; and
Aram or Syria, east. The whole world then
is dominated by Hand, self-righteous reason
(7:70–73; 8:6), and Hyle, false art—an
echo of Hayley, the popular poetaster. In
Blake's tracing of the genealogy of the
twelve generations backward from Nimrod
to Adam (ll. 19–26), to indicate perhaps
the basic confusion of the world or its
cyclic nature, not all the details are easily
explained. Nimrod, of course, is traditionally the world's first king as the founder
of Babylonia. This "mighty hunter before
the Lord . . . as in despite of Heaven,"
whose game was men rather than beasts
(*Paradise Lost*, XII, 24 ff.) in his physical
war and hunting fights against the two
eternal sources of life. As Blake says about
the material world, "the two Sources of
Life in Eternity, Hunting and War, / Are
become the Sources of dark & bitter Death
& corroding Hell" (43:31–32), whereas,
Los tells Albion,

  "Our wars are wars of life, & wounds of love
With intellectual spears, & long winged arrows of
    thought.
Mutual in one another's love and wrath all re-
    newing
We live as one Man."   (38:14-17)

Lines 19–20 refer to the Bible in that
Cush, grandson of Noah, son of Ham, and
the father (not the son) of Nimrod, was
thought to represent Ethiopia and was so
translated in Isaiah xi. 11; xviii. 1. Ethiopia
allied with Syria (Aram) against the Israelites, as inspired, for so Blake read the
Bible, by "the Daughter of Babel"—the
personification of evil. This Biblical evil

is linked with Blake's personal symbolism in the next lines (21–22), particularly to show (Udan-Adan) and not of the definite eternal life and its intellectual war. Kox is identified (ll. 23–24) as the Biblical Noah by being the father of his three sons; the Biblical flood is identified as "the Flood of Udan-Adan." Kox, who was the second, false accuser of Blake in his trial for sedition, is thus suggested as the type of person who would save his life or reputation at the expense of others. Hutton, possibly a judge at Blake's trial, the father of the first seven generations given backwards as was the genealogy of the twelve generations (ll. 24–25), may represent in Blake's mind the original "blueblood." In this way, Blake may be illustrating the degeneration of even "the finest people." Finally Schofield (usually "Scofield"), the prime cause of Blake's trial and a soldier, comes in for Blake's greatest wrath (ll. 25–26) if the reader can remember his Bible as well as Blake did. The Edomites, the descendants of Esau, who sold his birthright, were the subject of most violent invective in Obadiah, and one of the most contemptible tribes in the Bible. Fortunately such passages as the one just explicated are not too frequent.

The question, of course, remains: why did Blake establish his own set of symbols? Though I have tried to suggest that in a sense he was more conventional than some think, there is no doubt that he was also quite original with his symbols. Yet the fact remains that a careful study of his work often serves to explain even the most seemingly incomprehensible of them. Perhaps we have no right to quarrel with a poet who creates his own mythology unless we wish to contest the rights of any mythmaker. Few, if any, object to the mythmaking of Keats or Shelley, though their kind is somewhat different from Blake's (in that they often utilize and modify classical myth), and certainly not of his magnitude. Leigh Hunt ("Proem" to his 1844 edition of Keats's Poems) simply accepts Keats's

beholding a dryad behind every oak, and Keats himself often illustrates that the high imagination can "freely fly/ As she was wont of old." Regarding Shelley in this connection, I need only to cite Harold Bloom's *Shelley's Mythmaking* (1959). And even the most conservative of the great Romantics, Wordsworth, through the Wanderer in Book IV of *The Excursion* and often elsewhere, asserts the right of any imaginative man to create his own system —"If tired with system, . . . Let him build systems of his own." A Poet, however, should not have to be defended for fulfilling one of his traditional functions: to build "the stubborn structure of the Language, acting against / Albion's melancholy, who must else have been a dumb despair" (*Jerusalem*, 40:59–60). Still there are those who would have Blake use the established mythology, seemingly unaware of the fact that even Samuel Johnson had complained that the classical mythology was simply worn out from use; and for Blake it was not simply shopworn but tainted with the connotations of the world of time and space, with the centuries of light shed from the wrong world. As he put it in his *Vision of the Last Judgment:* "Let it here be Noted that the Greek Fables originated in Spiritual Mystery & Real Visions, which are lost & clouded in Fable & Allegory" and "Allegory & Vision ought to be known as Two Distinct Things, and so Call'd for the Sake of Eternal Life."

The use of the classic myth, then, is impossible to Blake because of its having been abstracted from vision or the eternal reality. Blake's recourse was to create his own system—"I must Create a System or be enslav'd by another Man's. / I will not Reason & Compare: my business is to Create" (10:20–21)—in order to communicate that eternal reality.

> I rest not from my great task!
> To open the Eternal Worlds, to open the Immortal Eyes
> Of Man inwards into the Worlds of Thought, into Eternity

Ever expanding in the Bosom of God, the Human Imagination.   (5:17-20)

We are not surprised, then, that for such
a task Blake could not "write for block-
heads" or those unwilling or incapable of
thinking beyond the spatial and temporal
limitations of this world. Perhaps, too, the
magnitude of this task explains why Blake
did not continue with such symbols as
that of the sick rose or the tiger—such
conventionally poetic symbols being not
sufficiently stimulating for his purpose,
and even perhaps being misunderstood. The
reader was not to be lulled into a vague
feeling that he apprehended the symbol;
he was to be shocked and thus led to
genuine understanding. He would be forced
to know what he did not know that he
might learn. "You say I want somebody
to Elucidate my Ideas. But you ought to
know that What is Grand is necessarily
obscure to Weak men. That which can be
made explicit to the Idiot is not worth my
care. The wisest of the Ancients consider'd
what is not too explicit as the fittest for
Instruction, because it rouzes the faculties
to act" (Letter to Rev. Dr. Trusler, August
23, 1799). "The Most Sublime Poetry" for
Blake must be "addressed to the Intellectual
Powers, while it is altogether hidden from
the Corporeal Understanding." The success
of this address will be determined by "the
Expansion or Contraction, the Translucence
or / Opakeness of Nervous fibres" (Jerusalem, 98:36–37) ; or as Eliot put it more
recently when writing of his Cocktail Party,
for those with sensibility "a meaning . . .
gradually reveals itself" according to "different degrees of consciousness."